7,50

Essay Index

OXFORD LECTURES
ON POETRY

OXFORD LECTURES ON POETRY

BY

E. DE SELINCOURT

Hon. Fellow of University College ; formerly
Professor of Poetry in the
University of Oxford

Essay Index Reprint Series

BOOKS FOR LIBRARIES PRESS, INC.

FREEPORT, NEW YORK

Essay Index

First published 1934
Reprinted 1967

PREFACE

THIS volume consists for the most part of lectures delivered during my tenure of the Chair of Poetry at Oxford; save for a few verbal corrections they are printed as they were spoken. To these I have added the 'Warton Lecture', read before the British Academy in celebration of the centenary of Keats, and an essay on the Preface to Wordsworth's *The Borderers*. This Preface only came to light a few years ago, and as it has never been printed with the poet's works, I have thought that students might welcome its inclusion here.

For leave to reprint the lectures on Keats and *The Testament of Beauty*, and the essay on *The Borderers* my thanks are due to the Council of the British Academy and to the Editors of *The Hibbert Journal* and *The Nineteenth Century and After*; my quotations from the poems of Robert Bridges are made with the kind permission of Mrs. Bridges and the Oxford University Press.

E. DE S.

CONTENTS

I
ON POETRY[1]

THE honour which the University has done me in electing me to the Chair of Poetry is deepened for me by the memory of what I owe to my predecessors. Looking back to my school-days, more than forty years ago, I recall the reading of *Culture and Anarchy* as a clear stage in my mental growth, whilst *The Scholar Gipsy* and the Preface to the *Essays in Criticism* prepared me to appreciate that strange beauty which is not the least precious of the gifts that Oxford lavishes on her sons, a gift that cannot, in these days, be too jealously preserved. To me as to so many others, *The Golden Treasury* was a revelation of the incomparable range and splendour of English lyric poetry, and Palgrave's lectures on Spenser, which I attended, a solitary and painfully conspicuous undergraduate in a select elderly audience, were the first discourses on literature I listened to. To Professor Bradley I owe a debt still deeper, and not only for the inspiration gained from contact with his rich and beautiful mind. When he was appointed to this Chair, the Honours School of English, in which I was a teacher, was in its infancy: with the linguistic studies in the hands of that great and learned scholar Professor Napier, and no one to give an equal prestige to the study of literature, the scales were heavily weighted against the humaner side of the curriculum. But Professor Bradley came to our aid; with the special object of helping the English School he voluntarily extended the scope of his office, and by delivering those lectures upon Shakespeare and Wordsworth, the like of which had not been heard since the days of Coleridge, he convinced a somewhat incredulous University that English poetry was worthy of a place among academic studies, and thus prepared the ground for a work so happily consolidated under the

[1] An Inaugural Lecture, delivered before the University of Oxford, March 1929.

guidance of Sir Walter Raleigh, the President of Magdalen, and Professor Nichol Smith. As I call these things to mind, and remember, too, my many obligations to those who have held this Chair during the last twenty years, I may well doubt my competence to 'follow in the footing of their feet'. For each of them, in his own way, and by his own individual method of approach, has upheld the claims of poetry to its place among the highest achievements of the human mind.

The abiding value of poetry is attested by the persistence with which generation after generation has attacked, defended, and discussed it. The Greeks, with their unrivalled sense of beauty and their piercing intelligence, might well have revealed, once for all, its essential nature; but their faith in reason as the sole avenue to truth forced them to distrust that incalculable element in it, which, according to their mood, they called either madness or inspiration. Plato expelled the poet from his Republic and himself assumed the poetic function; but although, when he wrote his myths, the poet within him gave the lie to the philosopher, his explicit doctrine darkened understanding for centuries after him. Despite Aristotle's recognition that poetry was creative of an ideal world of which the distinctive qualities were rhythm and an organic unity, much of his criticism was in reality an attempt to justify poetry rather than to define it; despite that flash of insight which led Longinus to speak of the effect of poetry as not pleasure but transport, and of words as the 'very light of the spirit', criticism tended to concentrate upon the didactic uses of poetry; its essential character was either taken for granted or misunderstood. The rationalist and the moralist were always at hand, insisting that poetry was only a means to an end outside itself; and the poet was more than half converted. Spenser, indeed, confident in the unity of truth and beauty, could safely accept the moral interpretation of his art:

> For of the soule the bodie forme doth take,
> For soule is forme, and doth the bodie make;

but only incidentally does Sidney refer, in his eloquent *Apologie for Poetrie* against its detractors, to 'that exquisite observing of number and measure in the words, and that high flying liberty of conceit proper to the poet, [which] did seem to have some divine force in it'. If the poets felt, with Milton, that they were truly inspired with a passion for the good and fair, they felt, with Milton also, that they had a divine message to the world, and gratefully accepted their role as 'mirrours of fructuous entendement'. Nor did poetry suffer any harm thereby. The danger only arose when the rationalistic spirit grew stronger than the creative impulse, and a fatal distinction was drawn between the content of a poem and its form, so that form came to be regarded not as inevitable expression, but merely as a pleasurable decoration of the subject-matter, a concession to that weakness inherent in man, by which he will listen more readily to the voice of reason if she appear before him tricked out in all the finery of fancy. From this heresy it was a clear logical deduction that such themes as need no extraneous ornament are unsuited for poetic treatment. 'Poetry', says Dr. Johnson, 'loses its lustre and its power applied to the decoration of something more excellent than itself. . . . In sacred poetry who has succeeded?' He forgot the *Psalms*; and he forgot too those moving lines which bring to a close his own *Vanity of Human Wishes*.

The true relation of reason to inspiration in poetry, and of substance to form, was first convincingly set forth by Dr. Johnson's successors. Poetry to them was simply the expression of the imagination, and the poetic imagination only another name

> For clearest insight, amplitude of mind,
> And reason in her most exalted mood;

they held the poet to be one who sees into the world of human experience with clear and comprehensive vision; the passion which stirs to life his creative instinct does not distort the truth, but reveals it; whilst his function is to communicate neither knowledge nor moral instruction, but power.

But man is an incorrigible moralist; and the finest critic among the Victorians, for all his rare perception of the greatest poetry, and of its power by a magical felicity of language to awaken in us 'a full, new, and intimate sense of things and their relations', could not escape the bias of his age. Setting up as the crucial test of poetry its application of ideas to life, he found Chaucer wanting in high seriousness, judged that Wordsworth would have been a better poet if he had read more books, and loftily dismissed Shelley as an ineffectual angel. What wonder, then, that some lovers of poetry, in exasperated revulsion from an attitude that bore no likeness to their own experience in reading Chaucer, or Wordsworth, or Shelley, retorted on a doctrine which seemed unduly to exalt content over form by claiming for form a value wholly independent of content? The peculiar emotion that poetry excites can, they urged, be felt with only an imperfect understanding of its meaning; a child can have it; we can have it by hearing poetry read to us in a foreign language, or by catching a beautiful line out of its context. Obviously, then, the poetic element in poetry lies in its music. It cannot be pure music, because it employs words which are primarily intellectual symbols, but it does its best to free itself from their encumbrance; at least it aspires to the condition of music, and it succeeds in so far as it attains its aspiration. Thus, distorting Pater's memorable phrase, they developed the theory that poetry works upon us by a kind of musical incantation with which the rational side of our nature has little concern.

But we can do full justice to the music of poetry without so uncompromising a disregard of its subject-matter. Indeed, the vital distinction between music and poetry lies just here, that whilst music enchants us by pure sound, the transport of poetry springs from the effect upon us of sound with a clearly defined intellectual content, so perfectly fused with it that we cannot distinguish sound from sense or sense from sound. To hear a poem read in a foreign language may excite an agreeable sensation, but that is partly because the human voice is itself the most lovely of musical instruments, partly because the poem can only be read to us by one who himself understands it, and hence by sympathy with him we catch some faint suggestion of its meaning; but even so the pleasure is different in kind from that which we gain from hearing a poem that we understand. Poetry in a foreign tongue is, in fact, not poetry to us, but music. If the essence of poetry lay in its music we should value poets chiefly for their metrical and melodic accomplishment, whereas nothing is more tedious in poetry than a music that has no meaning. If Spenser's exquisite melody has been the delight of all our greatest poets, it is because through that melody he is always presenting something that is in itself worth while, now a picture, now a delicate moral reflection, always some facet of his beautiful poetic self; whereas Swinburne, with a far greater melodic range, often irritates with mere virtuosity. That words have an intellectual significance from which the poet cannot escape is no disadvantage to poetry, it is simply the condition over which it triumphs; and the effect of the poet's music, as music, cannot be dissociated from its meaning. It is true, indeed, that lines can be found which haunt the ear with their melody:

And sweet, reluctant, amorous delay

Of Abbana and Pharphar, lucid streams

And on a sudden, lo! the level lake,
And the long glories of the winter moon,

though I doubt whether even here the melodic effect does not move us in proportion as we enter into the poet's thought, and accept it as worth the carriage. Would those lines upon the daffodils,

That come before the swallow dares, and take
The winds of March with beauty,

affect us even musically if we did not know what a swallow
or what a daffodil was? But the authentic thrill of poetry
is often gained from lines that make no special melodic
appeal:

> I tax not you, you elements, with unkindness;
> I never gave you kingdom, call'd you children
>
> Since there's no help, come let us kiss and part
> And never lifted up a single stone.

The musical effect of these lines is almost nugatory, yet no
one familiar with their context can doubt their supreme
poetic effect. And the true poet, where his melody is most
haunting, does not aim at lulling the intellect to sleep in a
kind of sensuous enchantment, but rather at kindling our
whole nature, so that we become intensely aware of things
and their relations.

   This conception of 'pure' poetry as it is called has, in
its crudest form, had little vogue in this country, but it
plays an important part in all those theories which find the
essence of poetry in its power to induce a kind of dream
consciousness or transcendental feeling. Professor Stewart,
with that persuasive charm that was natural to him, so employed it in his *Myths of Plato*, and it was a corner stone
of that brilliant argument with which some three years
ago M. L'Abbé Bremond (one of the most eminent of our
own Honorary Doctors) startled the French Academy.
M. Bremond accepts the view that poetry is a kind of
music, and that to appreciate it a full understanding of
its intellectual content is not sufficient or even necessary.
Poetry, he holds, has an obscure enchantment independent
of its sense; it is an incantation which gives unconscious
expression to the poet's state of soul, and in turn reveals
that state of soul to us. The poet's words, indeed, act as
a kind of electric current passing from his under-conscious-
ness to ours, so that we share with him a confused experience, inaccessible to distinct consciousness. And herein
lies the essential difference between poetry and prose, that
while prose excites our ordinary activities, poetry suspends

them. Poetry, therefore, in its essence, 'pure' poetry, is a mystic magic allied not to music but to prayer.

Before the audience to which this subtle and eloquent address was delivered its climax, *la prière*, was a splendid audacity, and it raised the storm that it was clearly intended to provoke. But while, if I had to choose between M. Bremond and his rationalist opponents, I should not hesitate, it is possible, I think, to hold as firm a faith in the spiritual value of poetry, and to admit the affinity of much poetry with mystical experience, without making that experience the touchstone which differentiates it from prose. For surely any human experience, if it be passionately felt and clearly imagined, can take its place in the ideal world of poetry. The Palace of Art has many apartments besides that lonely chamber in which the prophet communes with the stars, and the surest way of reaching the upper regions, and fitting ourselves to be their tenant, is to pass through the lower. It is significant that those two of our poets whose attitude to life is most profoundly mystical do not countenance this austere exclusiveness. Which of our writers is less of a mystic than Chaucer, who was hailed by the pioneer of a rationalistic age as 'the perpetual fountain of good sense'? Yet Blake sees in Chaucer 'the great poetical observer of men', and in his pilgrims 'visions of the eternal principles or characters of human life, as they appeal to poets of all ages'; whilst Wordsworth, who is often charged with caring for no verses but his own, acclaimed as true poetry alike the 'convivial exaltation' of Burns's *Tam o' Shanter*, and the careless gaiety of Suckling's *Ballad on a Wedding*. You remember Suckling's delicious description of the bride:

> Her feet beneath her petticoat,
> Like little mice, stole in and out
>   As if they feared the light;
> But O she dances such a way!
> No sun upon an Easter-day
>   Is half so fine a sight.

When Wordsworth came to this stanza he noted, with

pardonable exaggeration, in the margin of his copy, 'for grace and simplicity this stands unrivalled in the whole compass of ancient and modern poetry'. Indeed, the peculiar difficulty of the poet's art, that language, which is his medium, is normally an ill-used household drudge, brings with it this supreme compensation, that to him alone of all artists the whole of human experience is material, awaiting his creative energy. Nothing human is foreign to him, provided that he can relive it himself and feel it upon his own pulse. He is no less true to his poetic instinct when he fleets the time carelessly, as in the golden world, than when he probes the mysteries of existence, as if he were God's spy. He is no less a poet when he 'enjoys delight with liberty', as he watches the butterfly among the flowers:

> Now sucking of the sap of herbe most meete,
> Or of the deaw, which yet on them does lie,
> Now in the same bathing his tender feete,

than when he is wrapt in contemplation of our first parents in the garden of Eden; he can enter as whole-heartedly into Oberon's frenzy at the gallantries of Pigwiggen as into Othello's tragic passion; and the ecstasy of Romeo beneath Juliet's balcony is hardly more to him than a lover's rhapsody over his lady's costly apparel:

> Whenas in silks my Julia goes,
> Then, then, methinks, how sweetly flows
> The liquefaction of her clothes!

In conventional society he is at home as in nature's remotest solitudes. He is with Belinda playing cards at Hampton Court,

> Let spades be trumps! she said, and trumps they were,

and with Don Juan at the country seat of

> Lord H. Amundeville and Lady A.

'You have so many divine poems,' wrote Byron in his own defence, 'is it nothing to have written a human one?' And just as poetry can express the subtlest and deepest thoughts that enter into the mind of man, provided that they have passed through the crucible of passion, can even voice that artistically unpopular thing a great moral truth, so can it utter sheer nonsense, provided that the nonsense does not pretend to be other than it is, and that it conveys an irresponsible gaiety of heart. Nay, further, poetry can remain poetry when it is parodying itself. Swinburne mocking his own virtuosity is really more poetic than in some of that verse which for all its mellifluousness is empty of meaning; for here, at least, there is a genuine emotion, the delight of getting outside himself and revelling in his own absurdities. It is surely an error to deny to all this the name of poetry because it does not induce transcendental feeling.

And further, while we cannot thus limit the subject-matter of poetry, neither can we accept that mystical view of the poet's use of language which marks it off so sharply from our own, and makes into a difference of kind what is, perhaps, only a difference in degree. Our speech in ordinary life is as near as we can get it to what we mean: what the poet communicates in his poem is just what the poem says, and not some mystical state of soul which comes through the medium of his poem, above or apart from its meaning. The poet brings his imagination to bear upon his experience, and the breath of his passion

> winnows the light away,
> And what hath mass and matter, by itself
> Lies rich in virtue and unmingled.

This mass takes artistic shape in his mind as he finds the just and only words for its expression, and those words have a beauty of imagery and rhythm simply because his subject, which is not an abstract proposition or a common-place, but a living experience transmuted by imagination, can by its very nature only find voice in terms of beauty. It is true that he cannot explain this process to himself, that the subject seems to take control of him rather than he of it; but after all that is not a state of things peculiar to the poet. All our happiest thoughts and actions spring

spontaneously from us, without our being able to give a
reasonable account of their origin: we only know that some
power within us instinctively prompted them. This is,
indeed, a miracle in our constitution as human beings, but
it is no more a miracle than our power of thought or of
movement; it is an element in the supreme miracle of life.
And the poet, by a command of language approximate to his
power of vision, shares with us his imaginative experience.
But what some critics regard as magic in his use of words
is really only an extension of the natural power inherent in
language. I spoke earlier of words as intellectual symbols,
and they are, indeed, nothing else, so long as they are im-
prisoned in the dictionary; but as soon as they escape into
a living sentence, they gain individuality from the speaker's
voice and the expression upon his face, and catch subtle
shades of meaning which no dictionary can define, a meaning not purely intellectual, and capable of infinite variation according to the genius of him that uses them. We
say that such language suggests more than it expresses; but
it would be equally accurate to say that it expresses just
what it suggests. If, then, the poet's words convey to us
a transcendental feeling, over and above their logical significance, it is because the poet had that feeling and consciously expressed it. He may not be able to explain the
source of his inspiration, nor how the words came to him
in which he shapes it, but when the words have come he
knows what he means by them, and he is satisfied with them
in proportion as they correspond with his meaning. I feel,
therefore, that phrases such as 'obscure enchantment independent of the actual meaning', or 'incantation giving unconscious expression to a state of soul' do not help us to
understand even that mystical poetry to which alone they
could be applicable. The analogy between much of the
highest poetry and religion is clear enough in the doctrine
of the poetic imagination; but we learn more, as it seems
to me, of the distinctive character of both poet and mystic
if we contrast rather than seek to identify them. To the
mystic, experience is an end in itself; his sole desire is to

become merged in that divine life of which he is sublimely conscious. But what matters to the poet, as a poet, is not so much his experience as what he can create from it. He feels that

> if our virtues
> Did not go forth of us, 'twere all alike
> As if we had them not,

and he attests the divinity within him not by surrendering his personality, but by asserting the divine impulse to creation.

M. Bremond admits this, and sets down the poet as a mystic *manqué*; but surely that is to condemn him by the laws of a country not his own. The poet's business, whatever the nature of his experience, is to hand it on to others; and this he does by bringing to bear upon it all his powers to clarify and define. For the secret of art, as Blake saw, is definiteness.

> To see a world in a grain of sand
> And a heaven in a wild flower;
> Hold infinity in the palm of your hand
> And eternity in an hour;

no stanza in our poetry has more mystical depth than this; yet here is no 'obscure enchantment', no 'unconscious expression of a state of soul', but a beautifully clear statement of recognizable spiritual experience. If we want 'obscure enchantment' we shall find it in Blake's *Prophetic Books*, which are seldom poetry.

From all of which we conclude that if we would discover that abstraction, 'pure' poetry, i.e. the essentially poetic quality in a poem, we must seek it not in an alliance with music, nor in an alliance with prayer, but in the perfect rightness of its language to convey a passionately felt experience. The transport, as Longinus justly calls it, that the poet kindles in us springs from our instinctive recognition that his form, a term that includes both rhythm and diction, is an entirely faithful rendering of his experience, so that we gain from it a sudden clear sense of fulfilment, such as we can hardly hope to gain outside the ideal world of art. And the profounder the experience, provided that its form is adequate, the greater the poetic transport. But we can gain it without approaching to a mystical state, and if it is allied to prayer it is in the sense in which Fra Lippo Lippi met the Prior's complaint that his Madonnas did not instigate to devotion:

> If you get simple beauty and nought else,
> You get about the best thing God invents:
> That's somewhat, And you'll find the soul you have missed,
> Within yourself, when you return Him thanks.

Moreover, it is in the poet's struggle to find adequate expression for his experience that his experience acquires its true value, even for himself. Until he does this, all is confused and shapeless; power over language brings with it clarity of vision. Only when the stream is pellucid can the poet see into its depths. In a sense he hardly knows his subject till his poem is written; the character of Hamlet was not clearly defined, even for Shakespeare, before the play was complete; Milton's conception of Satan grew in strength and complexity as *Paradise Lost* took shape beneath his hands. Poetic inspiration lies less in the initial experience than in the creative act of translating it into fitting words. Shelley may seem to deny this. 'The mind in creation', he says, 'is as a fading coal; when composition begins inspiration is already on the decline; and the most glorious poetry that has ever been communicated to the world is probably but a feeble shadow of the original conception of the poet.' But this means no more than that the poet's world is inexhaustible in its beauty and resources, so that there will always hover o'er his restless head

> One thought, one grace, one wonder at the least
> Which into words no virtue can digest.

Art is emotion recollected in tranquillity, and relived imaginatively in an ideal atmosphere, wherein, if there is less heat, there is more light. The spontaneous overflow of powerful feelings in which it originates is itself too turbulent to find poetic form; it supplies at first no more than rough material from which the precise perfect record is yet to be created. This is a truth that dawned on Wordsworth at the time when he had just come into his poetic heritage, and when, as his sister tells us, his ideas were flowing faster than he could express them; and he jotted it down in a fragment of verse, found recently among his note-books:

> nor had my voice
> Been silent often times, had I burst forth
> In verse which, with a strong and random light
> Touching an object in its prominent parts,
> Created a memorial which to me
> Was all sufficient, and to my own mind
> Recalling the whole picture, seemed to speak
> An universal language. Scattering thus
> In passion many a desultory sound,
> I deemed that I had adequately clothed
> Meanings at which I hardly hinted, thought
> And forms of which I scarcely had produced
> An arbitrary sign . . .

rough notes, one might say, enough to enable the poet to 'recollect' his own emotion, but not an universal language, not poetry, because it was still formless. But the poet's art, he goes on, does not lie in these random effusions, but

> In that considerate and laborious work,
> That patience which, admitting no neglect,
> By slow creation doth impart to speech
> Outline and substance even, till it has given
> A function kindred to organic power,
> The vital spirit of a perfect form.

To give to impassioned experience that perfect form by which alone it can live on the lips and in the hearts of men, to give it *life by means of form*, that is the creative act of the poet. And it is, says Wordsworth, speaking naturally from his own experience, a slow and toilsome business. The poem does not spring from the poet's brain, like Minerva from the head of Jove; it comes gradually by a process that to his impetuous nature is often irksome and laborious. The extent of the labour varies with the genius of the poet and with his mood, but it is always greater than is implied in the common view of poetic inspiration. Wordsworth, as we know, found the effort to achieve equivalence of phrase and feeling far more exhausting to body and spirit than the earlier stages of composition, and in the end had often to admit defeat; whilst greater masters of language than he fall continually below themselves, either through a careless confidence in their own facility, or through reluctance to take those pains which are indispensable to poetic genius. Thus it was with Shakespeare; his friends, the players, might think it an honour to him that he never blotted a line, but Ben Jonson justly 'lamented their ignorance who chose that circumstance to commend their friend by wherein he most faulted'. To Shelley, too, it came easily; hence the number of fragments that he has left, desultory sounds scattered in passion we might call them, which would have become poems had he had the patience to complete them. Others, genuine poets, fail because they will not submit to that discipline which artistic creation demands. Thus it was that Collins, as Professor Garrod in a penetrating study has lately shown us, rarely secures that finality which his noble dirge and his exquisite *Ode to Evening* convince us to have been within his reach. And if we would gain insight into the process of poetic creation, we can do no better than study, where the material is available, the many changes through which the text of a poem passes, either before or after its first publication, and note what Keats has called the 'innumerable compositions and decompositions which take place between the intellect and its thousand materials before it arrives at that trembling, delicate, and snailhorn perception of beauty' which will satisfy its creator. If ever there was a poet to whom faultless expression seems to come without effort it is the Milton of *Comus* and *Lycidas*, yet a glance at his manuscript reveals how carefully he worked, rejecting lines in themselves without a flaw, if they seemed otiose, discarding here and there

words whose adequacy we should not question, had we not
the last consummate phrase with which to compare them.
Thus the lovely

> And every flower that sad embroidery wears

is only reached after the rejection of the less musical 'sad
escutcheon', whilst a line with which any poet might rest
content—

> And airy tongues that lure night wanderers

is so altered that it takes us to the very heart of romance:

> And airy tongues, that syllable men's names.

Similarly Keats, to whom poetry came like leaves to a tree,
and who before his death could almost rival the ripe felicity
of Milton, only gained it by the same process of scrupulous
refinement. All of which helps us to realize that the inspiration of a poem depends on a perfection of form in which
every phrase and cadence bears a significant part. A single
false note may ruin the harmony of a stanza. There is one of
Landor's charming epigrams in which a fatal flaw was only
healed years after its publication, when the poet, reliving
the experience which had prompted it, gave it the one
thing needful:

> The place where soon I think to lie
> In its old creviced nook hard by
>   Rears many a weed;
> If chance may bring you there, will you
> Drop slily in a grain or two
>   Of wall-flower seed?
>
> I shall not see it, and (too sure!)
> I shall not ever hear that your
>   Light step was there;
> But the rich odour some fine day
> Will, what I cannot do, repay
>   That little care.

So the poem runs in a copy corrected in Landor's own
writing; but for the phrase in the fourth line, 'If chance

may bring you there', all printed versions read 'If parties bring you there'. Parties! The suggestion is not of a friend drawn by some impulse she cannot explain to the grave of a once loved poet, but of personally conducted tours round Florence, 'putting in' the cemetery between visits to the Duomo and the Uffizi. With that one vile word the spirit of the poem evaporates.

But where the poet has attained to this perfect union of form and idea, though we recognize it by the power it has to move us, we cannot explain it, for therein lies the mystery of poetry. An exquisite feeling for words, for their associations, for their music, for their imaginative suggestion, have, we know, helped the poet to achieve it, but there is no sovereign rule to guide him, save sincerity to his vision; each poetic experience is unique and demands its own unique mode of utterance. Sometimes the crowning effect is gained by a fine extravagance, as in the cry of Iachimo, overcome by Imogen's matchless beauty,

> 'Tis her breathing that
> Perfumes the chamber thus; the flame of the taper
> Bows toward her.

Common sense might otherwise explain the flicker of a taper, and Ruskin would assure us that we have here a pathetic fallacy, yet surely Hazlitt is right in saying that 'this passionate interpretation of the motion of the flame to accord with the speaker's feelings is true poetry'. Sometimes an equally telling effect is gained by deliberate understatement, as in that superb final speech of Othello:

> When you shall these unlucky deeds relate,
> Speak of me as I am; . . . then, must you speak . . .
> Of one not easily jealous, but, being wrought,
> Perplex'd in the extreme.

What hyperbole of phrase could so poignantly bring home to our hearts the awful wreckage of Othello's life, and his agony of soul, as this ironic use of two wellnigh colourless

words, 'unlucky' and 'perplexed'? Sometimes the poet
attunes us to his emotion by putting before us images
which are in themselves of the rarest beauty, or by evoking the rich resource of musical suggestion, or of reminiscence far sought in history or romance,

> Aspramont or Montalban,
> Damasco, or Marocco, or Trebisond;

at other times he will draw his analogies from our daily
traffic with the world, raising the most mundane pursuits
to the level of poetry. What calling is more remote from
the imaginative life than the law? Yet Shakespeare's Sonnets are crowded with legal metaphor:

> When to the sessions of sweet silent thought
> I summon up remembrance of things past,

> Not mine own fears, nor the prophetic soul
> Of the wide world dreaming on things to come,
> Can yet the lease of my true love control,
> Suppos'd as forfeit to a confin'd doom.

These legal terms recur so often in the Sonnets, that when
I speculate, as we all do, upon the identity of Shakespeare's
friend, I am tempted to think that he must have been a
lawyer; for in no way can we more subtly suggest our
intimacy with one we love than by using language which
to him has special significance. But this use of prosaic
allusion needs such tact that none but the finest artists
are safe with it. Vaughan, a great poet but uncertain
artist, mars his sketch of a sunrise with the phrase 'Stars
shut up shop'; yet Milton can employ the same homely
metaphor with tender and delicate feeling:

> And set to work millions of spinning worms
> That in their green shops weave the smooth-hair'd silk.

But some of the greatest poetry is bare of either simile or
metaphor, piercing the heart by that strange spell that
lies in utter simplicity. Where does the pathos of frustrated

love find more plangent voice than in those few lines which fall from the lips of Troilus, when he sees on Diomed's coat the broach that he had given to Crisseyde?

> Through which I see that clene out of your minde
> Ye han me cast, and I ne can nor may,
> For all this world, within myn herte finde
> T' unloven you a quarter of a day!

'A quarter of a day'; why a quarter? you may ask. So Keats, viewing for a moment with playful detachment his own tragic passion in *La Belle Dame sans Merci*, comments on the line *With kisses four*, 'why four?' And there is no prosaic answer to the one query or to the other. And 'unloven you'; the phrase is one that a child might coin in momentary resentment at maternal reproof; and yet here we have the mystery of pure poetry, not to be explained on a theory of moral edification, or of musical enchantment, or of mystical suggestion. And similarly love's long-awaited fulfilment finds perfected utterance in that simple quatrain of Blake's, which seems to falter in its second line only to recover for a triumphant close:

> Dost thou truly long for me?
> And am I thus sweet to thee?
> Sorrow now is at an end,
> O my lover and my friend!

This coincidence of words and meaning can only move us poetically through our sense of beauty. Keats was surely right in insisting that to the poet a sense of beauty obliterates all other considerations. That is not to say that his aim is mere smoothness or grace. Beauty is Protean in its shapes, and may reveal itself even in the grotesque, when it is prompted by a genuine poetic impulse. But in the names of originality, sincerity, progress, it needs must be that offences come; and the loose form and ungainly phrase too often betray a state of mind in which thought and feeling are not wholly fused, as true poetry demands. So it was at times with the metaphysicals, and with

Browning; so it is often with our contemporaries. The result may be interesting, even exciting to the intellect, but if we are to be moved poetically, we must be transported beyond that state to which cleverness makes any appeal. Browning gave us some brilliantly unpoetic verse, justifying it with the triumphant query 'Do roses stick like burrs?' To which it is no paradox to retort that roses stick far better. A burr may stick for the moment, and we are annoyed for the moment, but picking it off we cast it from us and forget all about it. But roses, even when they die, and poets' roses do not die, 'live within the sense they quicken'. Only through beauty can the poet give permanent life to his creation.

And the value of poetry, from its lightest ebullition of fancy to its profoundest outcry of the spirit, lies simply in its power to communicate a sense of life in all its infinite variety and significance. The passion for life is the root instinct of our nature, and the poet differs from other men in that he has it more abundantly. It is this which inspires him to creative energy, and his creative power over language is itself the natural outcome of his intenser delight in life, and his keener sensitiveness to all its manifestations. His alertness to what is going on about him has often struck his more prosaic contemporary as something almost uncanny:

> He took such cognizance of men and things,
> If any beat a horse, you felt he saw;
> If any cursed a woman, he took note!
> Yet stared at nobody—you stared at him,
> And found, less to your pleasure than surprise,
> He seemed to know you, and expect as much.

It is, moreover, by this quick response to the world of sense that the poet enters into the world of spirit; indeed, to the world of spirit there is no other entrance. To the true poet spirit and matter in the universe are no more separable than idea and expression are separable in his poetry. Hence the most ordinary incident, which we might pass by unnoticed, may awaken in him thoughts and feelings which reach back

to the innermost recesses of his being. Let him but have
caught sight of a blind beggar in the street,

> who, with upright face,
> Stood, propped against a wall, upon his chest
> Wearing a written paper, to explain
> His story, whence he came, and who he was.
> Caught by the spectacle my mind turned round
> As with the might of waters; an apt type
> This label seemed of the utmost we can know,
> Both of ourselves and of the universe;
> And, on the shape of that unmoving man,
> His steadfast face and sightless eyes, I gazed,
> As if admonished from another world;

or he reads, in a friend's diary, of a peasant girl singing at
her work in the cornfield, and his imagination is set on fire:

> No nightingale did ever chaunt
> More welcome notes to weary bands
> Of travellers in some shady haunt,
> Among Arabian sands;
> A voice so thrilling ne'er was heard
> In springtime from the Cuckoo-bird,
> Breaking the silence of the seas
> Among the farthest Hebrides.

Thus it is that the poet has

> among least things
> An undersense of greatest, sees the parts
> As parts, but with a feeling for the whole.

And if 'least things' can cast this spell upon him, those
darker elements in life which loom so large in all human
experience, its sorrow, disillusionment, despair, offer him
a challenge from which he wrings his greatest triumphs.
Poetic tragedy has its source and inspiration in a passionate
conviction of the inherent worth of human life, a conviction which is roused all the more keenly by the spectacle of
the havoc and waste wrought by evil; and that beauty
which finds expression in the ordered scheme of the poem
and in the melody and imagery of its verse is but the out-

ward and visible sign of the temper in which the poet has viewed his subject and interpreted its significance. Hence, when his theme is tragic, he makes us feel it in a way that exalts rather than depresses. For his revelation is of

> Sorrow, that is not sorrow, but delight,
> And miserable love, that is not pain
> To hear of, for the glory that redounds
> Therefrom to human kind, and what we are.

What wonder, then, since the whole of life comes within the poet's ken, and since in his creation he gives us his reading of life, that we should tend to regard him as a teacher? He is, in fact, the only effective teacher, for not only does he present to us what he conceives to be the truth, but he presents it, as few teachers can, in such a way that it is carried alive into the heart by passion. And though some sensitive artistic souls may think it blasphemy to call him a critic of life, the functions of criticism and creation being so widely diverse, he has assuredly been to thousands, whether or not they admit it, life's fullest, most convincing interpreter. So, indeed, many of the greatest poets have regarded themselves, and Coleridge well said that 'great men are only wrong by being imperfectly right'. Their error is, after all, only an error in emphasis, mistaking an inevitable element in poetry for its real spirit. For the *distinctive* function of poetry is not interpretation. A poet's philosophy of life wears no better than that of the professional philosopher; systems of thought soon go out of fashion, and even though the poet may see deeper than his time, in much that he says he is inevitably the creature of his time. But what his imagination has created has a life independent of those very theories which may have prompted its creation. The ideas which inspired Dante and Milton may be out of date; *The Divine Comedy* and *Paradise Lost* retain their hold upon all who can read them poetically. Browning's Pippa convinces many who are not convinced that all's right with the world, and they can be stirred by the love of Pompilia and Caponsacchi without

caring overmuch for the moral that the Pope drew from it.
Indeed, Browning himself, who of all poets has been read
with most unction by unpoetic readers, and whose art so
often seems to invite prosaic comment, was under no delusion in the matter. The poet, he tells us, is not another
Boehme with a tougher book and subtler meanings of what
roses say, but is rather one who

> with a 'look you!' vents a brace of rhymes,
> And in there breaks the sudden rose herself,
> Over us, under, round us every side,
> Buries us with a glory, young once more,
> Pouring heaven into this shut house of life.

Every artist, however trivial his theme, lifts the shadow
from some tiny corner of the prison house that our dull
insensibility has erected about us: the great masters illumine for us the darkest recesses of human experience. That
profoundest of all attempts to justify the ways of God to
man, *The Book of Job*, suggests, I think, in its tremendous
climax, at once the supreme function of poetry and our
supreme need for it. To the fervid appeals of his outraged
reason Job obtains no response, and when at last an answer
is vouchsafed him argument is not met by argument, it is
transcended in a vision, a vision of the beauty and splendour of the universe and of the infinite power of God. And
Job's last words transport us into that world of our desire,
beyond the reach of reason, in which poetry and religion
are one:

> I had heard of thee by the hearing of the ear;
> But now mine eye seeth thee.

Vision, not interpretation, that is poetry. Only incidentally does the poet teach. But by the creative power of his
imagination, which gives to his passionate experience 'the
vital spirit of a perfect form', he reveals to us the wonder of
the natural world, the joys and the sorrows, the exultations
and agonies of man's unconquerable mind, so that we are
awakened for a time from our torpor, and seeing things

with the poet's eyes, see into their life. And when the vision fades, we are left with something of that serene sense of fulfilment which was Dante's at the close of his sublime pilgrimage:

> quasi tutta cessa
> Mia visione, ed ancor mi distilla
> Nel core il dolce che nacque da essa.

II
CHAUCER

IN my inaugural lecture I offered some objections to the
view that the poet is perforce a mystic. Poetry seems
to me to be the expression of any intense experience, in
language which, by its exact and vital correspondence with
the poet's vision, and by that beauty of form without which
the vision could not be conveyed, enables us to enter into
his world, to see it with his eyes and feel it with something
of his emotion. The life within ourselves is thus awakened
from its torpor, so that for the time we are quickened into
a more vivid sense of things and of their relation to one
another.

Those who insist on a mystical element in poetry must
assuredly coin some other word by which to denote the
work of Chaucer. His vision is of the world about him;
and he delights in 'life's daily prospect', not as an imperfect
shadowing forth of some higher reality, but simply for its
own sake, for its beauty of form and colour, its movement
and infinite variety; above all for its revelation of human
character. No man can have had a more varied experience
than he, none has used his experience to better purpose.
The son of a London merchant, bred up at court, in turn
a soldier, an envoy on foreign missions, controller of customs and clerk of the King's works, justice of the peace and
member of Parliament, he came into contact with all sorts
and conditions of men. Being from youth up a voracious
reader, he both enriched and tested his experience by that
of others. With the resources of classical and medieval
literature laid open before him he had as little need as
Shakespeare to invent his own plots:

> For out of oldė feldės, as men seith,
> Cometh al this newė corn fro yeer to yerė;
> And out of oldė bokės, in good feith,
> Cometh al this newė science that men lerė.

The world was already full of good stories, many of them

indifferently told, none of them told as he would have told
them; in reshaping them so as to express his own vision he
found all the scope he needed. And the 'science' that he
taught was indeed 'new' to the poetry of his country—it
was psychology, the knowledge of men and women, which
he revealed with an insight into the heart and an imaginative humour only equalled by Shakespeare.

And like Shakespeare's, his genius for life could triumph
over the most unpromising material. Dr. Johnson com-
mented with some asperity on the 'imbecility' of the plot
of *Cymbeline*, yet in this fantastic setting are that subtle
villain Iachimo, and Imogen, loveliest of heroines. So
from crudely miraculous legends Chaucer develops two
of his most intensely real and moving creations, Constance
and Dorigen: or if he would give us a searching comedy of
character, the life-like study of the highly-strung, imaginative man mated to a practical wife, he evolves it from the
popular farmyard fable of a cock and hen.

It was Chaucer's destiny to be a supreme master of poetic
narrative, but he had first to find and to perfect his artistic
medium. In acquiring the craft of verse his English fore-
runners gave him little help; for models he turned to
France, where courtly poetry, barren as it was of matter
or idea, had yet developed an elaborate and exquisitely
refined technique. To Machault and his followers Chaucer
put himself to school. It would have been easy for him to
render into their metres his own idle thoughts and fancies;
easier still, in the manner of the budding poet, to allow
metre or rhyme to suggest ideas; he chose the more difficult
task of literal translation. It was, as he tells us,

> a greet penaunce,
> Sith rym in English hath swich scarsiteé,
> To folowe word by word the curositeé
> Of Graunson, flour of hem that make in Fraunce.

But by grappling with the task he learnt his own technique, and in the process of acclimatizing his borrowed
metres he not only gave to English a new music, but at the
same time acquired a mastery over his own language.

But translation is never identical in meaning with its original. For poetry is no bare logical statement; its effect depends largely on cadence, and on those delicate nuances of feeling which the subtleties of verbal music alone can convey. In the choice of an equivalent for the commonest word the translator reveals something of himself. And this is truer of Chaucer than of most translators, for there was as yet no recognized poetic style, and he had to create one. Moreover the step from translation to adaptation is imperceptible. To his French admirers he remained to the end of his days 'Great translator, noble Geoffrey Chaucer', and, in fact, to the last he loved to weave into his fabric threads drawn from many a craftsman. Yet never is he more daringly himself than when, borrowing from others, he gives to their words a depth of feeling or of irony of which they were wholly innocent.

The vital independence of his genius is clearly shown in the emergence at once, along with a delicate metrical art, and an occasional high-wrought phrase, of a native English simplicity of style. His diction is everywhere vivid, nervous, racy—the language of prose raised to poetry by its vitality and by its music. He seems to be seeking only the aptest expression of his thought, to say everything just as one would wish to say it in talk, and yet, somehow or other, he finds it with rhyme and metre, giving it that graceful ease which is the highest art. At times, indeed, he achieves, irrespective of its meaning, an unforgettable melody:

> thou Polymnia,
> By Elicon, not fer from Cirrea,
> Singest with vois memorial in the shade;

and he can write a lyric which owes more to its music than to its intellectual content: but he avoids fine writing as studiously as many seek to achieve it. For the 'heigh style' he shares the deep-rooted objection of that incarnation of rich common sense, his own Harry Bailey, and when he is in danger of indulging in it he quickly pulls himself up:

> For th'orisonte hath reft the sonne his light;
> This is as muche to seye as it was night.

His style reflects everywhere his love of things real and natural. Hazlitt has noted that his metaphors are few, and that they are not for ornament but use. When he wishes to illumine his theme with simile or comparison, the image that flashes upon him has nothing recondite about it; it is drawn from the world of every day. In *The Prologue* to his *Canterbury Tales*, the Knight is 'as meke as is a mayde', the Squire is 'as fresh as is the month of May'; the Pardoner 'glarynge eyen hadde as an hare', the Friar's twinkle

> As doon the sterres in the frosty night.

The Franklin's beard is as white as a daisy, the Miller's is as red as a sow or a fox, and 'ther-to brood, as though it were a spade', whilst the hairs that adorn the wart upon his nose are like the bristles of a sow's ear. There is hardly an image in *The Prologue* that is not of this kind. They seem so simple and obvious that they might, we think, have occurred to any of us; but would they? When he indulges in longer description his analogies are similar. One of his most elaborate portraits is that of Alison in *The Miller's Tale*:

> Fair was this yongĕ wyf, and ther-with-al
> As any wesele hir body gent and smal.
>
> .   .   .   .
>
> Ful smale y-pullĕd were hir browĕs two,
> And tho were bent, and blake as any sloo.
> She was ful morĕ blisful on to see
> Than is the newĕ pere-jonettĕ tree;
> And softer than the wolle is of a wether;

and so on, for forty lines or more.

With a like homely vividness he makes his shrewdest comments upon life. The vanities of the world pass 'like shadows on the wall'; if he would convince us of the strength of natural instinct, this is how he does it:

> Lat take a cat, and fostre him wel with milk,
> And tendre flesh, and make his couche of silk,
> And lat him seen a mous go by the wal;
> Anon he weyveth milk, and flesh, and al,
> And every deyntee that is in that hous,
> Swich appetyt hath he to ete a mous.

In like manner he comments upon man's blindness to his essential good:

> We witen nat what thing we preyen here.
> We faren as he that dronke is as a mous;
> A dronkė man wot wel he hath an hous,
> But he noot which the rightė wey is thider;
> And to a dronkė man the wey is slider.
> And certes, in this world so faren we.

It is writing like this, that, despite some words and forms of words that are now archaic, puts Chaucer among the most modern of our poets. Tricks of fashion change with a generation, and, as we say, 'date', a writer. But the simple and the natural are never antiquated. The best of Chaucer has still the freshness of an April morning.

Even in his early work, while he moves in the tedious, formal world of allegory and romance, he shows the bent of his genius towards reality. His first long poem, *The Book of the Duchesse*, was written to commemorate the death of John of Gaunt's wife. Its dream setting recalls the *Romaunt of the Rose*, which he had already translated: much of its subject-matter is drawn from two poems by Machault. Yet in the poem, with its charming touches of naive and humorous autobiography, he sounds at once his own individual note. In the dream itself he puts a new life into the dead poetic conventions of the May morning with its flowers and singing birds, for he has felt as well as read about them; the hound that fawns upon him

> and creep to me as lowė,
> Right as hit haddė me y-knowė,
> Hild doun his heed and joyned his eres,
> And leyde al smothė doun his heres,

is a real dog, while the

> many squirelles, that setė
> Ful hye upon the trees, and etė,
> And in hir maner madė festės,

are familiar to us in many an English country-side.

A commemorative poem inevitably elaborates the pious fictions of the tombstone. But Chaucer's Blanche is no mere queen of the medieval Court of Love, an object of distant worship. She is frank and friendly with all good men, and yet no coquette; she is one who makes on her lover no extravagant demands of chivalric devotion, sending him

> To Pruyse and in-to Tartaryė,
> To Alisaundrė, ne in-to Turkyė,

to attempt impossible feats in her honour ('She ne used no suche knakkes smale', says Chaucer contemptuously). She is good, not from a child-like innocence, but from a knowledge of good and evil:

> I sey nat that she ne had knowing
> What was harm; or elles she
> Had coud no good, so thinketh me.

The ideal is strikingly modern; Chaucer's Blanche is a woman fit to play her part in the real world of to-day; and if her portrait, as he presents her, lacks the vivid colouring of his later work, it has at least the merit of simplicity.

> I have no wit that can suffysė
> To comprehenden hir beautė;
> But thus moche dar I seyn, that she
> Was rody, fresh, and lyvely hewėd.

Was it accident, or unconscious reminiscence, that led a later poet of the natural style to praise his *lovely maid* in the words

> Why should I fear to say
> That she is ruddy, fleet, and strong?

Finally, though the poem as a whole has something of the tedious prolixity of its models, the tale of Ceix and Halcyone, which he includes in it, proves him already accomplished in the art of narrative, and already a master of simple pathos. The body of her dead husband appears to Halcyone in a dream, and says to her

> 'my swetė wyf,
> Awak! let be your sorwful lyf!
> For in your sorwe ther lyth no reed;
> For certes, swete, I nam but deed;
> Ye shul me never on lyve y-see.
> But good swete hertė, (look) that ye
> Bury my body, at whiche a tydė
> Ye mowe hit finde the see besydė;
> And far-wel, swete, my worldės blissė!
> I prayė god your sorwe lissė;
> To litel whyl our blisse lasteth!'
>> With that hir eyen up she casteth,
> And saw noght; 'A!' quod she, 'for sorwe!'
> And deyėd within the thridde morwe.

Here is the first example in Chaucer of that acute sensitiveness to pain that has won him a place among the 'mighty poets of the human heart'. If he seldom plumbed the depths of great tragedy, few have equalled him in what Milton, in lovely phrase, has called 'the whole passion of pity'. In poignant sympathy with a mother's love for her child none of our poets, save Wordsworth, has approached him. True it is that

> Grisilde is deed, and eek hir pacience,

but her grief when her children are torn from her, and her ecstasy in their recovery, are immortal. Constance, cast adrift upon the sea with her babe, is among the sublime figures of poetry:

> Hir litel child lay weping in hir arm,
>> And kneling, pitously to him she seydė,
> 'Pees, litel sone, I wol do thee non harm.'
>> With that hir kerchef of hir heed she breydė,
> And over his litel yen she it leydė;
>> And in hir arm she lulleth it ful fastė,
> And in-to heven hir yen up she castė.

And then, after a touching prayer to the Virgin, that

Mother whose greater loss makes her pitiful to all human
mothers, Constance turns once more to her child:

> 'O litel child, allas! what is thy gilt,
>   That never wroughtest sinne as yet, pardée,
> Why wil thyn hardè fader han thee spilt?
>   O mercy, derè constable!' quod she;
> 'As lat my litel child dwelle heer with thee;
>   And if thou darst not saven him, for blamè,
> So kis him onès in his fadres namè!'

A poet's character is revealed by his favourite epithets.
You will have noticed how often in these stanzas, and with
what caressing tenderness, Chaucer repeats the word 'litel'.
'Yongè fresshè folkes', in their trustful confiding innocence
—life, fragile, delicate, unsmutched in its brightness by
contact with a rude world, made an appeal to him that
he could not resist. So, in his exquisite story of the 'litel
clergeon, seven yeer of age', who passed through the Jew-
ish quarter singing 'Alma Redemptoris mater', a habit that
might be deemed tactless in one of riper years, he dwells
lovingly upon the child's tender youth. And when, reading his Dante, he lights upon the tragic tale of Ugolino's
starvation with his sons in the Pisan prison, what arrests
him in the story is the thought of the guiltless children who
shared their father's cruel fate:

> Of the erl Hugelyn of Pysè the langour
>   Ther may no tongè tellè for pitee;
> But litel out of Pysè stant a tour,
>   In whichè tour in prisoun put was he,
> And with him been his litel children three;
>   The eldeste scarsly fyf yeer was of agè.
> Allas, fortune! it was greet crueltée
>   Swiche briddes for to putte in swiche a cagè!
>
> .   .   .   .
>
> And on a day bifil that, in that hour,
>   Whan that his metè wont was to be broght,
> The gayler shette the dorès of the tour.
>   He herde it wel,—but he spak right noght,

And in his herte anon ther fil a thoght,
  That they for hunger woldė doon him dyėn.
'Allas!' quod he, 'allas! that I was wroght!'
  Therewith the terės fillen from his yėn.

His yongė sone, that three yeer was of agė,
  Un-to him seydė, 'fader, why do ye wepė?
Whan wol the gayler bringen our potagė,
  Is ther no morsel breed that ye do kepė?
I am so hungry that I may nat slepė.
  Now woldė god that I mighte slepen ever!
Than sholde nat hunger in my wombė crepė;
  Ther is no thing, save breed, that me were lever.'

Thus day by day this child bigan to cryė,
  Til in his fadres barme adoun it lay,
And seydė, 'far-wel, fader, I moot dyė,'
  And kiste his fader, and deydė the samė day.

Nothing could be more significant of Chaucer's genius and character than his rendering of this episode. In Dante it is a tragedy of stark horror; in Chaucer its dominant sentiment is an exquisite pathos. One notices that whereas Dante, concentrating on Ugolino's anguish, does not even mention the children's age, Chaucer dwells upon it throughout, adding from his own heart the moving words of the youngest of them, 'that three yeer was of age'; whilst the touching comparison of these children to caged birds, which sums up for him the whole emotion of the story, has no counterpart in the *Inferno*.

For 'the grete poete of Itaille' Chaucer had a profound admiration; but he moved in a different sphere. 'Of heaven and hell he had no power to sing'; his world was the world of all of us. And just as he had not Dante's majestic range of vision, so had he a totally different outlook on that world that was common to them both. A man's art is fashioned from that part of his experience which counts for most in his emotional life. Chaucer lived in as stirring times as Dante, and was all his days a public servant in close touch with affairs; yet he had none of Dante's passionate interest in state concerns. National poet as he is, if we regard the matchless picture he has left us of the social life of his time, he is yet in no ordinary sense of the term a patriotic poet.

In wars he is not greatly interested. We owe, perhaps, to his observation on the field of battle that vivid touch which tells how Thisbe comes upon Pyramus in the throes of death, 'al blody',

> Beting with his helès on the grounde,

but he makes no patriotic capital out of military exploits. His 'verray parfit gentil knight' has borne no part in the triumphs of Crecy or Poictiers; he is a somewhat aimless knight-errant, who has ridden, no man ferrè,

> As wel in Cristendom as hethenesse;

the adventures of his squire are only vaguely alluded to; his yeoman, who bore a mighty bow, and had under his belt a sheaf of arrows bright and keen, typical of those sturdy archers who were the bulwark of the English army against France, has had no experience of battle; he is presented as a forester, a man of peace. On those troubles that distracted the country at home Chaucer is equally reticent. To the Black Death, so devastating in its effect that it actually halved the population, he merely refers as a source of considerable profit to his 'verray parfit practisour'. So the Peasants' Revolt, which threatened the very throne, is only recalled to his mind by the hubbub in the farmyard, when the fox carries off Chanticleer,

> So hidous was the noyse, a! benedicite!
> Certes, he Jakkè Straw, and his meynée,
> Ne madè never shoutès half so shrillè,
> Whan that they wolden any Fleming killè.

It is true that he makes some general reflections on the classes, and in his *Clerkes Tale* interposes an address to the

> stormy peple! unsad and ever untrewè!
> . . . .
> Delyting ever in rumbel that is newè,

and he warns us that he is a full great fool who puts his
trust in the people. Yet, unlike Spenser or Shakespeare,
he impresses on his work no political philosophy. And
though attempts have been made by both Protestant and
Catholic zealots to prove him a Wycliffite, his attitude to
the rise of Lollardry is not that of a partisan; his portraits
of different members of the Church are prompted by a
lively sense of contrast. It might be said that in all this
he was actuated by prudence, or that, depressed by the
gloomy national outlook, he averted his eyes from evils that
he had no power to cure. But the true reason is to be found
in his character and temperament. His heart lay other-
where.

There is not a trace in Chaucer of the spirit of the
reformer, either political or moral. He had no sense, like
his contemporary Gower, or like Milton, or Shelley, of a
message to the world, of wrongs that he must help to right.
Without believing that everything was for the best, his
instinct was to make the best of things. It is true that,
like many a comfortable conservative, he played with the
theory of the good old times:

> A blisful lyf, a paisible and a swetė
> Ledden the peples in the former agė,

he tells us, and he draws the inevitable contrast with his
own day, when there is nothing but 'covetyse'

> And doublenesse, and tresoun and envyė,
> Poysoun, manslauhtre, and mordre in sondry wysė;

but when he goes on, with the same unimpeachable gravity,
to give some details of that ideal simplicity of life, when
the fruits of the earth were devoured uncooked:

> They eten mast, hawės, and swich pounage,[1]
> And dronken water of the coldė wellė,

we shrewdly suspect that his sympathies were not entirely
with the golden age. For he loved the good things of this

---

[1] *pounage*: pig's food.

world. If he was an indefatigable student he was no less a bon-vivant, and, as he confesses, his abstinence was 'lyte'. Moreover the age of innocence was not nearly so lively and entertaining as the world he knew. Even Milton's Paradise was only saved from tedium by the arrival of the serpent; and if that enemy of mankind brought death into the world and all our woe, he brought with it, in rich compensation, that infinite variety from the norm of virtue which has made possible both morality and art. Chaucer loved the world for what it was, and his delight in observing all manifestations of human life took from him the desire to enact the moralist. He was, in fact, far more interested in discovering other people's points of view than in urging his own. He went through life not so much expressing himself as encouraging others to express themselves. His knowledge of man was not gained from the heights of a superior aloofness; he adapted himself to his surroundings, and whatever company he was in, he was sure, as at the Tabard, to be of their fellowship anon. As to his demeanour in company he has not left us in the dark. He was more a listener than a talker. He knew that most men gauge their enjoyment of a social gathering, not by the number of good things they have heard, but by the proportion of good things that they have been allowed themselves to contribute. We may admire the good talker, but the listener we love, and his tolerance of our ineptitudes we set down as intelligence. Chaucer allowed others to do the talking; and when he spoke it was with deference and modesty, to agree or to apologize, not to dispute or put his fellows in the right. When the jolly monk justified to this unassuming stranger whom he meets at the Tabard his preference of sport to the rules of St. Augustine:

> What sholde he studie, and make himselven wood,
> Upon a book in cloistre alwey to poure?

he little thought that he was addressing a student who read far into the night, 'til fully daswed' was his look. But it mattered little: 'And I seyde, his opinioun was good',

remarks Chaucer. It was thus that he made men and
women reveal themselves to him. Argue with a man, point
out his folly or his ignorance, you may possibly convert him,
though you will probably make him angry; more likely still
he will imitate the snail,

> whose his tender horns being hit
> Shrinks backwards in his shelly cave with pain.

Anyhow, you will not learn much about him. But en-
courage him with an interested and admiring acquiescence,
and he will lay bare to you the secrets of his soul. Such was
Chaucer's plan.

This self-depreciation and assumption of modesty, so
invaluable to Chaucer as putting his human material in
the mood for self-revelation, must have been intensely
humorous to those of the company who knew what he really
was, and had the insight to realize the subtle irony of his
attitude to the world about him. His work gains thus an
intimacy which suggests that he wrote for the delectation
of his friends; and much of its charm to-day springs from
our feeling, as we read, that we are admitted into the poet's
inner circle. No writer ever made such delicious fun of
himself. The proud boast of Horace, *Exegi monumentum
aere perennius*, has been re-echoed by poet after poet down
the ages. But Chaucer, of all our metrists gifted with the
most infallible ear, is content to record the Man of Law's
judgement upon him that he can 'but lewedly'

> On metres and on ryming craftily;

and the Eagle in the *Hous of Fame* assures him that he is to
be rewarded, not for his poetic achievement, but simply
for his good intentions:

> thou hast set thy wit—
> Although that in thy hede ful lyte is—
> To make bokes, songes, dytees,
> .   .   .   .
> *As thou best canst.*

In his own day, as in ours, he was doubtless criticized by
metrical purists for his habit of dropping a syllable in the
first foot of his line. He accepts the criticism as though
they were better judges of verse than he:

> Nat that I wilne, for maistrye,
> Here art poetical be shewèd;
> But, for the rym is light and lewèd,
> Yit make hit sumwhat agreable,
> Though som vers failè in a sillable.

Throughout the *Hous of Fame* he holds himself up to ridicule, in the same way as he belittles his art. At one time
it is an allusion to his terror at the sound of his wife's voice:

> 'Awak', to me he seydè,
> Right in the same vois and stevenc
> That useth oon I coudè nevene;
> And with that vois, soth for to sayn,
> My mindè cam to me agayn;
> For hit was goodly seyd to me,
> So nas hit never wont to be;

at another time he fears, as he is borne aloft in the eagle's
talons, that Jove intends to stellify him, and he thinks of
Enoch and Elias and Romulus and Ganymede, who had
all been thus borne heavenward, wondering, no doubt,
whether they found the transit as uncomfortable as he
does. But the eagle informs him with biting scorn that
as yet Jupiter has no intention to make of him a star. He
is whirled through the air so fast that he does not know
whether he is a body at all, or merely a disembodied spirit:

> I woot wel I am herè;
> But wher in body or in gost
> I noot, y-wis; but god, thou wost!

and the eagle sardonically has to reassure him:

> Nay, dred thee not therof, quod he,
> Hit is no thing wil byten thee.

This same humorous detachment from himself he will often
extend to his own deepest feelings and opinions, turning
the keen edge of irony against what he holds most sacred.

He might indeed be said to test the strength and the value of his most earnest convictions by their power to resist the shafts of his own ridicule, just as we can test the essential beauty of a poem by subjecting it to parody. As a student he is fully conscious of the dignity of learning, yet he loves to display it in an incongruous setting, quoting the arguments of Boethius on free will *à propos* of the fate of a cock, or putting St. Jerome on perpetual virginity into the mouth of the Wyf of Bath. One of the greatest of the world's love songs, the Song of Solomon, so haunts him with its beauty, that he echoes it in his own work:

> Rys up, my wyf, my love, my lady free;
> The turtles vois is herd, my douvé swete;
> The winter is goon, with alle his reynés weté;
> Com forth now, with thyn eyen columbyn!
> How fairer been thy brestés than is wyn!
> The gardin is enclosed al abouté;
> Com forth, my whyté spousé; out of douté,
> Thou hast me wounded in myn herte, o wyf!
> No spot of thee ne knew I al my lyf;

but he puts them in the mouth of a love-sick dotard, and adds the wicked comment 'Swiche oldé *lewed* wordes used he'. The line which occurs oftenest in his poetry, and expresses his deepest conviction, is 'pitee renneth sone in gentil herte'. But he will give it at times an outrageous context.

He is keenly sensitive to the havoc wrought on the world's happiness by inconstancy, recurring again and again with plangent beauty to the emotions of a heart-broken woman —in his early poem of Anelida's complaint, in one of his latest in the cry of the falcon in the *Squieres Tale*. *The Legend of Good Women* is not merely a poem written to order: it represents what was to him the most tragic cruelty in life. His dramatic picture of the forsaken Ariadne is among the great things in his poetry:

> Allas! for thee my herte hath now pité!
> Right in the dawening awaketh she,
> And gropeth in the bedde, and fond right noght.
> 'Allas!' quod she, 'that ever I was wroght!

I am betrayèd!' and her heer to-rentè,
And to the strondè bar-fot faste she wentè,
And cryed, 'Theseus! myn hertè swetè!
Wher be ye, that I may nat with yow metè,
And mightè thus with bestès been y-slain?'
  The holwe rokkès answerde her again;
No man she saw, and yit shynèd the monè,
And hye upon a rokkè she wentè sone,
And saw his bargè sailing in the see.
Cold wex her herte, and right thus seidè she.
'Meker than ye finde I the bestès wildè!'
Hadde he nat sinnè, that her thus begyldè?
She cryed, 'O turne again, for routhe and sinnè!
Thy bargè hath nat al his meiny innè!'
Her kerchef on a pole up stikked she,
Ascauncè that he sholde hit wel y-see,
And him remembre that she was behindè,
And turne again, and on the stronde her findè;
But al for noght; his wey he is y-goon.
And doun she fil a-swown upon a stoon;
And up she rist, and kiste, in al her carè,
The steppes of his feet, ther he hath farè.

Yet as Chaucer wrote *The Legend of Good Women* the conviction grew on him that the unrelieved gloom of this procession of nineteen deserted women was 'a thing out of nature's certain course', and his sense of humour broke in to disturb its melancholy tenor. With his task half completed he cast it aside, and even that part that he wrote he did not always treat with the seriousness which it demanded. It is significant that his solemnity gives way in that very story which, from his constant allusion to it, we know to have most deeply impressed him, the story of Dido. With an assumed naïvety he calls attention to the miraculous elements in the story:

Whan he was in the largè temple come,
I can nat seyn if that hit be possiblè,
But Venus hadde him maked invisible—
Thus seith the book, with-outen any lees;

in describing Dido's awakening passion he again plays the innocent:

> She waketh, walweth, maketh many a brayd,
> As doon thise loveres, as I have herd sayd;

finally, in the tempest scene, wherein the love of Aeneas and Dido is consummated, he adds, with a touch of sheer malice:

> She fledde her-self into a litel cavè,
> And with her wente this Eneas al-so;
> I noot, with hem if ther wente any mo;
> The autour maketh of hit no mencioun.

The story of the betrayal of Phyllis he brings to an unexpected conclusion:

> Be war, ye women, of your sotil fo,
> Sin yit this day men may ensample see;
> And trusteth, as in love, no man but me.

Chaucer wrote thus, not because he had not felt these tragedies, but because he saw that their theme, isolated from the fuller context of life, was untrue to the realities; and his sanity rebelled against a sentiment which might easily degenerate into sentimentality. Such things are, yet the world is not wholly a vale of tears. It was the very tenderness of his heart that prompted in him, as in his knight, the feeling that

> litel hevinessè
> Is right y-nough to mochel folk, I gessè.

There was much in him, as there was much in life, that could find no fit expression in *The Legend of Good Women*. He needed a wider canvas. He had found it before in *Troilus and Criseyde*, his one completed masterpiece, a tale of pathos and tragic passion, yet set in a background of comedy which gives it a true perspective; he found it again in *The Canterbury Tales*, where the Knight stands side by side with the Miller, the Friar by the poor Parson of the town, the Prioress by the Wife of Bath. *The Canterbury Tales* is only a fragment, yet here is the whole pageant of

human life, in all its colour and variety, its high romance
and matter-of-fact coarseness, its pathos and its humour.
And it is intensely alive. No significant detail escapes him,
and no detail is without significance—whether it is the
Wife of Bath's red stockings or the silk purse 'whyt as
morne milk' that hangs at the Franklin's girdle, whether
it is the peculiar pallor on the face of a man led 'toward
his deeth, wher-as him gat no grace', or the peculiar shine
on the face of a fresh country girl:

> So was it wasshen whan she leet hir werk.

With similar unerring acuteness he notes the ways of men
with one another and their varied attitudes to life, as the
readiness of the comfortably orthodox to scent heresy in
an uncomfortable sincerity, or the complacent aversion to
learning that stamps the ignorant:

> Ye, blessed be alwey a lewèd man,
> That noght but only his bilevè can!

He knows how men borrow money, not blurting out their
tiresome request, but paving the way to it by earnest solici-
tude for the welfare of their victim:

> I prey yow, cosin, wysly that ye rydè;
> Governeth yow also of your dietè
> Atemprely, and namely in this hetè.
>   .   .   .   .   .
> If any thing ther be by day or night,
> If it lye in my power and my might,
> That ye me wol comande in any wysè,
> It shal be doon, right as ye wol devysè.
>   O thing, er that ye goon, if it may be,
> I wolde prey yow; for to lenè me
> An hundred frankes.

There is no page of Chaucer without some such shrewd
revelation of the eternal comedy of life.

  'I see all the pilgrims in *The Canterbury Tales*,' wrote
Dryden, 'their humours, their features, and the very dress,
as distinctly as if I had supped with them at the Tabard.' We

might go further; for which of us, after passing an evening at an inn, would carry away so clear an impression of
our fellow guests, and that not merely of their outsides,
but of the character that their dress and manner in part
conceal, in part reveal? So life-like are their personalities
that recent criticism has been engaged in identifying many
of them with contemporaries of Chaucer with whom he
must have had a personal acquaintance. Criticism may be
right; every artist has his models, and takes his hints from
life. But his poetical characters are to be judged, not by
their closeness to a model, about which, when research has
done its worst, we care little, but by their essential truth to
human nature. Moreover, what Dryden says of the characters in *The Prologue* is even truer of Chaucer's other creations,
in *Troilus and Criseyde* and in the Tales told by the several
pilgrims. *The Prologue*, brilliant as it is, is no more than
the prologue to a real living and moving comedy. Great as
Chaucer is in significant description, he is at his greatest
when his characters reveal themselves in their action and
their talk. To his portrait of the Friar in the *Prologue* he
devotes more space than to any other character, and it is
one of the most complete and masterly; yet it pales beside
that other friar, whom we accompany on his visit to the
sick man and his good wife:

> 'Deus hic,' quod he, 'O Thomas, freend, good day,'
> Seydè this frere curteisly and softè.
> 'Thomas,' quod he, 'god yeldè yow! ful oftè
> Have I up-on this bench faren ful weel.
> Here have I eten many a mery meel;'
> And fro the bench he droof awey the cat,
> And leyde adoun his potente and his hat,
> And eek his scrippe, and sette him softè adoun.
>
> . . . .
>
> 'O derè maister,' quod this sykè man,
> 'How han ye farè sith that March bigan?
> I saugh yow noght this fourtenight or morè.'
> 'God woot,' quod he, 'laboured have I ful sorè;
> And specially, for *thy* savacioun
> Have I seyd many a precious orisoun,

And for our othere frendės, god hem blessė!
I have to-day been at your chirche at messė,

.   .   .   .

And ther I saugh our dame; a! wher is she?'
    'Yond in the yerd I trowe that she be,'
Seydė this man, 'and she wol come anon.'
    'Ey, maister! wel-come be ye, by seint John!'
Seydė this wyf, 'how fare ye hertely?'
    The frere aryseth up ful curteisly,
And hir embraceth in his armes narwe,
And kiste hir swete, and chirketh as a sparwe
With his lippės: 'damė,' quod he, 'right weel,
As he that is your servant every deel.
Thanked be god, that yow yaf soule and lyf,
Yet saugh I nat this day so fair a wyf
In al the chirchė, god so savė me!'
    'Ye, god amende defautės, sir,' quod she,
'Algatės wel-come be ye, by my fey!'

and she urges the friar to rate her husband on his irritable
temper:

    'O Thomas! Je vous dy, Thomas! Thomas!
This maketh the feend, this mostė ben amendcd.
Ire is a thing that hyė god defended,
And ther-of wol I speke a word or two.'

Before she goes off on her household duties the good wife
asks their guest whether he fancies anything for dinner:

    'Now damė,' quod he, 'Je vous dy sanz doute,
Have I nat of a capon but the livere,
And of your softė breed nat but a shivere,
And after that a rostėd piggės heed,
(But that I nolde no beest for me were deed),
Thanne haddė I with yow hoomly suffisauncė.
I am a man of litel sustenauncė.
My spirit hath his fostring in the Bible.
The body is ay so redy and penyble
To wakė, that my stomak is destroyėd.
I prey yow, damė, ye be nat anoyed,
Though I so freendly yow my conseil shewė;
By god, I wolde nat telle it but a fewė.'

'Now, sir,' quod she, 'but o word er I go;
My child is deed with-inne thise wykes two,
Sone after that ye wente out of this toun.'
   'His deeth saugh I by revelacioun,'
Seith this frere.

And so the scene proceeds, the friar now preaching his ser-
mon on anger, now urging on Thomas the efficacy of his
prayers because of his abstinence and neglect of the things of
the body, till at last the sick man's rage at his hypocrisy rises
to an ungovernable fury. The whole scene is conceived and
executed in the very finest and subtlest vein of comedy.

A like masterpiece of comic characterization is January,

             hoor and old,
And almost, god wot, on my pittès brinke,

who despite his years has learnt nothing from experience,
but after a life of debauchery thinks to renew his youth,
and make the best of both worlds by taking to himself a
young wife. And having already made up his mind he summons his friends to ask their advice, scorning the admoni-
tions of Justinus against his obvious folly, and applauding
as wisdom the transparent flatteries of Placebo. So elated
is he at the prospect of the felicity in store for him that he
fears it may imperil his chances of that future heaven which,
theologians have warned him, is only won by tribulacion
on earth; and he is hardly reassured by the suggestion that
even such a marriage as his may have its trials:

   She may be goddes mene, and goddes whippe;
   Than shal your soule up to hevene skippe
   Swifter than dooth an arwe out of the bowe!

The eager impatience with which he anticipates his happiness is drawn with irresistible humour; whilst the impending disaster is subtly suggested in that remorselessly vivid
picture of the old man as he sits up in bed and sings, obli-
vious of the scorn with which his young wife May regards
him:

   The slakkè skin aboute his nekkè shaketh,
   Whyl that he sang; so chaunteth he and craketh.

But god wot what that May thoughte in hir hertè,
Whan she him saugh up sittinge in his shertè,
In his night-cappe, and with his nekkè lenè.

Turn from this merciless exposure of a ludicrous senility
to that tragic portrait of an 'old man and a poor', vainly
seeking for that death on whom the three rioters, in the
insolence of a lustful youth, have vowed their vengeance:

Ne deeth, allas! ne wol nat han my lyf;
Thus walke I, lyk a restèlees caityf,
And on the ground, which is my modrès gatè,
I knokkè with my staf, bothe erly and latè,
And seyè, 'levè moder, leet me in!
Lo, how I vanish, flesh, and blood, and skin!
Allas! whan shul my bonès been at restè?'

And now turn to consider the serene old age of the 'verray parfit gentil knight', with his tender heart, his kindly
humour, his ripe wisdom, and you realize something of the
range and the penetration of Chaucer's vision of life.

The stories in which the Friar and old January figure as
protagonists, like several other Tales, are frankly indecent.
Chaucer had taken upon himself to depict all sorts and
conditions of men, and he gave to his churls such tales as
churls would indubitably tell. To do otherwise, as he truly
says, would be to 'falsen his materè'. He accepts from them
the dirty practical jokes and the time-worn jests at the expense of the hen-pecked or the jealous husband, and tells
them with a gusto and a brilliancy of art that testifies to his
own enjoyment. In him, as in Shakespeare, such things
were an ebullition of good spirits, and he was satisfied if he
made of them a pivot for the subtlest study of character.
As for their morality he urges that you must not make
earnest of game; whether or not you like the game is a
question of taste. It may be lamentable that such things
amuse; it may be incomprehensible; but it is a fact; and,
moreover, that they amuse not only those who are coarse
by nature but also those who have for themselves a lofty
and irreproachable standard of life. Chaucer's age was

franker than ours: after the Miller's vulgar tale we are told of the pilgrims that

> for the moré part, they loughe and pleydé,
> Ne at this tale I saugh no man him grevé,
> But it were only Osèwold the Revé,

and the Reve only objected because a fellow carpenter had been held up to ridicule. Here again, perhaps, Chaucer does not 'falsen his matere'. But I would suggest that if such things are comic they are only comic from a sense of incongruity, and that their whole humour depends ultimately upon that ideal which they seem to travesty or to outrage. Just as Falstaff's action in shamming death upon the battle-field can only be appreciated by a man with a high sense of honour, and his sublime ejaculation, 'Lord! how this world is given to lying!' by those who have a deep respect for truth, so the Wife of Bath's philosophy of life is only amusing to you in so far as you do not share it. Chaucer's indecencies, like Shakespeare's, differ from the dreary prurience of many a modern novelist in that they spring from a mind that pays full tribute to the nobler elements in life, and are not the outcome of a spurious philosophy which exaggerates the animal instincts as though they were the whole of man. No one has presented more faithfully than Chaucer the finer aspects of the relations of men and women: the spirit in which he had sketched the early portrait of Blanche the duchesse lived on through all the rough and tumble of a lifetime, till in his last period his conception of Dorigen drew from him that perfect exposition of the understanding on which alone a true love can be based:

> For o thing, sirés, saufly dar I seyé,
> That frendés everich other moot obeyé,
> If they wol longé holdén companyé.
> Love wol nat ben constreynéd by maistryé;
> Whan maistrie comth, the god of love anon
> Beteth hise winges, and farewel! he is gon!
> Love is a thing as any spirit free;
> Wommen of kinde desiren libertee,

And nat to ben constreyned as a thral;
And so don men, if I soth seyen shal.
Loke who that is most pacient in lovè,
He is at his avantage al abovè.

. . . .

Lerneth to suffre, or ellès, so moot I goon,
Ye shul it lerne, wher-so ye wole or noon.
For in this world, certein, ther no wight is,
That he ne dooth or seith som-tyme amis.

. . . .

On every wrong a man may nat be wreken.

But life is not lived uniformly upon the level of Dorigen and Arveragus; to some who fall below it Chaucer extends an infinite pity; for the most part he loses all desire to comment in sheer delight of imaginative creation. And the very comprehensiveness of his vision inspires a confidence in the truth of his ideal, which would be lost if he shrank from the baser elements of life, or presented them with the satiric bitterness of a conscious moralist, who weights the scales in favour of virtue. Moreover to him a healthier exercise than denunciation was laughter. His broad tolerance was born in part of that passion for life without which no artist can create, in part of that self-knowledge which awakened in him fellow feeling with all human frailty:

A man mot been a fool, or yong or old;
I woot it by my-self ful yore agoon.

The words and deeds of his churls call for no comment: the best criticism on the manners of the Reve or the Somnour is to be found in the bearing of the Knight who

never yet no vileinye ne saydè
In al his lyf, un-to no maner wight;

the best criticism of the morals of the Friar or the Pardoner is the life of the poor Parson:

But Cristes lore, and his apostles twelvè,
He taughte, and first he folwed it himselvè.

And let it not escape us that the gay surface of Chaucer's poetry is but the transparent veil of that deep seriousness which lies at the heart of all great artists. Just as the humour which he directed upon himself was a protection from his own intensity of feeling, so the gusto with which he threw himself into life's comedy concealed a profound sense of its inexplicable irony, and of the tears that are in human things:

> What is this world? what asketh men to have?
> Now with his love, now in his coldė grave
> Alone, with-outen any companyė.

What does it all mean? Chaucer's own reachings after an answer are evident in his absorption in astronomy, then thought to hold the secret of man's fate, in his eager study of the philosophers, with their arguments on free will and destiny. But tormented as he is at times by the mysteries he cannot solve, he has the wisdom to lay them by, and to lay them by in the spirit, not of scepticism but of humility:

> But god forbedė but men shulde levė
> Wel morė thing then men han seen with yė!
> Men shal nat wenen every-thing a lye
> But-if him-self hit seeth, or elles dooth.

Faith lies deeper than understanding. But he is no 'divinistre', his creative impulse as an artist is content with presenting the world that he knows: the wise cheerfulness with which he views it springs alike from his breadth of experience and the serenity of his faith. If the future is dark, and in the present

> this lif is as a faire
> That passeth soon as don the floures faire,

yet this he knows, that life, like the flowers, is beautiful and precious, and was meant by its Creator to be enjoyed; and he knows too, that it will only render up its full value to him who approaches it with something of the humourist's detachment.

And when we enter into his poetic world it is not hard to be convinced; for here, as Dryden said, is 'God's plenty'. There is the fresh countryside, with the 'softė greenė grass' whereon to lie and watch the spreading flowers, and with

the 'hord of apples leyd in hey or heeth', and with the
woods where the wind made

> in the leves grene a noise softe
> Acordant to the foules songe on-lofte;

and where squirelles and other bestes 'in hir maner made
festes'. And there is the rich inheritance of beauty and
wisdom in

> bokes, . . . of remembraunce the keye, . . .
> Through which that oldė thingės been in minde;

above all there are men and women, with their infinite
drollery and their noble passion, their love and faith
and courage and tenderness; and even if many of them,
like the man who 'dronke is as a mous', know they have a
home, but know not the way thither, and if a few, like the
Cook, fall into the mud by the wayside, there is also a
hearty good fellowship among them, with much pleasant
talk and laughter upon the road. It is the world of our
own experience, but richer and more vivid, moving to the
subtle and delicate music and lit up by the penetrating
vision of poetic genius.

III

TROILUS AND CRISEYDE

TROILUS AND CRISEYDE is Chaucer's first and greatest adventure in that world of every day where his genius found its natural home. Under the guidance of his French masters he had perfected himself in the technique of his art; and his irrepressible sense of actual life had broken ever more insistently through their prescribed conventions of dream and allegory: his advance towards a fuller freedom had received a marked impetus by his discovery of the great Italians, with their wider outlook and their more vital sense of the realities. With their help he had learned, among other lessons, how to tell a story directly and simply, with due emphasis on character and significant situation. But this art he had as yet employed only to give verisimilitude to the improbable or the miraculous. His Constance, indeed, compels poetic faith, but who can believe in her adventures? The patient Griselda he has portrayed with an exquisitely delicate pathos; yet, as he admits himself,

> It were ful hard to finde now a dayes
> In al a toun Grisildes three or two.

Troilus and Criseyde, despite its classical names and its medieval setting, is a page out of the book of modern everyday life, illuminated with an imaginative insight into character only rivalled by Shakespeare and Browning among our poets, and by a few of our greatest novelists.

The story was already popular before Chaucer handled it. It had first taken definite shape in the twelfth century, as one of the episodes with which Benoit de Sainte Maure had embellished his lengthy romance upon the Trojan war. There we read how Calchas, a Trojan priest, deserted to the Greeks, and left his daughter Briseida behind him in the city. 'She was very comely,' says Benoit, 'neither too little nor too big: she had wide open and beautiful eyes, and her wit was quick and ready. She was graceful and of a demure countenance. She was well beloved and could also love well, but her heart was changeable.' No sooner has she given her love to Troilus than her father sends for her to join him. At first she is inconsolable, but she is admired in the Greek camp for her sprightly wit, so that in four days she has no longer any desire to return to the city. Diomed makes advances to her, but she excuses herself courteously from granting him her love *at that time*. But a little later she relents, making to herself the charming excuse: 'I was in mortal anguish at receiving no comfort from Troilus. I should have died outright had I not sought to console myself.'

The popularity of Benoit's romance led Guido di Colonna, about a century later, to make a free Latin version of it. But when Boccaccio took up the theme in his *Il Filostrato* (1338), he moulded it afresh to suit his own purposes, and shifted its centre of gravity. What in Benoit was merely an episode introduced to diversify more important matter— the heroic exploits of Greeks and Trojans—becomes to him the sole plot, to which the war is but a faint background; and further, whilst Benoit concentrates his attention on the fickleness of Briseida, her intrigue with Diomed being as important to him as her love for Troilus, Boccaccio's sole theme is Troilo's constancy and tragic passion, to which Griseida (as he calls her) is entirely subordinated. He had his own personal reasons for this treatment of the story. He was himself deeply enamoured of Maria d'Aquino, wife of a Neapolitan noble and daughter of the Countess d'Aquino and Robert, King of Naples; and when she left the city Boccaccio wrote this poem for her in order to voice his ardent devotion, his longings in her absence, and the torments that he would suffer should she prove unfaithful to him. Naturally, therefore, *Il Filostrato* is a lyrical romance, with Troilo for its main character; the faithless Griseida, as he takes care to point out, bears no likeness to Maria save in her beauty, her courtesy, and all that is praiseworthy; but in the grieving of Troilo, he tells her, 'you may understand and recognize my very accents, my tears, and sighs, and anguish'. And whilst Benoit begins his story in *medias res*, when Briseida is summoned to join her father, concentrating upon the grief of the lovers at her departure, and on Diomed's subsequent wooing of her, Boccaccio devotes his three longest cantos to the birth, growth, and consummation of Troilo's passion, three more to that part of the theme elaborated by Benoit, and a further three to Troilo's anxieties in her absence and the growing anguish of his disillusionment.

Il Filostrato is a work of great poetic beauty; moreover it is essentially modern in spirit; and charged as it is with the poet's own sensuous passion, it contrasts forcibly with the spiritual idealism of the *Vita Nuova* or of Petrarch's affected Platonism, and finds fuller response in the unregenerate heart of man. With its wealth of realistic incident and its vivid psychological truth to the fluctuating emotions of its hero, one can readily understand how it would appeal to Chaucer, who had but lately escaped from the enchanted garden of the Rose. But though he closely followed Boccaccio in the main outlines of the story and in much of its detail, he had his own conception both of form and characters, and he reshaped the whole in his imagination. Taking a larger canvas than his model, he gave to his work a new perspective. It has been calculated that whilst his poem is nearly half as long again as Boccaccio's, less than a third of it is drawn from him; and even where Chaucer translates literally, he often gives his own turn to the meaning. He applies to three characters that full psychological analysis which the Italian had given to only one; two of them he entirely recasts; he allows himself a place as a commentator; gives to his scenes a still fuller and more vivid realism and to his dialogue a greater naturalness; and sets his tragic story in a background of comedy which enhances both its poignancy and its truth to life. The romance which Boccaccio had seen merely from Troilo's point of view Chaucer sees dramatically, as a rounded whole. The *Troilus and Criseyde* has justly been regarded as our first great psychological novel.

Yet modern as are the poems of both Boccaccio and Chaucer in their spirit and treatment, they can only be understood in relation to the set conventions of the *amour courtois* on which they are based. These *regulae amoris*, as codified by one Andreas Capellanus in his *De arte amandi*, regard love as a passion that can only exist outside the marriage tie. But that a woman is married is no valid excuse for her not loving, and she cannot rightly refuse her favours to a lover whom her beauty has enslaved. She must not, of course, yield to him at once; for we only prize what is hardly won. Hence, whatever the lady's real feelings, she must long maintain an indifferent, if not a haughty, demeanour towards her lover, thus putting to the test the seriousness of his devotion; only gradually, after a long suit, must she admit him to her favour; and this time of probation, in which the lover feels that his ultimate success is uncertain, is a time of anguish for him, wherein his sincerity is proved by his pallor, loss of appetite, and sleepless nights. But though infidelity to her husband is finally expected of her, infidelity in love, alike for man or woman, is the greatest of crimes against the code. The supreme virtue is not chastity, but constancy. For this love, though sensual, is not the mere gratification of animal passion, but draws into itself all the idealism of medieval woman-worship. It is distinguished from lust by its regenerating influence upon the whole of life. It is the motive force of every human excellence. The lover, conscious of his own unworthiness, is stimulated to higher endeavour: he is not only braver in battle, but modest, courteous, friendly to all men, and lavish in his generosity.

Another fundamental rule of the code, forced upon it doubtless by the fact that this love was illicit and anti-social, was that it must be secret. There must be no scandal. The act in itself is wholly praiseworthy, the only sin lies in its discovery. The man who boasts of his love and proclaims it is only less base than he who is unfaithful to it. Yet despite this, the lover is permitted a confidant and intermediary, and seeing that this love is so ennobling, it is the bounden duty of a brother knight to do all in his power to further the success of his friend. It was natural that Boccaccio, writing his poem for a lady of the Court, should wish to make it conform as far as possible with the conventions of the *amour courtois*. The exigencies of the plot he had chosen prevented him from giving his heroine a husband, but he turns the maiden Briseida of his original into a young widow, and adds to the story the character of Pandaro, the confidential friend. But it is clear also that he adopted the code because it gave an air of respectability to his own passion rather than from any real belief in its doctrines. Chaucer, as Mr. Lewis has recently pointed out,[1] took it far more seriously; he saw that with all its unrealities, it yet corresponded in its idealism with much that is deep and permanent in human nature: hence he altered whatever in Boccaccio seemed 'amiss', though, characteristically enough, he usually attributes to his 'auctor' just those points wherein he diverges most markedly from him.

The love which Boccaccio depicts is in reality the intrigue of an amorous woman who does not wish to be cumbered with a husband; and the normal attitude with regard to extra-marital relations is constantly breaking through his poem, to confound the principles of the *amour courtois*. When Troilo confesses to Pandaro that he loves Griseida, Pandaro's only fear is that she may prove too virtuous: when Chaucer's Pandarus receives the news, his knowledge of Criseyde's virtue gives him a ground for hope:

> That sith thy lady vertuous is al,
> So folweth it that ther is som pitee
> Amongès alle thise othere in general;

when Pandaro first broaches to Griseida the subject of Troilo's passion she meets him with the retort, 'Who has the right to have my love, if he should not first become my husband?' and when she decides to accept Troilo the thought of her impropriety and the necessary secrecy adds

[1] 'What Chaucer really did to *Il Filostrato*', by C. S. Lewis. *Essays and Studies by Members of the English Association*, 1931.

a spice of zest to her adventure. Chaucer significantly rejects both these incidents. It is significant, too, that the praise of love and its ennobling influence, put by Boccaccio into the mouth of Troilo in the ecstasy of triumph, is taken by Chaucer for the proem of his central book; and it thus expresses, not the sentiment of an interested actor in the story, but the accepted conviction of its narrator. To Chaucer there is nothing scandalous in the love of Troilus and Criseyde; his poem is a tragedy, not of immoral, but simply of inconstant love.

Inevitably, this affects his conception of the character of Pandarus, who is thereby relieved of much of the odium which his name suggests to modern ears. For just as this chivalric love, with its insistence upon faithfulness to the death, and its regenerating effect upon the lover, differs from mere lust—

> The expense of spirit in a waste of shame . . .
> Enjoy'd no sooner but despised straight;
> Past reason hunted; and no sooner had,
> Past reason hated,

so will those men differ who act as accessories to the one or to the other. As Troilus remarks, and Chaucer would have agreed with him:

> wyde-where is wist
> How that there is dyversitee requered
> Bitwixen thinges lyke, as I have lered.

Pandarus accepted the code no less than Troilus, and it is noteworthy that most of its doctrines are placed in his mouth. He has no qualms of conscience when he asserts that it is his niece's duty to love and cherish a worthy knight, and that unless she does so he 'holds it for a vice'. But he is also a man of the world; he knows the risks and the dangers; and these, indeed, seriously trouble him, and in the end confound him. There is always the chance of discovery; and again there is the danger that one or other of the lovers may prove false to the ideal, so that, in the issue, he will have performed no knightly service, but

betrayed his niece, and branded himself as a procurer.
Hence, though he is confident of his friend's integrity, he
does not forget to urge upon him the solemn duties of a
chivalrous lover, to

> keep hir out of blame,
> Sin thou art wys, and save alwey hir name.

But while Pandarus's attitude to the *amour courtois* is sympathetic, it is also ironical. Chaucer's consummate genius
saw in this third character the novelist's golden opportunity
for presenting the story from another angle. Boccaccio's
Pandaro is Griseida's cousin, a man of the same age as
Troilo, and wholly of a piece with him: Chaucer makes
him Criseyde's uncle, gives him the advantage of a few
years' experience, and endows him with his own matchless
gift of humour, thus opening the door of this hot-house of
romantic passion to let in the bracing air of the world of
common sense. Pandarus becomes in his hands the first
great triumph of English humour, to whom, in all the great
gallery of our comic characters, Falstaff alone is comparable for brilliance of conception and execution. And like
Falstaff he has been generally misunderstood. He is sometimes spoken of as though he were a battered man of the
world, a clever but unprincipled and cynical old jester.
But Chaucer saw him as a man of youngish middle age,
with principles of his own, even if they are not ours, highly
respected in Troy as a man of affairs, weighty enough in
counsel to be kept closeted for a whole day in conference
with King Priam. Nor is he a cynic, who regards love as
mere sensual appetite, and derides an emotion he cannot
understand. He knows the pangs of despised love, for he
has himself been long an unsuccessful suitor, and if his own
passion has not plumbed the depths known to Troilus, it
is at least so serious that he has kept faithful to it through
years of disappointment. Yet, for all this, he is a humorist,
and the true humorist does not confine his sallies to what
is in itself merely absurd: he turns his shafts against the
element of the absurd in what he himself accepts as both

serious and admirable. Pandarus can laugh at his own
thwarted passion, and accept with imperturbable good
nature the jests of others at his expense; whilst he is
realist enough to pierce through the subterfuges and illusions of lovers who, because they are conscious of the idealistic element in their passion, persuade themselves that it
is wholly Platonic, and either refuse to recognize its physical basis, or think that they will be content, or indeed
have the self-control, to stop short of its full satisfaction.
But, above all, his irony exposes the lover's preposterous
absorption in his own woes, as though nothing in the world
existed outside them. For Pandarus has himself the true
gusto for life, and his own experience has taught him that
even for a man crossed in love the world holds plenty that
makes it well worth while. First of all there are other, less
harrowing, affections. He has a kindly feeling towards the
world at large, he is genuinely fond of his niece, he is devoted to his young friend Troilus and finds a real pleasure
in accomplishing his happiness. The prayer of thanksgiving
that he offers, when at last Criseyde plights her troth to
Troilus, is not mere satisfaction at the success of his scheming, it springs from an overflowing heart. Moreover, he
loves the good things of this world, food and dance and
song and good company and talk; but, finally, he is really
pleased with himself, and in self-esteem lies a perennial
source of earthly happiness. He is delighted with his own
importance, with his shrewdness of observation and the
worldly wisdom that has accrued from it, with his ready
wit, and his stock of wise saws and modern instances, which
trip from his tongue both in and out of season, with that insight into character which gives him the power to mould the
fates of those who have less wit and experience than he; and
he plays his cards with the skill of an adept and the zest of
one who, playing keenly to win, yet loves the game for its own
sake. With his practical common sense and his humorous
but sympathetic detachment, he serves as an incomparable foil alike to Troilus, who is in the grip of an over-
mastering passion, and to the weak and yielding Criseyde.

The characters of both hero and heroine Chaucer has altered from Boccaccio's conception in such a way as to give Pandarus a fuller scope. In Troilus, indeed, he makes no radical change. But he endows him with a simpler nature, and a modesty, even shyness, which gives to him both charm and pathos, while at the same time it makes him more dependent upon Pandarus's support. Their relationship is brought out with a rich ironic humour in the first scene between them, where Pandarus, finding his friend lying grievously sick, worms from him his secret sorrow. Affecting to believe that Troilus is afraid of the Greeks, he tries first to rouse him by anger; then, when he learns that his malady is love, assures him that weeping and wallowing will not gain his mistress, reminds him of how Niobe wept herself to marble, and overwhelms him with reasons why he can safely make of him a confidant. And when this eloquence proves of no avail, he compares him to the ass that hears the sound of the harp, but through his bestiality, is deaf to the tune. His garrulousness at last takes effect:

> freend, (says Troilus) though that I stillè lye,
> I am not deef; now pees, and cry no morè;
> For I have herd thy wordès and thy lorè;
> But suffre me my mischef to biwaylè,
> For thy proverbès may me nought avaylè.
>
> Nor other curè canstow noon for me.
> Eek I nil not be cured, I wol deyè;
> What knowe I of the quenè Niobe?
> Lat be thyne olde ensaumples, I thee preyè.

But Pandarus is not thus to be put off: if Troilus dies without declaring his devotion, his lady will certainly think that fear of the Greeks, and not love for her, has killed him: it is clearly his duty to be fresh and green, and always eager to serve her: only let him make a clean breast of it and he (Pandarus) will help to win her. At last Troilus, struggling with his diffidence, confesses that his 'swete fo' is called Criseyde,

> And wel nigh with the word for fere he deydè.

Pandarus praises him for his choice of so virtuous a lady, and assures him of a happy issue; every one, he says, feels love either human or celestial,

> And for to speke of hir in special,
> Hir beautee to bithinken and hir youthe,
> It sit hir nought to be celestial
> As yet, though that hir liste bothe and couthe.

Throughout the whole scene the rich common sense and worldly wisdom of Pandarus throw into humorous relief the timid self-distrust of his lovesick friend.

The two characters stand out in the same vivid contrast in the last book of the poem, when Pandarus, from being the prime mover in the action, becomes little more than the spectator, powerless to stay the tragedy that he has helped to set in motion. After Criseyde has departed for the Greek camp Troilus sends for Pandarus, and declaring that he cannot live without her, gives elaborate instructions for his 'sepulture'. Pandarus justly points out that before this lovers have been parted a fortnight and have yet survived —and he recommends him to try a change of air. They go together to stay with Sarpedon in the suburbs, and are royally entertained; but on the fourth day Troilus says that he can't bear it any longer: he *must* go back to Troy. Pandarus, who is thoroughly enjoying Sarpedon's hospitality, points out how odd it would look, after promising a week's visit, to go away so soon, and he protests against cutting it short. They leave the day before Criseyde is due to return. As they approach the city Troilus's spirits rise:

> 'now god me grace sende,
> That I may finden, at myn hom-cominge,
> Criseyde comen!' and ther-with gan he singe.

Pandarus, with his fuller knowledge of Criseyde, already feels a little sceptical; but he pretends to agree, and jests with him to keep his heart up. They visit Criseyde's palace and find it desolate. Troilus is in despair. In his sorrow he gives himself up to fantasy, imagining that every one he meets by the way notices his deathly pallor, and feels pity

for his misery; he walks upon the city walls, looking towards the tent of Calchas; at one time the air that blows
from it is sweet and healthful, for Criseyde has breathed
it; at another it seems laden with his lady's sighs:

> for in non othere place
> Of al this toun, save onliche in this space,
> Fele I no wind that souneth so lyk peyne;
> It seyth, 'allas! why twinned be we tweyne?'

In the night before the tenth day he is unable to sleep;
and early the next morning he sends for Pandarus to go
with him to the walls to look out for Criseyde.

> Til it was noon, they stoden for to see
> Who that ther come; and every maner wight,
> That cam fro fer, they seyden it was she,
> Til that they coudé knowen him a-right,
> Now was his herté dul, now was it light;
> And thus by-japéd stonden for to staré
> Abouté nought, this Troilus and Pandaré.

Then Troilus explains that of course she cannot come
early—her old father will insist upon her dining before
she leaves; Pandarus jumps at the idea:

> it may wel be, certeyn;
> And for-thy lat *us* dyne, I thee biseche;
> And after noon than mayst *thou* come ayeyn.

But though Pandarus suggests, by his use of the pronoun
'us' when he speaks of dinner and 'thou' of the return after
dinner, that he is looking forward to a little time off, his
good nature overcomes his weariness, and he is back again
with his friend in the afternoon.

Troilus still clings to the idea that it is her father who is
detaining her, and he tells the porter not to close the gate:

> The day goth faste, and after that comth eve,
> And yet com nought to Troilus Criseydé.
> He loketh forth by hegge, by tree, by greve,
> And fer his heed over the wal he leydé.

At last he turns to Pandarus and says he understands how
it is. Criseyde is prudent, and has resolved to return by

night. He sees something move in the twilight and thinks it must be she, but it is only a cart. But Pandarus has already formed his own conclusions, though he keeps them to himself. And now Troilus thinks he must have miscounted the days, and on the morrow spends his time as before. And so for six days. Then he falls a hopeless prey to jealousy, and his distress becomes apparent;

> And who-so axed him wher-of him smerte,
> He seyde, his harm was al aboute his herte.

He has a dream, which he rightly interprets to signify that he is betrayed, yet when Cassandra supports his interpretation, he passionately refuses to believe her. He writes pathetic letters to Criseyde and receives ambiguous replies. But he is not fully convinced till the brooch which he had given her on parting is found on Diomed's armour. His lament is told with a touching beauty:

> 'Was ther non other broche yow listè letè
> To feffè with your newè love,' quod he,
> 'But thilkè broche that I, with terès wetè,
> Yow yaf, as for a remembraunce of me?
> Non other cause, allas, ne haddè ye
> But for despyt, and eek for that ye mentè
> Al-outrely to shewen your ententè!
>
> Through which I see that clene out of your mindè
> Ye han me cast, and I ne can nor may,
> For al this world, with-in myn hertè findè
> T'unloven yow a quarter of a day!
> In cursed tyme I born was, weylaway!
> That ye, that doon me al this wo endurè,
> Yet love I best of any creaturè.'

Boccaccio, in relating this incident, emphasizes the contrast between the ease with which Griseida has cast Troilo off, and the impossibility that he can ever forget her. 'You have cast me utterly from your bosom, and I against my will keep your fair face still pictured in my mind with tormenting sorrow.' But the language of Chaucer has an exquisite pathos, and a simplicity which, like so much of our greatest poetry, trembles on the verge of prose:

> and I ne can nor may,
> For al this world, with-in myn hertè findè
> T'unloven yow a quarter of a day!

and whereas Boccaccio's Troilo calls upon the thunder-bolts of Jove to destroy her in whose bosom are lies, deceit, and betrayal, the last words of Troilus are merely a tender, loving reproach:

> But trewely, Criseydè, swetè may,
> Whom I have ay with al my might y-served,
> That ye thus doon, I have it nought deserved.

And Pandarus, in the presence of this tragic sorrow, stands abashed, and can only stammer out a few broken words of helpless sympathy—he 'wolde amende it, wiste he how'.

Chaucer's Criseyde, likè his Pandarus, is a wholly original conception, and no less masterly in its subtlety and insight. Boccaccio's Griseida is deeply interested in Troilo from the first. Though she affects some reluctance, Pandaro has no trouble in pressing his friend's suit; and if she hangs back it is not from modesty but rather to stimulate her lover's longings. She soon becomes as eager as Troilo for their union, herself makes the assignation with him, and meets him with the frank and full-blooded abandon of the southern temperament. And though her affection for Troilo is genuine enough when she is with him, she yields to Diomed's persuasion with an equal readiness, and is in-capable of any remorse for her infidelity. Criseyde belongs to a wholly different world. If she is not, as some critics have tried to make out, an ignorant girl decoyed from innocence by an unscrupulous pandar, still less is she the practised coquette of a naturally sensual disposition. She is, indeed, something far more complex, more subtle, and one may add, more commonly met in life than either. With all that artless gaiety, naïve simplicity, and real tenderness that form so much of her charm, she is a woman who is perfectly aware alike of the current ideals of love and of the usages of society. But she is essentially timid and has, moreover, an innate modesty of nature which shrinks from the idea of any lover for herself. In marriage her heart has not been seriously engaged; now that she is a widow, young as she is, she is fancy free; and happy in the company of her friends, she has no desire to change her state. Yet in her very timidity lie the seeds of weakness. Vacillating in her moods, and unable to resist the impulse of the moment or resolutely to pursue a settled course of action, she is always prone, though she is herself unconscious of it, to turn to others for support, and, when she fondly imagines that she is making up her own mind, is swayed by the influence of characters stronger than her own.

Chaucer's delineation of her gradual yielding to Troilus is among the most masterly things in our literature. Pandarus has to use all his wiles to overcome her natural aversion to a lover, playing in turn upon her womanly fears, her curiosity, her affection for him and dependence on his judgement, her inherent tenderness of heart. Their first interview is presented in the finest vein of high comedy. Pandarus calls at her palace and finds her sitting in her paved parlour with her maidens, one of whom is reading aloud. When he enters she gets up, and greeting him with the remark that she dreamt of him the night before, sets him down beside her on the bench. 'I am sorry to interrupt your reading,' says Pandarus; 'what is the book? is it a tale of love?' Shaking her head at him and with a little laugh at his expense, 'Uncle, your mistress is not here', she tells him that it is the Tale of Thebes. 'Ah,' he replies, 'I know the book well enough, put it aside and let us have a dance in observance of May.' Criseyde's sense of the proprieties is a little shocked. 'Are you mad, uncle? is that a widow's life? Really, you frighten me sometimes, you are so wild.' 'Well,' he replies, 'yet coude I telle a thing to doon you pleye.'

> 'Now uncle dere', quod she, 'tel it us
> For goddes love; is than th'assege aweye?
> I am of Grekes so ferd that I deye.'

'Better than that,' says Pandarus. 'Better!' says Criseyde, 'you are joking as usual.' 'Well, anyhow, I am not going to tell you,' says Pandarus, 'it would make you too set up with yourself.'

Never before was Criseyde so bitten with curiosity, but with a sigh she promises that if he doesn't wish to tell her she won't annoy him by asking any questions, and they sit down, 'as freendes doon', to talk on all manner of things both grave and gay. In the course of conversation she asks after Hector. Pandarus at once seizes the opening:

> 'Ful wel, I thanke it god,' quod Pandarus,
> 'Save in his arm he hath a litel woundė;
> And eek his fresshė brother Troilus,
> The wysė worthy Ector the secoundė,
> In whom that every vertu list aboundė.'

'Ah yes,' agrees Criseyde, 'I like to see a king's son both brave and virtuous,

> For greet power and moral vertu here
> Is selde y-seye in o persone y-fere.'

'Only too true', says Pandarus, and he proceeds to draw a vivid portrait of the beauty and virtue and prowess of Troilus, and then gets up to go. Criseyde protests. What is the matter with him that he is so soon tired of her company? She has heaps of things to ask him about her private affairs. They sit down again to a long talk. At last Pandarus says he really must be off. 'But first,' he says, 'let's have a dance, and cast off your widow's weeds, so lucky a woman as you ought not to disfigure yourself.' 'Ah well bethought', says Criseyde, 'do tell me what you are driving at.' 'No,' he replies, 'these things need leisure, and besides, you might take it amiss, and I should be very sorry for that, for next to my mistress, you are dearer to me than any one.' 'Yes, dear uncle, and I love no one better than you, so do give up your strange speech and tell me; I promise not to be offended.' Pandarus coughs a little and after more beating about the bush looks at her so earnestly that she

feels quite uncomfortable. 'Lord,' she says, 'did you never
see me before?' At last he brings it out. 'Troilus is madly
in love with you and unless you take pity on him, he will
die. I need hardly say,' he adds, 'that I should not mention it unless his intentions were honourable.' Criseyde is
not deceived by this assurance, but in order to be quite
certain of his meaning she asks him what she ought to do
about it, and he replies 'Give love for love, while you are
yet young'.

Criseyde bursts out crying, for she is really distressed.
'What am I to do', she says, 'when my best friend gives me
such counsel? I should have thought you would have been
the first person to condemn me if I committed such folly.'
But he protests that he meant no harm or villainy. She
will be wicked to cause the death of Troilus; as for him he
will not survive his friend; and telling her that it will be a
long time before she sees him again, he starts up to go. But
Criseyde catches hold of him. She is terrified at the thought
of her uncle's death. She knows his devotion to Troilus;
she knows, too, the awful tragedies often brought about
by thwarted love. What a scandal it would be if Troilus
burst in upon her and killed himself in her presence! What
would people say of her? After all there is nothing 'un-
right' about her uncle's request. But she must play slyly:
perhaps by temporizing she may save her uncle, and yet
avoid taking a lover; and why not accept his proferred
devotion and yet keep him at a distance? But, she protests,
nothing will induce her to take a lover against her will, and
if more is asked of her than she can honourably give, she
will refuse, whatever the consequences. 'Of course,' replies
Pandarus; and they fall to other topics. But Criseyde's
mind naturally reverts to what her uncle has told her, and
after a little she asks him how he had discovered Troilus's
secret. 'Then Pandarus a litel gan to smyle', for he per-
ceives that her curiosity is fully awakened; and he goes
further, taking it for granted that she will accept his love:

> Ther werè never two so wel y-met,
> Whan ye ben his al hool, as he is yourè:

But she cuts him short:

> 'Nay, therof spak I not, a, ha!' quod she,
> 'As helpe me god, ye shenden every deel!'

(You spoil everything.) Pandarus protests that he meant nothing; and at last really takes his leave.

Criseyde goes up to her closet and sits down to think, 'as stille as any stoon', and the work which Pandarus had so cunningly begun pursues its natural course in her simple mind. After all, she reflects, there is nothing to be afraid of, a man may love till his heart bursts and a woman need not return it unless she likes; and as she sits thinking she hears a cry outside in the street. Troilus is returning in triumph from the battle. Her maidens rush to the window and throw open the lattice, and Troilus rides slowly by. The sight of him thrills her, 'who yaf me drinke?' (am I bewitched?) she asks herself; and as it flashes through her mind that this is the man who is dying for her love, she blushes, and pulls in her head from the window. She 'rolls up and down in her thought' his prowess, his renown and 'eek his gentilnesse', but most of all that his distress was all for her: assuredly, she concludes,

> 'it was a routhe
> To sleen swich oon, if that he mente trouthe.'

And now, Chaucer interposes, some people may object that she loved him too quickly, but

> I sey nought that she so sodeynly
> Yaf him hir love, but that she gan enclyne
> To lyke him first, and I have told yow why.

When Troilus has passed she sits down once more to think it out, and all the different reasons for and against accepting him pass in turn through her mind. 'Even if I don't give him my love I ought to accord him some slight show of favour: after all he is the king's son; if I rebuff him he may hold me in despite and his love turn to hate; would it be wise to risk this? There is measure in all things, drunkenness is no argument for total abstinence: after all he is virtuous and not a boaster; and suppose people did say that he was in love with me, what harm would there be in that? Plenty of women in the town have their admirers, and are they the worse for it? Anyhow, I can't prevent him.' And to this succeeds a charming little piece of vanity. 'He could have any one in the town that he liked and yet he has chosen me; and no wonder; for, though I shouldn't like any one to know I thought so, I *am* one of the most beautiful women in Troy. Moreover, I am my own mistress, a free woman; supposing I should come to love him, what then? I am not a nun. Provided I keep my honour and my name where would be the harm? But there is another side to the matter. What of the dredful joye, the constreynt, the peyne of the stormy life of lovers, the wicked tongues that slander them, the treachery and the betrayal so often a woman's fate?' Yet, she thinks, 'nothing venture nothing have', and so 'twixt hope and fear, now hot, now cold, she descends from her closet and joins her friends without. And as she walks round the garden arm in arm with them, Antigone starts singing, and her song is all in praise of love. 'Is there indeed such bliss among lovers?' asked Criseyde. 'Yea, surely', replies Antigone, 'when it is real love and not mere passion.' Criseyde prudently changes the subject—'it is getting late', she says; but the words of the song have sunk into her heart, and love frightens her less than it did before. And now evening comes on apace:

> And whytė thingės wexen dimme and donne
> For lak of light, and sterres for to appere,

and they go in to bed. All is hushed and still, and as Criseyde lies awake, the mysterious beauty of the night attuned to her mood of tenderness,

> A nightingale, upon a cedre grenė,
> Under the chambre-wal ther as she lay,
> Ful loude sang ayein the mone shene,
> Paraunter, in his briddes wyse, a lay
> Of love, that made hir herte fresh and gay.

At last she falls asleep, and dreams that an eagle swoops
down and rends out her heart, leaving his own in its place,
and yet she feels no hurt.

The next day Pandarus appears, and a scene follows, as
natural and delightful in its comedy as the former. He
enters with a jest at his own ill success in love, and Criseyde
gaily responds to his mood. They go out arm in arm into
the garden and he presents a letter from Troilus. Criseyde's
first instinct is one of fear; she draws back and refuses to
take it. Pandarus stares at her. Would he have brought it
if there were any harm in it? and he thrusts it into her
bosom, daring her to cast it away while all her women are
looking. 'I can abyde til they be goon', she says with a
smile, 'and anyhow *you* must answer it, for nothing will induce me to;' but she takes the first opportunity to slip away
and read it, and when she returns, the gaiety with which she
treats her uncle is proof that it has not displeased her.

They sit down to dinner, and when the meal is over
Pandarus, who has arranged that Troilus should pass along
the street, draws her to the window by putting her an innocent question about the opposite house. He asks her how
she liked the letter:

> Therwith al rosy hewėd tho wex she,
> And gan to humme, and seydė, 'so I trowe'.

She still makes some demur at answering it, she does not
know what to say, she has never written a love-letter, and
at last, when it is done, she gives it to her uncle with the
words,

> I never dide a thing with morė peynė
> Than wrytė this, to which ye me constreynė.

Then, just as Pandarus is urging her to play the tyrant no
longer, Troilus rides by and humbly salutes her. Pandarus
feels that the iron is hot and strikes at once:

> 'nece, I pray yow hertely,
> Tel me that I shal axen yow a lytė.
> A womman, that were of his deeth to wytė,

With-outen his gilt, but for hir lakked routhė,
Were it wel doon?' Quod she, 'nay, by my trouthė!'

But she is still determined to hold back, and to 'guerdon
him with no-thing but with sighte'. Pandarus, however, is
well content with his progress, for he knows her better
than she knows herself.

Days pass; the lovers salute each other in the street and
exchange letters and messages; but whilst Criseyde has no
desires beyond this distant homage, the longings of Troilus
become more and more unbearable. At last Pandarus plots
for him a surprise meeting with Criseyde at the house of
Deiphebus. Troilus has prepared an elaborate address, but
as soon as he sees her, he blushes violently,

And sire, his lesson, that he wendė connė,
To preyen hir, is thurgh his wit y-ronnė,

and he can bring out nothing but 'mercy, swete herte!'
Criseyde, however, likes him none the worse for that. After
a while he summons up courage to beg her to accept his
humble service, and overcome as she is by his distress and
by his evident sincerity, her pity melts into love; if he will
swear to attempt no more sovereignty over her than is
right in such a case, and will submit to her chiding when
he does amiss, she will return his devotion:

'And shortly, derė herte and al my knight,
Beth glad, and draweth yow to lustinessė,
And I shal trewėly, with al my might,
Your bittre tornen al in-to swetnessė;
If I be she that may yow do gladnessė,
For every wo ye shal recovere a blissė;'
And him in armės took, and gan him kissė.

Pandarus is in ecstasies, and promises that as soon as may
be he will arrange a secret meeting for them at his house.
And Criseyde, who is now completely won, makes no
demur.

Yet when he invites her to come and sup with him,
her fears again get the upper hand, and she makes

excuses—the weather is too bad, and . . . will Troilus be
there?

> He swor hir, 'nay, for he was out of towne,'
> And seydė, 'nece, I posė that he were,
> Yow thurfte never have the morė fere.
> For rather than men mighte him ther aspyė,
> Me werė lever a thousand-fold to dyė.'

He takes it for granted that fear of discovery is the
reason for her reluctance; and in the end she consents
to come, though she knows, of course, why she has been
invited.

But at night, when she learns that Troilus is concealed
in the house, she has another access of real fear and distress,
and she would draw back if she could: she wants to call
her maidens, to put off seeing him till the morning, to
send him her ring in token of her affection; and Pandarus
has much ado to get her to receive him. It is not coquet-
tishness; it is a genuine and to her temperament a wholly
natural shrinking from the consequences of the course into
which she has allowed herself to drift. And yet she is no
less sincere when she breathes into the ear of her lover, as
he calls upon her to yield to his caresses:

> Ne haddė I er now, my swete herte dere,
> Ben yolde, y-wis, I werė now not herė!

Now that she has taken the plunge, and there is no going
back, Troilus is the only precious thing in her life. No
lover in this world of change ever spoke words more tender
or more sincerely from the heart, nor spoke them in a
fuller confidence of their immutable truth:

> Ye be so depe in-with myn hertė gravė,
> That, though I wolde it turne out of my thought,
> As wisly verray god my soulė savė,
> To dyen in the peyne, I coudė nought!
> And, for the love of god that us hath wrought,
> Lat in your brayn non other fantasyė
> So crepė, that it causė me to dyė!

And that ye me wolde han as faste in mindè
As I have yow, that wolde I yow bi-sechè;
And, if I wistè soothly that to findè,
God mightè not a poynt my joyès echè!
But, hertè myn, with-outè morè spechè,
Beth to me trewe, or elles were it routhè;
For I am thyn, by god and by my trouthè!

When she is forced to depart to the Greek camp Troilus is
not more heart-broken than she. The idea that she could
be inconstant never crosses her mind. On recovering from
her first shock of grief her lover's despair seems to her unreasonable—a weakness to which *her* love can rise superior.
After all, their separation will only be for a time; and she
can easily arrange to be back in ten days. His suggestion
that they should flee together she rejects as shameful; he
would be deserting his country in its sore need; and their
love, of which the beauty lies partly in its secrecy, would be
branded as a public scandal; and when he reiterates his
prayer she feels that it implies a wholly unwarranted reflection upon her;

I see wel now that ye mistrusten me;
For by your wordès it is wel y-sene:

if he knew how sorely he wounded her he would 'cease of
this'. She is quite confident of her ability to wheedle her
father into letting her return:

I am not so nyce a wight
That I ne can imaginen a way
To come ayein that day that I have hight.

In all this, says Chaucer, she 'spak right as she mente'.
And so, sad as she is when Diomed conducts her to the
Greek camp, she is convinced that she will soon return to
the city. But Diomed has neither the diffidence nor the
chivalry of Troilus. Astute and self-confident, his attitude to life is summed up in his reflection: 'he is a fool
that wol for-yete himselve'; and acting in accordance with
his cynical creed, he takes every advantage of Criseyde's

weakness, and the instinct which prompts her to lean upon any available support. He wastes no time in beating about the bush. Pretending at first to sympathize with her grief at leaving Troy, he asks her to look upon him as a brother. He will devote himself to her service, for he loves her at first sight. She pays little heed to him; indeed, so wrapt is she in her sorrow that she only hears a word or two of what he is saying; yet her instinctive fear for the future, just as for long it had kept her from the arms of Troilus, now draws her insensibly to Diomed. Afraid of making an enemy, she thanks him for his friendship and promises to do what she can to please him. In her father's tent she bewails bitterly that she is powerless to return to Troy. For resourceful as she was before the event, when she is faced with opposition and danger she has neither courage nor initiative. If she does not keep her promise to the day Troilus will think her false. But if she is caught stealing away at night she may be taken for a spy; nay worse, she may even fall into the hands of a ravisher. But she does not give up hope, and rehearsing in her mind all the goodly words of Troilus 'sin first that day hir love bigan to springe', she resolves that 'bityde what bityde', she *will* make her escape. Then Diomed visits her and definitely urges his suit. Playing on her fears, he draws a relentless picture of the imminent fate of Troy. When the city falls, as fall it must, and all are put to the sword, she will be in sore need of a protector. She replies pathetically,

> O Diomede, I love that ilkè placè
> Ther I was born; and Joves, for his gracè,
> Delivere it sone of al that doth it carè!
> God, for thy might, so leve it wel to farè!

She prays him to speak no more of love; if he promises this, he may come to see her again. But she dares not tell him she has a lover. She had once a husband, she says, but he is dead. And she begs him not to mock her. Boccaccio here puts into the mouth of his Griseida words which really are more of encouragement than of rebuff. 'I am

surprised that you can set your heart on a little woman
like me. I am in sorrow now and not disposed to hear
such talk.' Chaucer's Criseyde, with a pathos not un-
mingled with womanly dignity, appeals to his sense of
chivalry—

> And that doth me to han so gret a wonder,
> That ye wol scornen any womman so.
> Eek, god wot, love and I be fer a-sonder;

but then, fearing to anger him she adds:

> What I shal after doon, I can not seye;
> But trewely, as yet me list not pleye.
> Myn herte is now in tribulacioun.

It is the picture, not of a coquette, but of a woman piti-
fully weak, resenting the advances of Diomed, and in her
sore straits using what seemed to her her only weapon of
defence, her 'uncertain sickly appetite to please', in the
fond hope that by putting him off from day to day she may
be able to retain her faith.

But at last her courage entirely breaks down, and Diomed gains his desire. For she cannot live without some
one on whom to lean. Yet she has no joy in her new love.
She bitterly reproaches herself, even at the time of her
faithlessness:

> But trewely, the story telleth us,
> Ther madé never womman more wo
> Than she, whan that she falsed Troilus.
> She seyde, 'allas! for now is clene a-go
> My name of trouthe in love, for ever-mo!
> For I have falséd oon, the gentileste
> That ever was, and oon the worthieste!

> . . . .

> And certes, yow ne haten shal I never,
> And freendés love, that shal ye han of me,
> And my good word, al mighte I liven ever.

> And, trewely, I woldė sory be
> For to seen yow in adversitee.
> And giltėlees, I woot wel, I yow levė;
> But al shal passe; and thus take I my leve.

The resolve with which she tries to console herself will
arouse scorn in those who think their love immutable because its constancy has never been severely tested, yet it is,
in reality, infinitely pathetic:

> But sin I see there is no bettre way,
> And that to late is now for me to rewe,
> To Diomede algate I wol be trewe.

The letter which she writes afterwards in reply to Troilus's
passionate appeal for her return to Troy, in its mixture of
artifice and nature, its attempted dissimulation and excuses,
its instinctive love and pity, and excuses again for what
after all cannot be excused, is a masterpiece of subtle characterization—especially the last stanza, with its apology for
writing so shortly:

> Yet preye I yow on yvel ye ne take,
> That it is short which that I to yow wryte;
> I dar not, ther I am, wel lettres make.
> Ne never yet ne coude I wel endyte.
> Eek greet effect men wryte in place lyte.
> Th'entente is al, and nought the lettres space;
> And fareth now wel, god have you in his grace!

'It isn't safe for me to write much. Besides, I never was
good at letter-writing. And then you know one may put
much meaning into few words. The spirit is what counts
in a letter not the length.' The very fact that she gives
three excuses suggests that none is valid. How indeed
could Criseyde tell the truth without cruelty? If she had
had the courage for that, she might have had the courage
to keep her faith.

And Chaucer does his best to extenuate her fault. We
do not know, he says, how long she resisted Diomed. And
again, it was only after he came back from battle sorely

wounded that she gave way to him, pity bringing her to
his arms, as before it had brought her to the arms of Troilus.
Boccaccio's last comment on his Griseida is the cruel word
villana. Chaucer views his Criseyde in a very different
spirit:

> Ne me ne list this sely womman chyde
> Ferther than the story wol devyse.
> Hir name, allas! is publisshed so wyde,
> That for hir gilt it oughte y-now suffyse.
> And if I mighte excuse hir any wyse,
> For she so sory was for hir untrouthe,
> Y-wis, I wolde excuse hir yet for routhe.

To Chaucer this woman, who has become a byword for
light and heartless infidelity, is by nature neither sensual
nor fickle. In happier circumstances her life might have
been irreproachable. But the trial which she is called upon
to surmount, which would have been as nothing to a
Griselda or a Dorigen, is for her too hard. For she is a
'woman naturally born to fears', with that clinging dependence upon others which, by its implied flattery of
the strength of those on whom she leans, adds, more often
than we admit it, a subtle charm to character; and with a
'beauty' 'whose action is no stronger than a flower', how
could she hold out 'against the wrackful siege of battering
days'?

It has been urged against Chaucer that the more he
dwells upon Criseyde's modesty, and on the sincerity of
her love for Troilus, the more inexplicable does her subsequent treachery appear. But if he had presented her simply
as the light woman there would be nothing to explain. It
would have been easy enough for him to follow his Italian
model and draw a portrait with a family likeness to his
Alison or May, or to make of Criseyde a study for the youth
of the Wyf of Bath. But he chose a harder task, and trium-
phantly accomplished it. Realist though he was, he wrote
in full sympathy with the nobler side of chivalric love, and
though the heroine of his story had sinned against its fundamental laws, it suited his own mood of 'gentilesse' to depict

her as one whose fall stirred him to pity rather than to contempt; for

> pitee renneth sone in gentil herte.

Shakespeare, as we know, reverted to the more obvious conception. His Cressida is one whose

> wanton spirits look out
> At every joint and motive of her body.

His Pandarus has nothing to redeem him from the vice and nastiness that the name implies. He sets the tragedy of Troilus's disillusioned love in a dark background of treachery and shame. The noble Hector, unarmed, is butchered by Achilles. The Greeks are as lustful as Paris, whose rape of Helen they are come to avenge. 'Nothing but lechery! all incontinent varlets' is the just comment of Thersites. The drama is a remorseless satire upon chivalric pretensions in both love and war.

The sense of the pathos and the irony of life is both subtler and deeper in Chaucer, whose main characters have a more normal intermixture of good or bad, and who, by his background of exquisite homely comedy, with its intimate detail and natural conversation, makes us feel that his story, despite its chivalric setting, is, after all, a piece of normal human experience.

Yet modern as he is in his psychology and in his subtle realism, he is medieval in his love of 'doctrine and sentence'; and to introduce them into a work of art is to him no flaw, but rather its justification. While he viewed the world as it is with the keenest delight in its vagaries, he saw it also from the vantage-ground of an orthodox and wholly sincere religious faith. Hence, just as in the course of his poem he had not scrupled to introduce sententious matter which to the modern critic seems an irrelevant intrusion, so at the close, after relating how Troilus, slain by Achilles, looks down from the seventh sphere and laughs within himself at the vanity of all human desires, he appeals, in verses of an exquisite tenderness, to all 'yonge fresshe

folkes, in which that love up groweth with their age' to set
their affections on things heavenly:

> And loveth him, the which that right for lovė
> Upon a cros, our soules for to beyė,
> First starf, and roos, and sit in hevene a-bové;
> For *he* nil falsen no wight, dar I seyė,
> That wol his herte al hoolly on him leyė.
> And sin he best to love is, and most mekė,
> What nedeth feynėd lovės for to sekė?

'What nedeth', indeed, except that human nature is what
it is? This question, in the mouth of Chaucer, the profound but tender and loving student of life and character,
implies, perhaps, the deepest irony of all.

IV

TROILUS AND CRESSIDA

No play of Shakespeare's is more beset with problems than *Troilus and Cressida*. In the Quarto of 1609, its first published form, it is described upon the title-page as 'a famous historie', and in the Preface as a 'comedie'. The editors of the Folio were uncertain where they should place it; their first thought was to put it after *Romeo and Juliet* (and, indeed, if they sought the piquancy of contrast, none could be more effective), then they changed their minds and decided to insert it between the History plays and the Tragedies; and on the title-page called it *The tragedie of Troilus and Cressida*. When we get beyond the title-page the problems thicken. Few modern critics would accuse Shakespeare of writing the Prologue, or the soliloquy of Pandarus with which the play concludes; some readers, and I am one of them, see little of Shakespeare in the last six scenes; and though the bulk of the play is indubitably Shakespeare's, it is obvious that it contains work of widely different periods. Part of the love theme is handled in the style of the early comedies: the camp scenes, as certainly, are late; and farther, the loose construction of the play, in which two strands of interest are somewhat casually drawn together, betrays a more than usual carelessness; nowhere in his dramas is the time scheme more hopelessly confused; and despite Johnson's approval of *Troilus and Cressida* as correctly written, in no other play is the language more often contorted and obscure. Shakespeare seems at times to be feeling after a new vocabulary, wrapping up his thought in an obscurity which would be a fatal barrier to its comprehension on the stage; and this over-intellec-tualized diction, at times pregnant and suggestive, at times merely troublesome, is the more noticeable by its juxtaposition with phrases, whether of prose or verse, that have the inflection and accent of homely modern speech, and with lines that flash straight to the heart with the thrill of inevitable poetry.

Stranger still is Shakespeare's handling of his theme, which, indeed, seemed to Swinburne 'insolubly enigmatic'. As a rule, when he dramatized a story which had already been even competently treated, we are struck by his fidelity to his source; here he had before him a poem by his one predecessor who was in the least comparable to him, either in depth of psychological insight or genius for expression; yet he deals with his subject in a manner and in a spirit wholly different from Chaucer's; and not only so, but different from that which we usually associate with Shakespeare himself. *Troilus and Cressida*, indeed, is more akin to the imaginative temper which is reflected in fiction of our own time.

The bulk of the play, as we have it, is attributed with some certainty to the years 1602–4, and it thus represents a phase in the development from the Elizabethan to the Jacobean Shakespeare.

Shakespeare's interests had never been confined to those intimate, domestic aspects of a man's life, with which the artist is usually concerned. Even to his slightest comedy he loved to give a significant national setting. He wrote for a society in which political and national affairs were closely intertwined with the more private relationships, and often reacted upon them; but up to now, whilst his treatment of both was penetrative and illuminating beyond the reach of his fellows, his attitude towards them had reflected the optimistic outlook of the normal, healthy Elizabethan. He had passed his youth in a time wherein imminent dangers of dissension at home and attacks from abroad had gradually been surmounted, till the defeat of the Spanish Armada had seemed to prove the essential unity and strength of the people. He had fully shared the national enthusiasm; and in his history plays had been its most eloquent mouthpiece. He had not glossed over the darker pages of the past; he had driven home their obvious political moral; but he had felt that, on a long view, England had been true to herself, and he had fitly brought his series to a close with *Henry V*, in whose famous victories, and the spirit which achieved them, he saw a picture of the England of his own day.

The same optimistic spirit had inspired his comedy. He had delineated the relations of men and women with the convictions of an uncompromising romantic idealist; through all adversity and mischance he had traced the fortunes of his pairs of lovers and celebrated their triumph; even in *Romeo and Juliet*, though the end may be tragic, there is no sense of defeat, but rather of the consummation of an ideal.

And in these comedies, be it noted, where love had been shallow, or wavering, or inconstant, the failing had always been the man's; the depth, constancy, fidelity had been the woman's, and her love the redeeming force by which a rather unheroic hero is brought to realize his better self. The stories of Proteus and Julia, of Orsino and Viola, of Claudio and Hero, of Helena and Bertram, are all of them variations played on this one simple theme. And the fact already admitted, that the love scenes in *Troilus and Cressida* have in them traces of early composition, strengthens rather than weakens my contention; for if they contain some early work, the most piercing of Troilus's utterances are as certainly late; and what could be more significant than that Shakespeare took up the subject after, say, writing *Romeo and Juliet*, of which there is often in *Troilus and Cressida* an ironic echo, and finding it little to his taste, threw it aside? In all the earlier plays one feels that the scales are, perhaps too chivalrously, weighted in favour of the heroines. With his deeper and more intimate knowledge of men than of women, it is natural that it should be so; and it is noteworthy that in his later plays, in his Posthumus and Imogen, his Leontes and Hermione, he returns to the same point of view.

But immediately after he has brought his historical plays to their triumphant climax in *Henry V*, and his comedy to its zenith in *Twelfth Night*, there comes a sudden reversal of his outlook upon the two worlds he had surveyed in them. He enters his tragic period, and becomes for the time, and with a growing sense of disillusionment, obsessed with the problem of the man who, nurtured in that attitude to life of which his earlier plays are the expression, is confronted by an actuality which gives the lie to his faith.

How far external circumstance wrought this change in him we may speculate, but we cannot know. The chorus in *Henry V* had looked forward to another national triumph, with the general of our gracious empress,

> As in good time he may,—from Ireland coming,
> Bringing rebellion broachèd on his sword;

but the ignominious return of Essex, and the miserable intrigues and disaster that followed, may well have led him to probe more deeply the motives and actions of soldiers and politicians; whilst close upon the heels of this rude awakening to the realities of public life, he may have been, in his own most intimate circle, the victim of some horrible disenchantment. Yet it is well to bear in mind that whereas such imagination as the ordinary man may possess is only stirred by a blow struck directly at himself, the slightest suggestion may start the poet on a train of thought and feeling which carries him far beyond the present, and once possessed by it he cannot himself foresee to what heights or depths it may sweep him.

But whatever may have been its cause, the change in Shakespeare is clear enough. It appears first in his treatment of the world of political intrigue, with the study of Brutus the idealist called upon to act in a world with which, by the very aloofness of his idealism, he is unfitted to cope. The tragic irony of the situation lies in the paradox that whilst the conspirators need the support of Brutus in order to give a semblance of disinterestedness to their rebellion, Brutus's lofty inability to live in their lower world and understand the motives which actuate them brings all their plans to ruin. Yet it is significant that in this, Shakespeare's first study of the idealist broken on the wheel of harsh reality, he is more tender to his hero than in later studies of a similar theme. Brutus is not defeated or disillusioned. Tricked as he has been into becoming the tool of an unscrupulous conspiracy, he dies with his faith unbroken either in his cause or in his fellow men:

> My heart doth joy that yet, in all my life,
> I found no man but he was true to me.
> I shall have glory by this losing day,
> More than Octavius and Mark Antony
> By this vile conquest shall attain unto.

In *Hamlet* Shakespeare strikes deeper; his hero is confronted with a world that is rotten in both its public and its private life. A heroic monarch has been superseded by an easy-going drunkard; the chief statesman of the realm is as ready to serve the one as the other, the fickle populace to accept and to applaud him. But this public aspect of affairs is only the background to the essential tragedy; the worst blow to Hamlet has been the shattering of his faith in the purity and fidelity of woman. His mother has changed Hyperion for a satyr, and in Ophelia, he finds, or thinks he finds, a treachery which betrays him in his need; in his bitter words 'Get thee to a nunnery . . . or, if thou wilt needs marry, marry a fool; for wise men know well enough what monsters you make of them', Hamlet voices his revulsion from that whole theory of life which before he had never questioned,—that theory on which, as we have seen, Shakespeare had built his earlier romantic comedies.

In *Troilus and Cressida*, which immediately follows *Hamlet*, the theme of disillusionment is worked out even more remorselessly, and with an emphasis equally divided between the private and the public aspects of life; and the manner in which the play falls into two parts, imperfectly welded together, strengthens our impression that Shakespeare is here making a definite attack upon the too facile optimism in which, hitherto, he had conceived both comedy and history plays. For both themes he found material in Lydgate and Caxton's two versions of Guido de Colonna's long and rambling Latin History of Troy, in which the love of Troilus and Cressida forms an episode.

Long before Shakespeare's day Cressida had already become proverbial as a type of the frailty of woman. Chaucer's subtle and profound apologia for her had never been understood; as I attempted to show in a previous lecture, it was built up on an elaborate moral code drawn from the medieval Courts of Love, a code which had never enjoyed a wide currency, and by the fifteenth century would be quite incomprehensible. Neither Caxton nor Lydgate were psychologists; they were content simply to narrate the facts and leave the reader to draw his own conclusions. 'O how soon is the purpose of woman changed', is Caxton's comment:

> I can non other excusacioun
> But only kindes transmutacioun,

remarks Lydgate, leaving it at that. But Henryson, a greater poet than Lydgate, and something of a psychologist, had been fired with all the moral fervour of the Scot; he felt that Crissyde had been let off too easily; and he wrote her *Testament* to correct his Master Chaucer's reprehensible tolerance of a woman who had

> changed in filth all [her] feminitee,
> And be with fleschelie lust sa maculait.

He had punished her with leprosy, and condemned her to live in a spittal house and beg with 'cop and clapper'. From Shakespeare's allusions to Cressida in earlier plays it is clear that even if he had not read Henryson he had accepted Henryson's version of her life and character; it is clear also that his Elizabethan audience had accepted it, for otherwise his allusions would have missed fire. What he thought of Chaucer's Criseyde we can only conjecture. It is probable that ignorance of medieval conventions would preclude him from realizing the beauty and the truth of the portrait; but even if he had appreciated it to the full it would have been as impossible for him to follow it in a play destined for an Elizabethan audience as it would have been to represent Richard III as a national hero or Henry V as a coward. And, anyhow, in his present mood, he had no inclination to do so.

In his Cressida, therefore, he turns his back upon Chaucer, and is content to illuminate with the insight of genius the popular tradition. There is in literature no more relentlessly faithful portrait of the calculating, heartless coquette; with the beauty and the ready wit that make her dangerous, yet without a trace of modesty in her composition. Animal desire is in her divorced from any uplifting or generous emotion. She has not even the excuse of strong passions; her predominating instinct is simply to seduce and to enthrall. In her first soliloquy she reveals to us her settled code of life:

> Women are angels, wooing:
> Things won are done; joy's soul lies in the doing:
> That she belov'd knows nought that knows not this:
> Men prize the thing ungain'd more than it is.

Acting on this principle she holds off as long as she feels it politic to do so. The persuasions of Pandarus have played little part in her choice of Troilus for her victim, but she realizes her uncle's value to her as a tool; for she is aware that his sense of self-importance will make him exaggerate the difficulty of winning her, and thus add fuel to her lover's passion. So she allows him to think that he is influencing her, and delights to draw him out by pretending to hold Troilus in small esteem. 'What sneaking fellow comes yonder?' she asks as Troilus passes over the stage; then, after listening to his ecstatic praise of her lover's virtues, she dismisses him with the contemptuous, 'you are a bawd'. She knows her uncle through and through, but by her readiness to bandy indecent jests with him she shows clearly enough that in reality she belongs to his world.

When she decides that the time has come to give herself to her lover, while Troilus is overcome with the intensity of his passion, she remains complete mistress of herself, and plays with consummate skill the part of the bashful, modest woman. She appears before him veiled, she draws back. To Troilus's ejaculation

> O Cressida! how often have I wished me thus!

she stammers out:

> Wished, my lord! The gods grant,—O my lord!

yet a moment later she can turn with a coarse aside to Pandarus. Affecting to be carried away by her feelings she confesses her love, and then counterfeits confusion at her immodesty:

> Why have I blabb'd? who shall be true to us
> When we are so unsecret to ourselves?

By an obvious ruse she leads him on to kiss her, and then feigns distress at the forwardness:

> I am asham'd: O heavens! what have I done?

and she makes a pretence of leaving him:

> I would be gone:
> Where is my wit? I speak I know not what.

At length, realizing that Troilus is so completely under her spell that she can say anything with safety, she ventures on the truth:

> Perchance, my lord, I show more craft than love;
> And fell so roundly to a large confession,
> To angle for your thoughts.

These are the only sincere words she ever speaks, and she did not intend them to be believed. At daybreak, when Troilus has to leave her, her mind harks back once more to her settled policy:

> O foolish Cressid! I might have still held off,
> And then you would have tarried;

but on her uncle's entry she responds to his ribaldry with the zest of evident enjoyment.

When she hears the news that she must return to her father her distress is genuine enough; she is loth to resign so soon a lover completely in her power, and a prince to boot, for whom she has angled many months. She will be, she says, 'A woeful Cressid 'mongst the merry Greeks!' But her grief is of a totally different order from his, and she is quite incapable of comprehending the depth of his anguish. On his first prayer to her to be 'true of heart' she expostulates,

> I true! how now! what wicked deem is this?

and when, in an agony, he repeats his prayer: 'But yet, be true'; she is simply bored—'O heavens! "be true" again!' A moment afterwards, when Diomed pays her extravagant compliments, treating Troilus with a studied insolence, she shows no resentment, and before she reaches the Greek camp she has already promised him her love. In the company of the Greek chieftains she is all sprightly wit and badinage, cracking an immodest joke at the expense of Menelaus. 'A woman of quick sense', remarks Nestor. But Ulysses sees through her at a glance:

> Fie, fie upon her!
> There's language in her eye, her cheek, her lip,
> Nay, her foot speaks; her wanton spirits look out
> At every joint and motive of her body.

With her interview that night with Diomed Shakespeare's biting sketch of her is complete. She is playing her old game of luring her lover on by pretending to hold back, though she realizes that with a very different man to ensnare she must play it with less modesty and more seductiveness:

> Sweet honey Greek, tempt me no more to folly.
> .   .   .   .
> I prithee, do not hold me to mine oath;
> Bid me do anything but that, sweet Greek.

But the cynical and practised Diomed, unlike the innocent Troilus, does not labour under the delusion that she is 'stubborn-chaste'. 'Foh, foh! adieu; you palter', he says, and she has to exert all her charms to keep him. She strokes

his cheek and reasserts her promise: 'In faith, I will, la;
never trust me else'; and as a pledge of good faith she presents to him the sleeve that was Troilus's last gift to her,
affecting grief at parting with it; then, counting on having
aroused Diomed's jealousy, she once more plays at holding
back, and retracts her promise. But Diomed is not thus
to be trifled with: he has only to threaten to take her at her
word, and she makes a definite assignation with him, taking
leave of him with the entreaty,

> Good-night: I prithee, come.

Left alone, her only regret is that she cannot have them
both; she has not a trace of remorse, exclaiming with a little
sigh

> Troilus, farewell! one eye yet looks on thee.

She is, in fact, quite satisfied with herself, and trots out a
little platitude in which she throws all responsibility for
her treachery upon the natural frailty of womankind:

> Ah! poor our sex; this fault in us I find,
> The error of our eye directs our mind.
>
> .   .   .   .
>
> Minds sway'd by eyes are full of turpitude,

a remark which Thersites bluntly interprets:

> A proof of strength she could not publish more,
> Unless she said, 'My mind is now turn'd whore;'

and he is probably not far wrong in his conjecture that she
will soon be eager to welcome the advances of Patroclus.

With this conception of Cressida, Pandarus loses all the
importance he held in Chaucer's poem. But Shakespeare
degrades him even more than his version of the story requires. His Pandarus, unlike Chaucer's, shows no affection
for either his niece or Troilus; he has neither heart, nor
brains, nor dignity, nor genuine humour. He is just a
fussy busybody with a dirty mind, enjoying the self-
importance that Troilus's helpless passion gives him. No

one but Troilus takes him seriously. Cressida, as we have
seen, despises even while she employs him. Helen and
Paris mock him as a buffoon. The servant treats him with
familiarity. Shakespeare could not, indeed, help giving
him one or two good remarks, simply because he is Shakespeare. Such is that marvellously vivid picture of Cressida's nervous excitement before she gives herself to her
lover—'It is the prettiest villain: she fetches her breath as
short as a new-ta'en sparrow'; but as a whole he seems to
have felt too much disgust at Pandarus to have made of
him a genuinely comic character.

This ruthless portraiture of Cressida and Pandarus
throws into stronger ironic relief the tragic passion of
Troilus. Nowhere in the comedies of romantic love, not
even in *Romeo and Juliet,* is the soul of the infatuated lover
laid bare with such profound psychological insight. Where
Cressida is not in question Troilus has all the heroic virtues;
more than Chaucer, Shakespeare emphasizes the virility of
his normal temper. Aeneas, who knows 'the youth even
to his inches', describes him to Ulysses as 'the second hope
of Troy',

> Not yet mature, yet matchless; firm of word,
> Speaking in deeds and deedless in his tongue;
> Not soon provok'd, nor being provok'd soon calm'd:
> His heart and hand both open and both free;
> For what he has he gives, what thinks he shows;
> Yet gives he not till judgement guide his bounty;

but under the spell of Cressida he gives his love with a
bounty that no judgement has guided, and he confesses
himself

> Tamer than sleep, fonder than ignorance,
> . . . .
> And skill-less as unpractis'd infancy.

So skill-less is he that he misreads Pandarus as fatally as he
misreads Cressida, thinking that

> he's as tetchy to be woo'd to woo
> As she is stubborn-chaste against all suit.

His passion has exalted him into a world remote from theirs. His love is not mere sensual desire, it is a religion of which Cressida is enthroned the goddess, in which is concentrated all the romantic aspiration of his chivalrous nature; and he yearns to its fulfilment as to the consummation of an ideal. When at last Cressida yields to his entreaties he awaits her

> Like a strange soul upon the Stygian banks
> Staying for waftage.

He is giddy, 'expectation whirls him round'; his spirit, he fears, is too dull and gross to fathom the supreme mystery, and taste its full significance. In Cressida's presence he is at first tongue-tied: and when he speaks, it is not to urge his suit but to lose all sense of the present in a rapt contemplation of the 'monstruosity in love, that the will is infinite, and the execution confined; that the desire is boundless, and the act a slave to limit'; and Cressida has herself to do the wooing. Twice she has to say to him 'Will you walk in, my lord?' Brought down to earth his ecstasy is crossed by the presentiment that love such as he feels can find no mortal counterpart; and he speaks those wonderful words which haunt the mind not merely with the pathos of Troilus's appeal to Cressida, nor even as the cry of every lover to his beloved, but with the deeper pathos of all relationships in a finite inconstant world;

> O! that I thought it could be in a woman—
> As if it can I will presume in you—
>
> .　　.　　.　　.　　.　　.　　.
>
> To keep her constancy in plight and youth,
> Outliving beauty's outward, with a mind
> That doth renew swifter than blood decays:
> Or that persuasion could but thus convince me,
> That my integrity and truth to you
> Might be affronted with the match and weight
> Of such a winnow'd purity in love;
> How were I then uplifted!

When, after a brief night of ecstasy, he is called upon to

surrender her to Diomed, he yields her as a priest at the altar, 'offering to it his own heart'. A presentiment of impending tragedy again assails him; he feels subconsciously that Cressida inhabits a different world from his, yet he will not acknowledge it to his conscious self: he persuades himself that his fears for her loyalty spring from his own unworthiness; his heart assures him that Cressida could not be false. And yet—

> something may be done that we will not:
> And sometimes we are devils to ourselves
> When we will tempt the frailty of our powers,
> Presuming on their changeful potency.

The truth of this psychology is attested by the terrible fascination which the play had over Keats, to whom Shakespeare was 'the miserable and mighty poet of the human heart'. Separated from Fanny Brawne, Keats was mastered by an agony of mistrust which reason and his better nature could not still, and in Troilus's divided soul he saw his own anguish, painted to the life.

As penetrating in its psychology is the scene where Troilus, in company with Ulysses, watches Cressida act out her treachery with Diomed. Nowhere else shall we find so vivid a picture of the distraught mind of the idealist confronted with the damning reality, a reality which with one side of his nature he passionately rejects, for it shatters to its foundations the whole fabric of his life, and which yet his reason forces upon him. His emotion is not merely that of the lover who finds his mistress false, for he has universalized his passion; his is the bewildered conflict of one who in a moment is called upon to surrender the keystone of his faith:

> Cressid is mine, tied with the bonds of heaven:
>
> .   .   .   .
>
> The bonds of heaven are slipp'd, dissolv'd, and loos'd.

His lot is more tragic than Hamlet's, for he has not Hamlet's power of thought, of finding escape from a shattered faith in intellectual speculation. His whole universe is tottering, and as before the consummation of his ideal he was giddy with expectation, so now he reels before the inexorable cruelty of fact. Cressid is his whole world; if this fail,

> 'The pillar'd firmament is rottenness,
> And earth's base built on stubble.'

Against this he must struggle even in defiance of the clear evidence of his senses:

> there is a credence in my heart,
> An esperance so obstinately strong,
> That doth invert the attest of eyes and ears,
> As if those organs had deceptious functions,
> Created only to calumniate.
> *Was* Cressid here?

There is no madness in this denial of his eyes and ears: it is a last effort to be sane; and when Ulysses insists, he can only reply:

> Let it not be believ'd for womanhood!
> Think, we had mothers.

It is easy for Ulysses, the dispassionate observer, who had never been deluded by Cressida, and knows the world a place of mingled good and evil, to keep what faith in humanity he had:

> What hath she done, prince, that can soil our mothers?

he asks. And to the lips of Troilus, to whom Cressida was at once the type and ideal of woman, rises the bitter answer:

> Nothing at all, unless that this were she;

he begs for time to readjust himself to the whole cruel fact,

> To make a recordation to my soul
> Of every syllable that here was spoke.

But when he has digested his experience he emerges a

hardened man of the world. Chaucer's broken-hearted lover, in like case, cannot bring himself to utter more than a gentle reproach at the treachery that has laid his life in ruin:

> But trewely, Criseyde, swete may,
> Whom I have ay with al my might yserved,
> That ye thus doon, I have it nought deserved.

Despite everything, it is his fate to love her still, the 'best of any creature'. In place of this we have from Shakespeare's Troilus the fierce denunciation:

> O Cressid! O false Cressid! false, false, false!
> Let all untruths stand by thy stained name,
> And they'll seem glorious.

And so, when Pandarus brings a letter from 'yond poor girl', he makes on it a scornful comment:

> Words, words, mere words, no matter from the heart;

and he tears the letter into shreds. And when Pandarus, with no knowledge of the scene which had opened Troilus's eyes, would fain expostulate,

> But hear you, hear you!

Troilus turns on him with fury:

> Hence, broker lackey! ignomy and shame
> Pursue thy life, and live aye with thy name!

He knows Pandarus at last as fully as he has learnt to know Cressida.

In the modern text this final dismissal of Pandarus is reserved for the concluding scene of the play, where it is followed by a bawdy soliloquy from Pandarus, obviously not Shakespeare's. But in the Folio the lines occur here also, and this is undoubtedly their proper place. It was only a base desire to please the groundlings that led the botcher of Shakespeare's work to give Pandarus the last disgusting word.

With Troilus's illusions of love his illusions of chivalry go too. Athirst for vengeance he now sees war as the cruel bloodthirsty thing it is. Hector's 'vice of mercy' appears to him mere fool's play:

Let's leave the hermit pity with our mothers,

he says contemptuously, and to Hector's reproof, 'Fie, savage, fie!' he retorts with a stern sense of the realities: 'Hector, then 'tis wars.'

The tragedy of Troilus and Cressida, which was the whole theme of Chaucer's poem, occupies little more than a third of Shakespeare's play; the rest is devoted to a portrayal of the corrupt society of the Greeks and Trojans, in which Cressida's infidelity is merely a sordid, but characteristic episode. Readers have often resented Shakespeare's belittling of the Homeric world; they forget that his material was drawn from medieval sources—that the only Homer he knew was seven books of Chapman's translation, which probably suggested to him his conception of Thersites; and that his attitude to the Trojan war and its heroes was that commonly held for more than a century before him. No stories were more popular in England than the Arthurian cycle and the tale of Troy; both were read as romances of chivalry, delighted in for their wealth of warlike and amorous adventure, but judged, when they were judged at all, by the stern standards of normal contemporary life. Shakespeare accepted those standards; unlike so many writers of to-day it was never his aim to set up a new code of morals, but rather to transfigure the old and give it a deeper reality. Popular opinion was not much more lenient to Helen than to Cressida. Though the medieval chronicler was always favourable to the Trojans he made no attempt to justify their cause. Lydgate denounces the love of Paris and Helen as an adultery, for which Cassandra had foretold divine punishment; whilst the various exploits of Greeks and Trojans, readable enough as mere incidents, if taken seriously as an index of character, create an impression which Caxton and Lydgate hardly intended to convey. In the fierce light of a searching common sense, this world of chivalry, as they had depicted it,

could only appear as a world of petty passions, criminal
intrigue, and distorted values; and it gave Shakespeare
just the material he needed, to set forth the sordid realities of love and politics and war as, in his present mood
of disillusionment, he saw them enacted in the society
about him.

Shakespeare had never harboured illusions about the
causes of the Trojan war, and he attributes none to its
participants. In his early poem, the *Rape of Lucrece*, he
had dismissed Helen as 'the strumpet that began this stir',
and in the only scene in the play in which she figures, she
is pert and flippant—a striking contrast to the gracious
portrait of her which is among the most delightful things
in Chaucer's poem. The war, as he views it, is fought for
a cause which neither side believes in, or thinks worth the
sacrifice. Hector admits that the Trojans, in keeping
Helen, are opposing the law of nature and of nations; the
Greeks, who might be supposed to vindicate that law,
have no such motive, they are themselves entirely cynical
about it, infected with the vice they are ostensibly punish-
ing. Diomed is the mouthpiece of the spirit in which they
engage in the conflict:

> Who, in your thoughts, merits fair Helen best—
> Myself or Menelaus?

asks Paris, and he replies with a bitter scorn:

> Both alike:
> He merits well to have her that doth seek her—
> Not making any scruple of her soilure—
> With such a hell of pain and world of charge,
> And you as well to keep her that defend her—
> Not palating the taste of her dishonour—
> With such a costly loss of wealth and friends:

and on Paris's protest—'You are too bitter to your country-
woman,'—he breaks out:

> She's bitter to her country. Hear me, Paris:
> For every false drop in her bawdy veins
> A Grecian's life hath sunk; for every scruple

Of her contaminated carrion weight
A Trojan hath been slain.

But that he speaks, not from righteous indignation, but from cynical contempt, is clear enough from his own intrigue with Cressida. And Diomed is no exception. Achilles is kept from battle by a secret passion for Polyxena, the daughter of his enemy Priam. Agamemnon and Patroclus, if we are to believe Thersites, are equally licentious. 'Nothing but lechery! all incontinent varlets.' Thersites the railer, who gloats over the depravity of his superiors and finds in their stupidity and vice his one topic of discourse, is the natural product of a corrupt and decadent civilization. He is the most revolting character that Shakespeare ever drew, and the enjoyment which Ajax and Achilles get out of his society is in itself a damning proof of the disgust with which Shakespeare viewed the whole moral atmosphere of the Greek camp.

There is as little true chivalry in their war as in their loves. When the two camps mingle during the truce their elaborate courtesies are the mere cloak for savage hatred. Achilles, 'the sinew and forehand' of the Greek host, views Hector limb by limb, that he may discover in which part of his body he may destroy him; and he plans to 'heat his blood with Greekish wine' in order that on the morrow he may prove the easier prey. He does not even seek the glory of overcoming his foe in fair combat, for he falls upon Hector unarmed, and summons his Myrmidons to aid him in the slaughter. No trace of martial virtue redeems this 'great-sized coward' from the most brutal passions that war engenders.

A further glimpse into the characters of these men who guide the destinies of nations, and of the motives which actuate them, is afforded us by the councils of war held in Troy and in the Greek camp. In Troy a cabinet of five, Priam, Hector, Helenus, Paris, and Troilus, meet to consider the Greek offer, that if Helen be returned they will abandon the siege and conclude a peace. Troilus is the chief advocate against its acceptance. He reviews with perfect frankness the causes which led up to the war, and his arguments are typical of the belligerent frame of mind. The Greeks took away our aunt Hesione. We sent Paris to avenge the theft,

> And for an old aunt whom the Greeks held captive
> He brought a Grecian queen, whose youth and freshness
> Wrinkles Apollo's, and makes stale the morning;

that is, to avenge a wrong we did a greater wrong, but gained the advantage. We approved the act at the time, if we went back on it now, we should be resigning our advantage; it would be weakness and look like fear. The quarrel is therefore a good one, for our honours are bound up with it. Then, with a wholly unconscious irony, he concludes, as though his cause were just:

> Jove forbid there should be done amongst us
> Such things as might offend the weakest spleen
> To fight for and maintain.

Paris, naturally enough, supports this argument. We did Helen a wrong by snatching her away from her husband, we must make it up to her, not by restoring her—that would look as if we did not value her—but by keeping her honourably; anyhow it would be disgraceful to yield her up 'on terms of base compulsion'.[1] Against the conclusion of Troilus and Paris the other three dissent. Helenus objects with justice that their speeches are empty of reasons; but he is silenced by the contemptuous rejoinder that he only asks for reasons because he is a priest and cannot fight. He is therefore a coward and can be ruled out. Priam exposes the obvious flaw in Paris's position, that he is 'besotted on his sweet delights', but Priam is too weak to enforce his own conviction. Hector is worse still; for he sins wilfully against the light he has. With masterly clarity he exposes his brothers' failure to

> make up a free determination
> 'Twixt right and wrong;

[1] One is forcibly reminded of Falstaff's refusal to give reasons 'upon compulsion' (1 Hen. IV, II. iv. 270).

and points out that they are simply blinded to truth by the ignoble passions of pleasure and revenge; and he sums up the case against them:

> thus to persist
> In doing wrong extenuates not wrong,
> But makes it much more heavy.

Yet though he sees thus clearly the right he is eager to persist in the wrong. This war, which he has denounced as both useless and unjust, must continue, for on it depend 'our joint and several dignities'. And he concludes the conference with the announcement that he has just sent a roisting challenge to the dull and factious Greeks. It is worth noting that Lydgate represents Hector as having sent the challenge with the honourable purpose that upon the issue of the combat the war should be decided: Shakespeare takes from Hector this worthy motive and sees the challenge as an empty act of chivalry, to make good his boast that he

> hath a lady wiser, fairer, truer,
> Than ever Greek did compass in his arms.

This debate has been criticized as pointless, but what could be a more caustic comment on the distorted sense of values always fostered by an actual state of war, and peculiarly incident to men whose professional code trains them to value their honour 'above the right'.

In the Greek camp the big three, Agamemnon, Nestor, and Ulysses, meet to confer upon the situation. The war has dragged on indecisively for seven years, and they are as far as ever from bringing it to a successful issue. What is to be done?

Agamemnon opens the debate, and as commander-in-chief might be expected to have some thing vital to contribute; yet his speech amounts to no more than the statement that these reverses they have suffered are merely a test of courage and endurance. Nestor then takes up the word, but with all the experience of his many years he can only repeat in different language the point already made by

Agamemnon. They have both expressed high sounding
moral platitudes with force and conviction, but have not
one whit advanced the discussion. Then Ulysses, after
elaborate compliments to both of them on the value of
their remarks, proceeds to unravel the true causes of the ill
success. Into his mouth Shakespeare puts his own ripest
political wisdom, gained from the study of his country's
troubled fortunes alike in his own lifetime and in the past,
and already clearly set forth in his history plays; it is the
moral summed up in *Henry V* in the Archbishop's comparison of the state to a beehive, and later pressed home
by Menenius to the rebellious Roman plebs in his fable of
the belly. The state, Ulysses argues, is an organism of
which each part has its distinctive function to perform.
Only by the observance of 'degree',

> Which is the ladder to all high designs,

can any enterprise prosper. But the Greek camp is split
into factions, none of which recognize a central authority.
Their foremost warriors, Achilles and Ajax, show open
contempt for the high command. With the typical scorn
of the brainless soldier for anything but brute force, they
call policy cowardice; strategy and forethought they dis-
miss as 'bed-work, mappery, closet-war',

> So that the ram that batters down the wall,
> .   .   .   .
> They place before his hand that made the engine,
> Or those that with the fineness of their souls
> By reason guides his execution.

This disaffection has spread through all ranks:

> The general's disdain'd
> By him one step below, he by the next,
> That next by him beneath.

But even the wisdom of Ulysses cannot prescribe a remedy
for the disease. For the conception of 'degree' presupposes
at the head of the state a mind capable of directing the

organism with a true genius for leadership, and this, it is clear, Agamemnon lacks. And we feel that Ulysses knows it. For the zest with which he recounts to Agamemnon the way in which Patroclus is burlesquing him and Nestor for the amusement of Achilles, and his evident enjoyment of their discomfiture, though he professes to be scandalized at the insult, suggests that his own respect for degree is not entirely unimpeachable. Nor is his recital likely to help the cause of unity, by easing the strained relations between Agamemnon and his refractory generals. And it is significant that the practical policy which he puts forward to meet the crisis, and bring both Ajax and Achilles to that 'observance of degree' without which all 'enterprise is sick', is as empty of result as the pious platitudes of Agamemnon and Nestor. Achilles is to be goaded into action by setting up the blockish Ajax as his rival, and by transferring to Ajax the honour and pre-eminence that Achilles had come to regard as his due. It is a clever plot, and its execution affords us the only good scenes of comedy in the play. Led by Ulysses the Greek chieftains flatter Ajax to the top of his bent, and Ajax, puffed up with his newly acquired importance, swallows their ironic praise with a sublimely fatuous self-complacence: 'Why should a man be proud?' he asks, 'How doth pride grow? I know not what pride is.' 'I do hate a proud man, as I hate the engendering of toads.' When Agamemnon suggests that Ajax should be sent to reason with Achilles, Ulysses protests with elaborate irony:

> No, this thrice-worthy and right valiant lord
> Must not so stale his palm, nobly acquir'd;
> Nor, by my will, assubjugate his merit,
> As amply titled as Achilles is,
> By going to Achilles:
> That were to enlard his fat-already pride.
>
> .   .   .   .
> This lord go to him! Jupiter forbid,
> And say in thunder, 'Achilles go to him'.

The whole scene is superb comedy. Shakespeare with his

genius for drawing immortal half-wits, never surpassed his portrait of the blockish Ajax.

The other part of Ulysses' plan for humbling Achilles is carried through with equal gusto. The chieftains who were wont to court his favour pass him by with insulting nonchalance, and then Ulysses himself follows, to point the moral of their neglect. In a fine speech he exposes to Achilles the shortness of human memory, and impresses upon him that honour is only kept untarnished by perseverance in valiant action:

> to *have* done, is to hang
> Quite out of fashion, like a rusty mail
> In monumental mockery.
>
> .   .   .   .
>
> [For] all with one consent praise new-born gawds,
> Though they are made and moulded of things past,
> And give to dust that. is a little gilt
> More laud than gilt o'er-dusted.

For a moment he almost persuades Achilles to take the field again. But in reality his clever scheming achieves nothing. For though Achilles may be galled at the rise of Ajax and the loss of his own prestige, his secret love for Polyxena is stronger in him than his desire to restore his reputation. When the truce is over and the Trojans launch their offensive, neither the 'snail-paced' Ajax who, thanks to Ulysses, is now grown prouder than Achilles, nor Achilles himself answers the call to arms. It is late in the day, after Hector and Troilus have already worked deadly havoc among the Greeks, when they don their armour; and then, not to fulfil their public duty, but merely because they are maddened by the lust for private vengeance. And after the battle, there is no more of that 'degree' of which Ulysses had been the eloquent exponent than there was before. What success the Greeks had won came not from policy but from accident, and from the vilest treachery. Agamemnon may flatter himself that, with the murder of Hector,

> Great Troy is ours, and our sharp wars are ended,

but they have in store for them three more years of loss of
time, travail, expense,

> and what else dear that is consum'd
> In hot digestion of this cormorant war.

This final impression, which Shakespeare leaves upon us,
of inconclusiveness, of futility, betokens an outlook on life
far more depressed and depressing than any to be found
elsewhere in his dramas. In those tragedies wherein his
hero's battle with fate is reflected in the disordered state
of the world about him, the malignant forces of evil, always
potent, gain, indeed, for the time full mastery, and work a
terrible havoc. Yet at the close, when evil has done its
worst, a more normal course of events is resumed, and we
are left with a sense of peace and restoration; the forces
that work for good, after however cruel a struggle, are in
the end justified. The strong rule of Fortinbras brings
order to distracted Denmark, Malcolm succeeds Macbeth;
after the death of Lear, Albany and Edgar are left to 'rule
in the realm and the gor'd state sustain'; even in *Timon of
Athens* the corrupt senators have learned their lesson, and
they admit Alcibiades to establish 'regular justice in the
city's bounds'. But the world, as reflected in Troy and in
the Greek camp, has little to redeem it or make it worth
redemption. There is no cause worth fighting for, and no
faith in any cause. Those few who show themselves
possessed of understanding are either false to it, like
Hector, or, like Ulysses, are rendered ineffective by the vice
and stupidity of their associates. So things just muddle on,
without real policy, or true leadership; the world is a
stage on which the petty ambitions, the treachery, the
lust, the cruelty of man pursue their endless, aimless course.
Shakespeare views the spectacle with disgust.

The same gloom pervades his outlook on the life of the
individual. Troilus, it should be noted, comes of that same
noble family from which Shakespeare drew all his tragic
heroes. Different as they are in other respects, while in
the world of practical affairs they are potent forces, in the

higher sensibilities, in their greater capacity for joy and suffering, they all have the poetic temperament. Their tragedy comes upon them because, despite their inherent nobility of soul, they are unable to cope with some danger or temptation peculiarly incident to their temper, which a smaller man might easily avoid. And when they fall and the world falls in ruins about them, though we realize that the germ of the catastrophe is inherent in themselves, we glory in the splendour of the human spirit, noblest in its suffering, triumphing in apparent defeat, and often gaining its fullest life and its clearest vision in the presence of death.

But the effect of Troilus's tragic experience is to impeach the validity of those very ideals which spring from the higher side of his nature. This is clear enough if, for a moment, we revert to the obvious analogy of his situation with Hamlet's. The words given to Troilus in the agony of his disillusionment:

> Let it not be believ'd for womanhood!
> Think, we had mothers,

takes us right to the heart of Hamlet's tragedy. Hamlet is confronted with a world in which his dearest faith has been outraged, but the sanctity of his ideal is not questioned, even by the offender whose crime has outraged it. Whereas Cressida shelters herself complacently under the general corruption of her sex, Gertrude's heart is cleft in twain by her son's passionate pleading, and Hamlet in his appeal to her,

> O! throw away the worser part of it,
> And live the purer with the other half,

shows that his own faith in the ideal is, in reality, as firm as ever. Ophelia, he felt, had been in league with his enemies, yet that bitterness passes with which he had coupled her with his mother as a type of woman's frailty; and his last thought of her is no repudiation:

> I lov'd Ophelia: forty thousand brothers
> Could not, with all their quantity of love,
> Make up my sum.

In how different a tone rings out the last despairing cry of Troilus:

> O Cressid! O false Cressid! false, false, false!

None of Shakespeare's tragic heroes is defeated as Troilus is defeated. Othello passes through an agony greater indeed than his, because his soul is greater, but he 'dies upon a kiss'. Troilus is left to his despair, to learn the folly of all faith in human nature, and to become more like the cruel, loveless world into which he had been born. Shakespeare seems to be turning, with a fierce irony, upon the deepest convictions of his manhood. And the 'hero' now held up for our admiration is Ulysses, the man of no illusions, of shrewd practical sense, who knows the world through and through, but whilst he is above its meaner vices has no spiritual insight. He can diagnose the weakness of a divided state, but his keen political wisdom is untouched by that sense of a great cause which moves both men and nations, as nothing else can move them; he can detect the inherent nobility of Troilus and stand by him in his trial, but he views his passion as the folly of an impressionable young man, and he is wholly unable to understand its intensity:

> May worthy Troilus be *half* attach'd
> With that which here his passion doth express?

he asks incredulously (i.e. can you possibly be moved to half the extent that your words imply?). Such depth of passion is quite beyond his ken. And if he is not soured by his experience it is because he expects little of life, and can enjoy it as a comedy of which he is himself the hero; playing upon the crass stupidity of an Ajax, or reading Achilles a salutary lesson on the fickleness of human fame and the ingratitude of men. His greatest speech,

> Time hath, my lord, a wallet at his back,
> Wherein he puts alms for oblivion,

is the epitome of worldly wisdom: no man is fit to play his part in the world unless he has learnt its lesson. For who can deny that, as life is lived upon the lower levels of normal human intercourse,

> Love, friendship, charity, are subjects all
> To envious and calumniating time?

And yet who is willing to accept this as the final word on human relationships, a creed by which to live? Not Shakespeare, in any other play. No one can question the relentless exactitude with which, in *Troilus and Cressida*, he has exposed the seamy side of life and character. It is all terribly true, but it is not the whole truth. For the time he has narrowed his outlook, shutting out from his work not only those qualities of mind and heart that led his fellows to speak of him as the 'gentle Shakespeare' and have made him of all our poets the most beloved, but those also by reason of which he takes rank among the world's supreme artists—the discourse that looks before and after, the reason that is godlike, the imagination that illumines and does not merely expose. Bereft of these, his reading of life bears a striking likeness to that of some of our ablest writers to-day. Their bitter disillusionment is easy to explain as the natural reaction of sensitive minds to the war, the peace, and all the social chaos and misery that have been the result of both. To speculate upon what drove Shakespeare to this mood is perhaps less important to us than to note its transience. Not indeed that he ever recovered the radiant buoyancy of spirit that marks his earlier work. On the contrary, he plunged deeper and deeper into life's resistless tragedy, slurring over nothing of its horror, offering no solution of its inscrutable mystery, yet lighting up its darkest recesses with an imagination that pays its tribute to the essential glory of the human spirit. Unlike Troilus, the soul of Lear undergoes no shrinkage as the result of his awful sufferings: it 'unfolds through blood and tears'. The love of Cordelia, of Hermione, of Imogen, outsoars the philosophy of Ulysses: it is not subject to 'envious and calumniating time', but 'looks on tempests and is never shaken',

and 'bears it out even to the edge of doom'; and the truth
of Shakespeare's later reading of life is attested by our
deepest experience. With such a vision he passes out of
that mood in which the earth had seemed to him 'a sterile
promontory', and 'all the uses of this world', 'weary, stale,
flat, and unprofitable'; for he has recaptured his faith in
the diviner elements in our nature; with an insight as
keen as ever into mortal crime and folly, man, 'this quint-
essence of dust', once more becomes for him a creature
'noble in reason . . . infinite in faculty . . . the beauty of
the world'.

V

SPENSER

SPENSER has justly been called the poet's poet. By his contemporaries he was acclaimed as the immortal Spenser, the English Virgil. In the seventeenth century Milton acknowledged that he was his original, Dryden called him master, and Cowley tells how from reading a volume of *The Faerie Queene* that was wont to lie in his mother's parlour he was made a poet while yet he was a child. In the eighteenth century, when the restricted ideals of the poetic art were furthest removed from the looser romanticism of the Elizabethans, Spenser did not lose his fascination. With the correct, concise Pope he was ever a favourite, like a mistress whose faults we see, but love her with them all; and the countless Spenserian imitations perpetrated in that age, tedious most of them, when they are not amusing, bear witness to the potency of an ideal which even when it was not understood, could not be repudiated. The rebirth of a more imaginative spirit was heralded by a growing sensitiveness to Spenser's inherent charm and a deeper appreciation of his meaning; and Wordsworth and Coleridge, Shelley and Keats, all came in different ways under his spell. Later still, he exercised a profound influence on the early writings of Tennyson, was echoed in the cadences of Robert Bridges, and became the idol of that much underrated poet Charles Doughty. To the essentially prosaic mind, indeed, he has often been an offence and a stumbling-block. But despite Addison, who loftily dismissed his 'mystic tale' as able 'to please an understanding age no more', or Horace Walpole, who complained of 'wading through Spenser's interminable drawling stanzas' as the severest penance, or that modern verse writer to whom *The Faerie Queene* is 'the work of a lunatic poet, with no co-ordination, an appearance of moral earnestness, and long dullness, lit up by flashes of nearly good', the consensus of authoritative opinion is with W. P. Ker when he says that *The Faerie Queene* is 'the truest sort of poetry, a poem in which the poetic genius declares itself most truly, as distinct from other kinds of genius'.

This judgement does not imply that Spenser cared for nothing but beauty, or that, provided he had a theme to embroider, the nature of the theme did not greatly concern him. He had, indeed, an unvarying grace of style that gave to the merest trifle or commonplace an individual charm; but if that were all, he would not have been specially beloved of those poets who have taken their art most seriously. Great poetry is not mere filigree, however exquisite; it is expression; and its mysterious beauty of thought and word can only rise from depths of emotional experience. Spenser's passion for beauty was not his sole passion, indulged to the neglect of other elements in his being: it was rather the condition under which, as an artist, he saw all that he loved; through which alone, as an artist, he could express his feeling for it. No man was ever more finely sensitive to the many and varied interests of his time. 'Poets,' says Shelley, 'are a chameleonic race, they take their colour not merely from the food they eat, but from the very leaves under which they pass.' It is sometimes forgotten that Spenser, idealist and dreamer, the fervent Platonist, the tireless explorer of all the wealth of humanistic art and knowledge, followed with a breathless eagerness every turn in the fortunes of his country, and bore an active if humble part in promoting them; that he was a keen partisan, with staunch personal loyalties, that he was known to those in authority as a man 'expert in the wars', the author of businesslike dispatches and of a closely reasoned political pamphlet. His ideal of life was, in fact, the same that inspired many a cultured, high-minded Elizabethan:

> What good is like to this,
> To do worthy the writing, and to write
> Worthy the doing, and the world's delight?

He differed from his fellows in a genius which early awakened his ambition to be the supreme poet of his time. At the age of twenty-seyen this ambition was in part achieved.

The Shepheardes Calendar is rich in interest, both as a bold experiment in poetic language and as a part of Spenser's autobiography, but its chief significance and its lasting value lie in its poetic melodies. Since the days of Chaucer, English verse had limped and halted; and though, with the help of Italian models, Wyatt, Surrey, and Sackville had restored some of its lost dignity, it still lacked suppleness and liquid ease; and there were learned critics who roundly asserted that only by adopting a classical prosody could it ever hope to rival the harmonies of Greece and Rome. Spenser, for all his love of Homer, of Ovid, of Virgil, looked back, with a sure artistic instinct, to Chaucer, and recaptured at once a music that had been lost for a century and a half:

> through infusion sweete
> Of thine owne spirit, which doth in me survive,
> I follow here the footing of thy feete.

In variety and subtlety of rhythm, he excelled even his master. Of the light delicacy of his April Eclogue there is no suggestion in our earlier poetry; whilst in the Eclogue for November he gave a first foretaste of that stately processional music, deeply charged with pathos, which was to be, perhaps, the consummation of his own metrical art:

> Why doe we longer live, (ah why live we so long)
> Whose better dayes death hath shut up in woe?
> The fayrest floure our gyrlond all emong,
> Is faded quite and into dust ygoe.
> Sing now ye shepheards daughters, sing no moe
> The songs that Colin made in her prayse,
> But into weeping turne your wanton layes,
> O heavie herse,
> Now is time to dye. Nay time was long ygoe,
> O carefull verse.

In *The Shepheardes Calendar* Spenser was but trying his wings for a loftier flight. There was good precedent for making the pastoral a prelude to work of bolder design and scope. In the years that followed he poured forth occasional verse sufficient both in quality and bulk to rank him next in his age to Shakespeare; but this was merely the by-product of an unresting poetic activity that was already engaged on a great national poem, in which he hoped to rival, perhaps to overgo, the masterpieces of Italy and France.

The form of *The Faerie Queene* was an almost inevitable outcome of the confluence of literary tradition. To the Platonic doctrine that poetry was a 'divine fury' it seemed to the Renaissance critic an obvious corollary that poetry must serve high moral ends; and as the Elizabethan read the great literature of the past, that end was most nobly realized in the national heroic poem. This conception persisted in Europe from the days of Petrarch for wellnigh three centuries. 'A heroic poem', said Dryden, introducing his translation of the Aeneid, 'is undoubtedly the greatest work which the soul of man is capable to perform. The design of it is to form the mind to heroic virtue by example.' And when Spenser states as the general end of his *Faerie Queene* 'to fashion a gentleman or noble person in vertuous and gentle discipline', and justifies himself by the precedent of Homer and Virgil and Ariosto, he is taking a line which none of his contemporaries would wish to challenge. It is significant, indeed, of the temper of his age that it is not his moral purpose, but his poetry that he feels called upon to defend. 'To some I know,' he says, 'this method will seem displeasant, which had rather have good discipline delivered plainly in way of precepts, or *sermoned at large*, than thus cloudily enwrapt in allegorical devices.' And Milton obviously had in mind these words, as well as the poem which prompted them, when he spoke of poetry as 'the inspired gift of God . . . of power, *beside the effect of the pulpit*, to imbreed and cherish in a great people the seeds of virtue and public civility, to allay the perturbations of the mind and to set the affections in right tune'.

Later aesthetic has poured scorn on this crude poetic theory; but fortunately ignorance of aesthetics, and a misconception of his own psychology, has never hampered a poet when he had the mind to write a masterpiece; and the desire to 'justify the ways of God to men', and to 'fashion a gentleman or noble person in vertuous and gentle discipline', has produced nobler results than have been achieved on the most correct aesthetic principles. To Spenser, indeed, this error was probably a help rather than a hindrance. He was full of poetry; he had a passion for chivalry, for pageantry, for all mythologies, and he had been taught to view them as symbols of fundamental truth; but he had no original constructive power. His moral intention suggested to him a scheme which would give him something of a plot on which to work, and so aid in directing the progress of his poem.

The manner in which the allegory directs the plot of *The Faerie Queene* I shall not now elaborate, for I have dealt fully with it in another place.[1] Dryden remarked that Spenser 'wanted only to have read the rules of Bossu', but the genius of a poet is a law to itself: it is enough for him and for the poetic reader if he find a form, however elastic, in which he can truly express himself. Spenser found it in his fairy land of chivalrous adventure, where every event had some moral significance, and where many an incident glanced at current public affairs. Thus he satisfied at once his vital interest in the world about him and his ideal yearning after physical, moral, and spiritual beauty. The poetic result is an allegory, and in the hands of an inferior artist allegory may be a poor enough thing: to Spenser's imagination it was an incentive. It starts him on his course, but once started allows him a loose rein. Allegory, after all, is a primitive human instinct: for what is metaphor but allegory in the making? Spenser's intellect was essentially of that type in which allegory was born. Abstract thought was impossible to him; his mind worked instinctively by images. When an idea possessed him, it took life in his imagination; he did not consciously, like a philosopher, reason it out, and then

[1] *v.* Introduction to Spenser in the *Oxford Poets.*

rack his brains for an illustration by which to drive it home:
the idea and the illustration were inseparable. He is often
called a philosophic poet; but he is only so in the loose
sense that he was deeply interested in moral ideas; for in
point of fact no writer could illustrate more clearly the
essential quality of the poetic as distinct from the philosophic type of mind. In the age succeeding Spenser's,
Hobbes justly pointed out that metaphors were the *ignes
fatui* of scientific reasoning: Spenser thought in metaphor
and picture. Thus when he conceives of false pride as
having its deepest root in Ignorance, Ignorance becomes
at once incarnate for him in the person of the porter to the
castle of Orgoglio:

> At last with creeping crooked pace forth came
> An old old man, with beard as white as snow,
> That on a staffe his feeble steps did frame,
> And guide his wearie gate both too and fro:
> For his eye sight him failed long ygo,
> And on his arme a bounch of keyes he bore,
> The which unused rust did overgrow:
> Those were the keyes of every inner dore,
> But he could not them use, but kept them still in store;

and to every question that Arthur puts him, his only
answer is *He could not tell*. Or, to take another illustration,
Spenser is fascinated, as who has not been? by the wonders
of memory, that inexplicable faculty to which man owes
all his mental and spiritual growth. But in place of arid
speculation, a picture rises before him of an aged scholar
in a library:

> And therein sate an old old man, halfe blind,
> And all decrepit in his feeble corse,
> Yet lively vigour rested in his mind,
> And recompenst him with a better scorse:
> Weake body well is chang'd for minds redoubled forse.

> This man of infinite remembrance was,
> And things foregone through many ages held,
> Which he recorded still, as they did pas,
> Ne suffred them to perish through long eld,

As all things else, the which this world doth weld,
But laid them up in his immortall scrine,
Where they for ever incorrupted dweld:
The warres he well remembred of king Nine,
Of old Assaracus, and Inachus divine.

The yeares of Nestor nothing were to his,
Ne yet Mathusalem, though longest liv'd;
For he remembred both their infancies:
Ne wonder then, if that he were depriv'd
Of native strength now, that he them surviv'd.
His chamber all was hangd about with rolles,
And old records from auncient times deriv'd,
Some made in books, some in long parchment scrolles,
That were all worme-eaten, and full of canker holes.

Amidst them all he in a chaire was set,
Tossing and turning them withouten end;
But for he was unhable them to fet,
A litle boy did on him still attend,
To reach, when ever he for ought did send;
And oft when things were lost, or laid amis,
That boy them sought, and unto him did lend.

Here we have, instead of abstract reflection on ignorance
and memory, two finely contrasted portraits of old age.
And even when the allegory is most forced and mechanical,
the imaginative picture is true enough. What could be
more ludicrous as an intellectual concept than the *personnel* of the House of Temperance, with its dinner steward
hight Diet, its marshal Appetite, its cook Concoction, and
its kitchen clerk Digestion? Yet the kitchen itself is presented with the genius of a Chardin or van der Meer:

It was a vaut ybuilt for great dispence,
With many raunges reard along the wall;
And one great chimney, whose long tonnell thence
The smoke forth threw. And in the midst of all
There placed was a caudron wide and tall,
Upon a mighty furnace, burning whot.

By the side of the furnace stands a huge great bellows and
about the caudron
>   many Cookes accoyld,
>   With hookes and ladles, as need did require;
>   The whiles the viandes in the vessell boyld
>   They did about their businesse sweat, and sorely toyld.

Such must have been the scene in the great kitchens of
Kenilworth Castle, when a banquet was preparing for
Queen Elizabeth.

This pictorial imagination, innate in Spenser, was
doubtless fostered and developed by his close and ardent
study of works of plastic and decorative art, and of those
pageants, so popular in the 'merry London' of his youth,
which might properly be described as living pictures.
One would gladly know what paintings Spenser had seen,
for his England was not rich in them; but if paintings
were scarce, there were woodcuts and engravings in plenty,
tapestries and illuminated missals. For their reproduction
in poetry he had precedent in his master Chaucer; and he
took every occasion his poem offered to translate into his
own medium what the decorative artist achieved in line
and colour. On the gate to the Bower of Blis, framed of
precious ivory, is carved the tale of Jason and Medea and
the wondered Argo
>   which in venturous peece
>   First through the Euxine seas bore all the flowr of Greece.
>
>   .   .   .   .
>   Ye might have seene the frothy billowes fry
>   Under the ship, as thorough them she went:
>   That seemd the waves were into ivory,
>   Or ivory into the waves were sent.

So the walls of the Castle Joyeous are adorned with costly
cloths of Arras and of Tours, depicting in different scenes
the love of Venus for Adonis:
>   And whilst he slept, she over him would spred
>   Her mantle, colour'd like the starry skyes,
>   And her soft arme lay underneath his hed,
>   And with ambrosiall kisses bathe his eyes;

And whilest he bath'd, with her two crafty spyes,
She secretly would search each daintie lim,
And throw into the well sweet Rosemaryes,
And fragrant violets, and Pances trim,
And ever with sweet Nectar she did sprinkle him.

Such works 'of rare device and wondrous wit' made an
irresistible appeal to him, and their study taught him
much of the art of pictorial composition. No poet has
greater power of unfolding his story in a series of lovely
pictures. When Venus surprises Diana as she is bathing
with her handmaidens in a forest pool we have a painting
that might have come from the hand of Titian:

Soone her garments loose
Upgath'ring, in her bosome she comprized,
Well as she might, and to the Goddesse rose,
Whiles all her Nymphes did like a girlond her enclose.

The guardian angel who watches over the sleeping Guyon
might have sat for his portrait to Mantegna. Spenser's
more homely scenes are equally effective. When Arthur
forces his way into Corflambo's castle,

There he did find in her delitious boure
The faire Poeana playing on a Rote,
Complayning of her cruell Paramoure,
And singing all her sorrow to the note;

it is a life-like Elizabethan interior. So too, with a painter's
eye for the essential, he can depict a landscape. Florimell
looks down from a hill-side into a thickly wooded valley,
and

Through the tops of the high trees she did descry
A litle smoke, whose vapour thin and light,
Reeking aloft, uprolled to the sky:

he has the keen eye of the painter for significant details:
Arthur, visited in a dream by the Queene of fairies,
awakes to find

her place devoyd,
And nought but *pressed* gras, where she had lyen,

and in the same way we are made to feel the fury of the
dragon's onset upon St. George by reference to the *brusëd*
grass over which he has bounded. But like the Renaissance
painters his passion for beauty finds its deepest satisfaction
in depicting the human form; and no one of them has
surpassed Spenser's full-length portrait of Acrasia. Even
where his pictures are less detailed he knows instinctively
on what features to lay the emphasis. He realizes, for
example, like the painter, how rich a source of expression
is a woman's hair, both as a thing of beauty in itself, and
as indicative of the whole mood of his study. Belphoebe's
hair streams down her shoulders, and

> As through the flouring forrest rash she fled,
> In her rude haires sweet flowres themselves did lap,
> And flourishing fresh leaves and blossomes did enwrap;

but the staid matron-like Medina, whose 'gravitie is above
the reason of her youthly yeares,' wore what is, I believe,
called to-day a hair-net:

> Her golden lockes she roundly did uptye
> In breaded tramels, that no looser heares
> Did out of order stray about her daintie eares.

And, like the painter, Spenser delights in the hair for its
colour and its light: when Britomart's helmet is sheared
away the hairs about her face

> Having through stirring loosd their wonted band,
> Like to a golden border did appeare,

and they glisten like the sands of Pactolus; whilst when it
falls to her feet it is 'crested all with lines of fiery light'.

No effect of colour or light or shade escapes him. When
Duessa faints, the Red Cross Knight notes not merely her
ghastly pallor, but the *blue* upon her eyelids. The ferry-
man on the Idle Lake detects the quicksand by the checkëd
wave and the discoloured sea. In the cave of Error the
knight's glistening armour makes 'a litle glooming light,
much like a shade'. Britomart's beauty when she vents her

umbrière suggests to him the moon breaking through a cloud:

> As when faire Cynthia, in darkesome night,
> Is in a noyous cloud enveloped,
> Where she may find the substaunce thin and light,
> Breakes forth her silver beames, and her bright hed
> Discovers to the world discomfited;
> Of the poore traveller, that went astray,
> With thousand blessings she is heried;
> Such was the beautie and the shining ray,
> With which faire Britomart gave light unto the day.

The many descriptions of morning and evening scattered through the poem, whilst they bear witness to his naïve delight in classic myth, are also studies in colour:

> Now when the *rosy*-fingred Morning faire,
> Weary of aged Tithones *saffron* bed,
> Had spred her *purple* robe through deawy aire,
> And the high hils Titan discovered.

But this unique gift for evoking a picture is not reserved for the delineation of beauty. Spenser is equally master of the grotesque. When his giant laughs

> all his teeth wide bare
> One might have seene enraung'd disorderly,
> Like to a rancke of piles, that pitched are awry;

and the pictures of the Deadly Sins, or the figures in the masque of Cupid, afford many a vivid example of realistic power:—Lechery with his 'whally eyes', Doubt who

> lookt askew with his mistrustfull eyes,
> And nicely trode, as thornes lay in his way,
> Or that the flore to shrinke he did avyse,

or Fear

> all arm'd from top to toe,
> Yet thought himselfe not safe enough thereby,
> But feard each shadow moving to and fro,
> And his owne armes when glittering he did spy,
> Or clashing heard, he fast away did fly,
> As ashes pale of hew.

One could illustrate this gift of Spenser's from almost every page of *The Faerie Queene*.

But poetry is not painting; and if it evoke an image it is by means of sound that the image is evoked. Spenser brought to perfection that mysterious pre-established harmony which exists between the rhythm and colour of words and the varied human emotions. The music of our speech is not an accidental ornament, it is a vital element in language; as soon as we use language not merely as a vehicle for ideas, but as a medium for intimate feeling, rhythm and harmony are of its essence. Spenser was the first of our poets to realize this in its full significance, and consciously and consistently to explore the hidden mysteries of musical utterance, giving us his pictured thought in words whose melody creates within us that mood in which alone it can be apprehended. This is clear enough, I think, in many of his descriptions of works of art. An ordinary prose description of a painting, however meticulously accurate, merely acquaints us with its content; and however much it may *talk* of rhythm gives us no real *sense* of it. But the poet's rhythms make us feel the whole as an artistic composition.

> Then was he turnd into a snowy Swan,
> To win faire Leda to his lovely trade:
> O wondrous skill, and sweet wit of the man,
> That her in daffadillies sleeping made,
> From scorching heat her daintie limbes to shade:
> Whiles the proud Bird ruffing his fethers wyde,
> And brushing his faire brest, did her invade;
> She slept, yet twixt her eyelids closely spyde,
> How towards her he rusht, and smiled at his pryde.

By his music, too, Spenser gives unity to that strange and varied world of his *Faerie Queene*. His melodies, with their even flow and rarely broken rhythms, suggest the atmosphere which pervades his imaginative kingdom, contrasting with the world of harsh noises and hoarse disputes without, and bringing that sense at once of security and freedom that we experience, after the tumult and

incoherence of much modern music, in listening to the
rhythm and melody of Bach or Mozart. His music, like
theirs, is sometimes thought monotonous, for only a trained
ear can detect, within so close and definite a structure, the
exquisite nuances of which it is capable: like theirs, it is said
to be soporific; but the sleep into which it lulls is not a
senseless torpor, it is a reverie which unfolds dream after
dream of magic beauty. In the stanza which bears his
name he invented a metrical structure adaptable to all his
moods. Critics have seldom noted how swift and vigorous
it can be when he so desires it:

> But Artegall him after did pursew,
> The whiles the Prince there kept the entrance still:
> Up to the rocke he ran, and thereon flew
> Like a wyld Gote, leaping from hill to hill,
> And dauncing on the craggy cliffes at will;
> That deadly daunger seem'd in all mens sight
> To tempt such steps, where footing was so ill:
> Ne aught avayled for the armed knight,
> To thinke to follow him, that was so swift and light.

It can roll with a magnificent fullness of sound, as in the
stanzas on memory that I have already quoted. Best of
all does it convey the enchantment of 'soft peace'.

> And more, to lulle him in his slumber soft,
> A trickling streame from high rocke tumbling downe
> And ever-drizling raine upon the loft,
> Mixt with a murmuring winde, much like the sowne
> Of swarming Bees, did cast him in a swowne:
> No other noyse, nor peoples troublous cryes,
> As still are wont t'annoy the walled towne,
> Might there be heard: but carelesse Quiet lyes,
> Wrapt in eternall silence farre from enemyes.

Spenser has many devices by which to avoid the mono-
tony that might beset a stanza form repeated through so
many cantos. Throughout his poem he plays off gram-
matical construction against the metrical, ending his sentence anywhere within line or stanza, so that while the
rhythm is maintained, the verse neither becomes too

insistently regular nor imposes itself unduly upon his
thought. In this, as in so many ways, Milton, the supreme
master of the verse paragraph, learnt a lesson from Spenser.
He is the first, too, of our poets to explore the melodic effects
of repetition of word and phrase. This was doubtless
suggested to him by his study of Virgil and Ovid, and none
but Virgil has used it with as telling an effect. Beautiful
examples are to be found in *The Shepheardes Calendar*; it
is brought to perfection in *The Faerie Queene*. At times
he employs it merely for emphasis, an artistic extension
of its use in common speech; at times it takes the form of a
wistful parenthesis:

> And all this was for love of Marinell,
> Who her despys'd (ah, who would her despyse?),

at times it is carried through a whole stanza, each line as it
were catching up its predecessor, so that he seems, like the
stock-dove, to brood over his own sweet voice.

> The joyous birdes shrouded in chearefull shade,
> Their notes unto the voyce attempred sweet;
> Th'Angelicall soft trembling voyces made
> To th'instruments divine respondence meet:
> The silver sounding instruments did meet
> With the base murmure of the waters fall:
> The waters fall with difference discreet,
> Now soft, now loud, unto the wind did call:
> The gentle warbling wind low answered to all.

The musical effect gained by repetition is more subtly
carried out in the studied recurrence of sound which knits
into a closer texture the whole metrical fabric. Alliteration
is a means of emphasis natural to ordinary speech, and in
our earliest poetry it was the basic principle of verse construction. But in Spenser it is not mere hunting the letter;
to him its value lies in the fact that while the metrical
structure depends on its rhythm and regularly recurrent
rhymes, the alliteration is merely an undersong, appearing
and disappearing, now insistent, now faint, sometimes
running on for a word or two, sometimes persisting

through a whole stanza, at times carried out on one letter only, but more often interlacing one alliterative letter with another, and supported by a careful use of assonance; and this 'linked sweetness long drawn out' has not merely a melodic value, it is controlled by the emotional content of the passage.

Spenser knew instinctively, as few poets have done, the emotional correspondences of the different sounds, and he exploited them to the full—the sense of space given by long open vowels and by the semi-vowel *w*—'wide and wasteful wilderness', the harsh effects of the guttural and the medial *r*, the sense of peaceful beauty brought by the letter *l*:

> My senses lulled are in slomber of delight.

Indeed, when Marinell, sorely wounded by Britomart, is visited by the physician, and

> the lilly handed Liagore,
> (This Liagore whylome had learned skill
> In leaches craft, by great Appolloes lore,) . . .
> Did feel his pulse,

our anxiety is relieved, for we know already he is on the road to health. The sibilant is of all sounds the most difficult to render musically, as any one may testify who has listened to a public singer. But Spenser can triumph with it:

> Soft Silence, and submisse Obedience;

there is a hush in the whole line.

It will be noticed that in all these quotations alliteration is not merely on the initial letter; it is sustained by the recurrence of the alliterative letter in the middle of words that follow. And the effect depends not merely on alliteration, which can be crude enough by itself, but rather upon its combination with the other consonant and vowel sounds that surround it, and on the variation of pause and rhythm. Thus it will be felt how in the line

> 'Let me not die in langour and long teares'

the pathos is enforced, after the rapid movement of the

opening words, by the slowing down of the pace at the close, with these two long syllables which disturb the iambic rhythm; or, again, take the line

And on the rocke the waves breaking aloft,

and note how the effect of a breaking wave is suggested by the break in the iambic flow in the fifth foot, and by the cunning disposition of the two long *a* vowels in the middle, *waves breaking*, with the shorter vowels at the beginning and at the end. By the infinitely varied effects gained by variation of pace, and by this subtle juxtaposition of the different vowel and consonant sounds, Spenser gives to his verse that quality justly described by Miss Sitwell as texture, without which mere rhythm and rhyme can achieve little of real melodic beauty.

On the fusion of these two aspects of his genius, the pictorial and the musical, depends the individual charm of his poetic narrative. His gift for telling a story is sometimes questioned. He is said to be too languid and desultory. But surely the object of telling a story is not to get it over. There are, in fact, two contrasting methods in narrative, which, to borrow Schiller's famous distinction, might be termed the 'naïve' and the 'sentimental'. In the first the tale is simply told for its incidents, without comment or embroidery; in the second the story is made the medium for the teller's own thought and feeling, and he elaborates at will any features of it which have vividly caught his imagination. The distinction is clear enough in a comparison, say, of Boccaccio's story of *Isabella and the Pot of Basil* with Keats's retelling of it. Spenser's is the second method; when he does not actually comment on his theme, he makes us feel throughout his own attitude towards it, why he tells it, and what to his eyes is its peculiar fascination. He could often, indeed, have put things more tersely; but beauty counted with him for more than speed, and a lovely elaboration of detail did not, he thought, deflect the mind from his main drift, but rather helped to create the mood in which it could be

seized. This is the reason for those frequent periphrases
which are a prominent feature of his poetic style—'Mul-
ciber's devouring element' for 'fire', or, 'nought under
heav'ns wide hollownesse', when it would unquestionably
be shorter to say 'nothing on earth'. But Spenser cannot
even tell the time prosaically:

> What time the native Belman of the night,
> The bird, that warnèd Peter of his fall,
> First rings his silver Bell t'each sleepy wight,
> That should their mindes up to devotion call.

Even the crudest machinery of his story he will invest
with an unexpected beauty. It is the immemorial romantic custom to identify a stolen or long-lost child by a
birth-mark, and so it is with Spenser's Pastorella; yet who
but he would have thought of referring to a birth-mark as

> a litle purple mold,
> That like a rose her silken leaves did faire unfold.

Thus does he delight to load every rift with ore. And if we
love his story less for its own sake than for what he makes
of it, is the story the worse for that?

Of course some tales suit his method better than others;
but who could wish shorter and brisker his account of
Sir Guyon at the Cave of Mammon, or on the Idle Lake,
or on his journey to the Bower of Acrasia, or, to take a
very different example, the exquisite myth of the birth of
Amoret and Belphoebe? And if his best narratives move
slowly we should at least admit the vigour and rush of his
knightly encounters. Doubtless we wish them fewer, but
their frequency does not impugn the merits of any one of
them taken by itself. And the Elizabethan, who delighted
in the tournament, who himself fought hand to hand, and
knew all the fine points of swordsmanship, must have followed these Spenserian duels with a zest like that with
which we enter into the niceties of skill and resource evoked
by our less venturous athletic contests.

Spenser's stories have also been called confused, chiefly
because, in his later books, instead of finishing off one tale

before he turns to another, he keeps too many running at the same time. Thus he begins the story of Florimell in the first canto of the third book, drops it till the fourth, takes it up again in the seventh and eighth, and then breaks it off till near the close of the next book, leaving poor Florimell in the depth of her misfortunes in order that he may pick up the threads of another story:

> It yrkes me leave thee in this wofull state,
> To tell of Satyrane, where I him left of late,

he explains to his heroine, with his unfailing courtesy. Perhaps it irks us too, but we have only to piece the tale together to find that it moves with perfect lucidity.

But to enjoy this, as so many of Spenser's stories, you have to accept the conditions of fairyland: it is vain to turn upon them the searching light of common sense. To enter into the richest provinces of the kingdom of poetry you must become as a little child, with a child's passion for make-believe and something of the child's credulity. The Elizabethan, like the ancient Greek, could do this. Ovid's *Metamorphoses* was among his favourite books; he could read with delight the wildest medieval romance. And when he wrote romances himself he gave them all Spenser's impossibilities without achieving his beauty. Yet Shakespeare thought it no shame to plunder them for plots. The 'childish absurdity' of Spenser was the discovery of the rational eighteenth century. It did not disturb Ben Jonson, who disliked Spenser's diction, yet declared that he should be read for his matter; it did not trouble Milton. 'Allah', says a modern poet, 'gave men dreams by night that they might learn to dream by day.' But we are for the most part too sophisticated, and there is a modern tendency to relegate the dream to the psycho-analyst's laboratory. Spenser is for those who can still delight to wander in that world of his imagination

> exceeding spacious and wyde,
> And sprinckled with such sweet variety,
> Of all that pleasant is to eare or eye,

a world which prosaic reason may reject, but which, for all that, is shot through with vivid glimpses of our waking life. For the 'ear and eye' of the sane man do not find 'pleasant' that which is meaningless; and below and through the shifting stream of dream-like imagery flashes a poet's vision of that world 'which is the world of all of us'. Though Arthur's love is for the queen of fairies, who has only visited him in sleep, the stirrings of his heart under sudden passion are revealed with realistic penetration. Dragons may not nowadays be one of the terrors we are called to face; yet the behaviour of the crowd when they come out to view the dead monster is not the less true to life:

> And after, all the raskall many ran,
> Heapèd together in rude rablement,
> To see the face of that victorious man:
> Whom all admirèd, as from heaven sent,
> And gaz'd upon with gaping wonderment.
> But when they came, where that dead Dragon lay,
> Stretcht on the ground in monstrous large extent,
> The sight with idle feare did them dismay,
> Ne durst approch him nigh, to touch, or once assay.

> Some feard, and fled; some feard and well it faynd;
> One that would wiser seeme, then all the rest,
> Warnd him not touch, for yet perhaps remaynd
> Some lingring life within his hollow brest,
> Or in his wombe might lurke some hidden nest
> Of many Dragonets, his fruitfull seed;
> Another said, that in his eyes did rest
> Yet sparckling fire, and bad thereof take heed;
> Another said, he saw him move his eyes indeed.

> One mother, when as her foolehardie chyld
> Did come too neare, and with his talants play,
> Halfe dead through feare, her litle babe revyld,
> And to her gossips gan in counsell say;
> How can I tell, but that his talants may
> Yet scratch my sonne, or rend his tender hand?
> So diversly themselves in vaine they fray;
> Whiles some more bold, to measure him nigh stand,
> To prove how many acres he did spread of land.

Or again, we may not think of Care as a blacksmith, but
who has not experienced a night such as Scudamour passes
in Care's gloomy dwelling?

> There lay Sir Scudamour long while expecting,
> When gentle sleepe his heavie eyes would close;
> Oft chaunging sides, and oft new place electing,
> Where better seem'd he mote himselfe repose;
> And oft in wrath he thence againe uprose;
> And oft in wrath he layd him downe againe.
> But wheresoever he did himselfe dispose,
> He by no meanes could wished ease obtaine:
> So every place seem'd painefull, and ech changing vaine.
>
> And evermore, when he to sleepe did thinke,
> The hammers sound his senses did molest;
> And evermore, when he began to winke,
> The bellowes noyse disturb'd his quiet rest,
> Ne suffred sleepe to settle in his brest.
> And all the night the dogs did barke and howle
> About the house, at sent of stranger guest;
> And now the crowing Cocke, and now the Owle
> Lowde shriking him afflicted to the very sowle.

These are but obvious examples of a constant penetration
into the things of life to be found in a poem that is sometimes dismissed as a mere succession of lovely pictures.

As the *Faerie Queene* proceeds its character undergoes
some change, and in place of pure allegory it develops a
more intimate psychology. This was partly because the
virtues which Spenser comes to treat—Love, Friendship,
Courtesy—called for a different handling, partly also because his interest in the subtleties of human nature grew
with the passage of the years. Britomart, whose character is developed through three books of the poem, is not,
like Una, a mere allegorical idealization; though she is a
warrior, whose enchanted spear lays every foe upon the
green, she has all the complex emotions of a living woman.
The way in which she struggles with her nascent passion
and strives to hide it, disparages her lover that she may
have the exquisite joy of hearing his praises sung; her

bearing when she meets him, and then, when they have to part, her ingenuity in devising pretexts to keep him a little longer, are all delineated with a subtle knowledge of the heart. Most wonderful of all is that later scene, which depicts the jealous fears that crowd upon her when she is waiting alone, 'after the utmost date assigned' for his return:

> Yet loth she was, since she no ill did heare,
> To thinke of him so ill: yet could she not forbeare.

She first resolves to send and seek him out; then she decides that she must go herself:

> One day, when as she long had sought for ease
> In every place, and every place thought best,
> Yet found no place, that could her liking please,
> She to a window came, that opened West,
> Towards which coast her love his way addrest.
> There looking forth, she in her heart did find
> Many vaine fancies, working her unrest;
> And sent her winged thoughts, more swift then wind,
> To beare unto her love the message of her mind.
>
> There as she looked long, at last she spide
> One comming towards her with hasty speede.

It is Talus, with the tidings of Artegall's subjection to Radigund. And with the same unerring instinct Spenser lays bear her torment when called upon to face this new trial of her love. It is throughout a marvellous portrait; for its equal outside Shakespeare there is no woman in our literature between Chaucer's Criseyde and Clarissa Harlowe.

Equally masterly in its psychology, and startlingly modern in its theme, is Spenser's contrasting picture of the eternal triangle of jealous husband, light woman, and heartless rake. Malbecco, torn between love for his wife and for his money, Paridell, accomplished in all the arts of the seducer, and when he has had his pleasure casting her off, 'so had he servèd many one', Hellenore encouraging him, then hesitating, then becoming utterly dissolute, are all revealed in the most telling and subtle strokes. Guy de Maupassant has given the story a different setting, but has not made it more true to life. Then, in the final episode, Spenser reverts from realism to fantasia, and in his conception of Malbecco's transformation from a jealous, covetous man into jealousy itself, he gives us one of his most daringly imaginative flights. And as in a dream those situations which bear upon our waking life stand out most clearly in their strange unreal setting, so in Spenser the juxtaposition of the realistic with the romantic lends force to each. After the story of Malbecco he brings us back for a time to the world of allegorical romance, and we accompany Britomart as she passes through the flames to rescue Amoret from the toils of the enchanter. But once more, on her triumphant return, we return to our own world; and with that insight into the heart of reality which belongs to the imaginative poet, and to him alone, Spenser lays bare in a perfect picture the emotions of two noble lovers, reunited after a long and bitter separation:

> Lightly he clipt her twixt his armes twaine,
> And streightly did embrace her body bright,
> Her body, late the prison of sad paine,
> Now the sweet lodge of love and deare delight:
> But she faire Lady overcommen quight
> Of huge affection, did in pleasure melt,
> And in sweete ravishment pourd out her spright:
> No word they spake, nor earthly thing they felt,
> But like two senceles stocks in long embracement dwelt.

Spenser, with all his exquisite artistic proficiency, would not have been the 'poet's poet' had he lacked knowledge of the deepest human emotions, or failed to cast the light of beauty upon the motive forces of our being. His faith in man's inherent nobility never wavered, and he delighted to pay it homage. He chose the world of chivalry for his *mise en scène* because those virtues which chivalry held most in honour—loyalty, courage, tenderness to the weak, unfailing courtesy—were most precious to him also. The gay mockery which flickers over the surface of Ariosto's world, or Chaucer's ironic detachment were alike alien to his grave idealistic temper. He follows the fortunes of his characters with an intense sympathy, and their perils and distresses stir him to his noblest moral reflection.

Critics have objected that in these reflections he has only proclaimed with sonorous voice obvious moral truths. And let us admit that he made no ethical discoveries: he tells us nothing that we did not know before. But to bring this as a charge against him is to misconceive the whole function of poetry. Shelley was surely right when he asserted that we have more wisdom than we know how to reduce into practice; we want the creative energy to imagine what we know and to feel what we imagine. The truest things in life are the most obvious, but their very familiarity deadens our sense of them, if it does not actually breed contempt. Seen through the poet's eyes, and moving to his music, what we had accepted as a commonplace is 'felt in the blood, and felt along the heart'.

The Faerie Queene is the 'intimate echo' of a nature singularly rich and lovable. No poet has exercised a more potent personal spell: his very style reveals a graciousness of temper that is irresistible. For all the far sought opulence of his art there is in him a winning simplicity. If he entered with zest into the splendours and pageantry of his age, his poem makes it clear enough, by slight incidental touches, that his heart still lay open to the most elemental of human pleasures. When Sir Calepine recovers from his wounds his first longing is 'to heare the thrushes song'. After the magnificent procession of Deadly Sins the company go forth 'to take the solace of the open aire', and be 'with pleasaunce of the breathing fields yfed'. Spenser had too an exquisitely tender feeling for all creatures that are young, or helpless, or fragile: the foundling child is to him 'a lovely litle spoile'; a gnat is 'the litle noursling of the humid ayre'. The prevalent mood in which so delicately sensitive a nature looks out upon this harsher world, is inevitably tinged with a profound melancholy. The eternal

warfare waged between the life of every day and the life
of the spirit weighed heavy upon him; he was conscious
of the discord not merely outside himself but in his own
divided nature. Though right may triumph in his dreams,
in his experience the struggle was hard and the issue doubt-
ful. Even his absorbing passion for beauty he knew to be
a snare as well as an inspiration. The creator of Acrasia
and the Bower of Bliss would have found it hard to enact
the ruthless part assigned to his knight of Temperance.
As a true son of his age he accepted its ideal of strenuous
action, but he was baffled by its contradictions and com-
plexities. And further, he was haunted by a sense of the
vanity of wordly ambitions, even while he pursued them,
above all by the transitoriness of all human things:

> So passeth, in the passing of a day,
> Of mortall life the leafe, the bud, the flowre.

What could man achieve against 'Time with his consuming
sickle'? Life holds out to every man a challenge that none
but the coward can refuse, yet the poignant cry of his
heart, which re-echoes through his most lovely poetry, is
for 'careless quiet', and it is significant that the subtlest
bait with which Despair can tempt man to self-destruction
is the lure of peace:

> He there does now enjoy eternall rest
> And happie ease, which thou doest want and crave,
> And further from it daily wanderest:
> What if some litle paine the passage have,
> That makes fraile flesh to feare the bitter wave?
> Is not short paine well borne, that brings long ease,
> And layes the soule to sleepe in quiet grave?
> Sleepe after toyle, port after stormie seas,
> Ease after warre, death after life does greatly please.

But the poet who could translate into language, so exquisite
in image and melody, the deepest questionings of his heart,
had within himself the resource with which to combat
them. Though all things on this earth, even beauty, were
transitory, yet in his yearning for that 'central peace

subsisting at the heart of endless agitation', he could look
forward to a future

> when no more change shal be,
> But stedfast rest of all things, firmely stayd
> Upon the pillours of Eternitye;

and in the meantime, he found abiding solace in the loveliness of the world about him as it was reflected in his own
mind; and with a faith that was never shaken he saw in it
a symbol of the divine beauty after which he aspired:

> For of the soule the bodie forme doth take:
> For soule is forme, and doth the bodie make.

VI

BLAKE

THE art of the eighteenth century is never happier than when it draws its inspiration from contemporary life. The very limitations of its horizon gave an ordered perfection to its achievement. Pope, Fielding, Hogarth—all its greatest artists—recognized in man their proper study, and by man they understood man in his social relations. None better than they could

> shoot folly as it flies,
> And catch the manners living as they rise;

their art reflects as in a mirror of unrivalled clarity and brilliance the world in which they lived.

But with that world Blake had no concern. 'Inspiration and vision' were his 'eternal dwelling place'. The man who has never in his mind travelled to heaven was to him no artist. From early childhood he saw visions and he dreamed dreams: he did not confuse the world of vision with the world of every day, and in this world he often showed a shrewd practical sense; but poetry, painting, music belonged for him elsewhere—they were simply 'the three powers of conversing with Paradise'. To the eighteenth century, poetry was the finest of accomplishments; and if you had the gift, its practice was merely a matter of industry and application. Dr. Johnson condemned as 'fantastic foppery' Gray's notion that he could not write but at certain times and in happy moments: Blake held with Milton that poetry was 'the gift of that eternal spirit who can enrich with all utterance and knowledge, and sends out his Seraphim with the hallowed fire of his altar to touch and purify the lips of whom he pleases'. 'The ancients', he writes, 'did not mean to impose when they affirmed their belief in vision and revelation. Plato was in earnest, Milton was in earnest. They believed that God

did visit man, really and truly.' And the contemporary
distrust of enthusiasm he countered by asserting that
'enthusiastic admiration is the first principle of knowledge,
and its last'.

Naturally, therefore, he was recalcitrant to the lessons
which his age might have taught him. To formal education he owed even less than Chatterton, but unlike Chatterton he rejoiced in his escape:

> Thank God! I never was sent to school
> To be flogg'd into following the style of a fool.

From the first his genius found its own models and followed
its own impulse. At ten years old he attended a drawing
school, and at fourteen he was apprenticed to an engraver,
to learn that profession which was to be his livelihood;
but whilst the models set before him were chiefly classical
in design and spirit, the Gothic monuments at West-
minster Abbey gave him something of the inspiration that
Chatterton had gained from St. Mary Redcliffe, and at
a time when the more florid later Italian painters were
all the rage, the drawings he eagerly studied were copies
of Raphael, Michael Angelo, and Dürer. 'I am happy',
he wrote later, 'I cannot say that Raphael was from my
earliest childhood hidden from me. I saw and knew
immediately the difference between a Raphael and a
Rubens.' In poetry he showed the same revolt from contemporary fashion. At twelve years old he was a poet, and
his *Poetical Sketches*, privately issued in 1783, were all
written before he was twenty. It would be natural to
assume that the cruder of them were the work of early
boyhood, yet the one poem we can date, written before
he was fourteen, reveals the sure touch of an accomplished
artist.

> How sweet I roam'd from field to field
> And tasted all the summer's pride,
> Till I the Prince of Love beheld
> Who in the sunny beams did glide!

He show'd me lilies for my hair,
And blushing roses for my brow;
He led me through his gardens fair
Where all his golden pleasures grow.

With sweet May dews my wings were wet,
And Phoebus fir'd my vocal rage;
He caught me in his silken net,
And shut me in his golden cage.

He loves to sit and hear me sing,
Then, laughing, sports and plays with me;
Then stretches out my golden wing,
And mocks my loss of liberty.

Only one line, 'And Phoebus fir'd my vocal rage', savours
of current taste: the rest resumes the purer style of an
earlier period. In one of the lyrics, indeed, he captures the
finely controlled form and balanced music of his time; but
he employs them, significantly, to lament the evil days
on which poetry has fallen:

How have you left the ancient love
That bards of old enjoy'd in you!
The languid strings do scarcely move!
The sound is forc'd, the notes are few!

For the most part his music is as individual as is the spirit
which impelled him to sing. Where he can be said to have
a model he harks back to Shakespeare and the Elizabethan
and Carolingian songsters, catching echoes that had long
grown faint. 'My silks and fine array', 'Love and harmony
combine', 'I love the jocund dance', *To Memory*, recall
those happy days when words and notes were coupled
lovingly together. Such, indeed, was Blake's own practice.
He delighted, we are told, to sing his songs to airs of his
own invention, and doubtless tune and words came into
being together, his mood or idea guiding him to the tune,
the tune moulding the words to their peculiar cadence and
melody. Finest of all, both metrically and imaginatively,
is the *Mad Song*. In this wonderful poem he gives individual and haunting music to the turbid passion of the

maniac, who finds in the wildness of the night a sympathy
with his own disordered state, and hugging his anguish,
turns in horror from the sweet comforts of day:

> The wild winds weep,
> And the night is a-cold;
> Come hither, Sleep,
> And my griefs unfold:
> But lo! the morning peeps
> Over the eastern steeps,
> And the rustling birds of dawn
> The earth do scorn.
>
> Lo! to the vault
> Of pavèd heaven,
> With sorrow fraught
> My notes are driven:
> They strike the ear of night,
> Make weep the eyes of day;
> They make mad the roaring winds,
> And with tempests play.
>
> Like a fiend in a cloud,
> With howling woe
> After night I do crowd,
> And with night will go;
> I turn my back to the east
> From whence comforts have increas'd;
> For light doth seize my brain
> With frantic pain.

But if this first volume reveals what Blake could do
supremely well, it shows too, his limitations. In those
forms of poetry in which the narrative, the dramatic, the
meditative predominate over the lyrical impulse, and prescribe a stricter verse-form, he is less happy. His *Imitation
of Spenser* has six stanzas; in three of them he does not
even hit the right number of lines to the stanza; in none
of them is his verse-scheme correct, in none is his music
comparable to that of his great model. His mastery of
blank verse is hardly surer. Despite his passion for Milton,
the Miltonic harmonies awakened in him no echoes. His

attempted drama, *Edward III*, is clearly inspired by Shakespeare's historical plays, but its verse, at times mechanically
correct, often becomes so chaotic that the metrical scheme
is wholly lost—only where the feeling is lyrical is his ear
true. So too, when, drawn for a boyish moment to the
bastard romanticism of Walpole's *Castle of Otranto*, he
wrote in blank verse his crude ballad of *Fair Elenor*, his
real voice only breaks through in Elenor's lyrical cry:

> 'My lord was like a flower upon the brows
> Of lusty May! Ah, life as frail as flower!
>
> .   .   .   .
>
> 'My lord was like a star in highest heav'n
> Drawn down to earth by spells and wickedness;
> My lord was like the opening eyes of day
> When western winds creep softly o'er the flowers.

But the laxity of his sense of form, when his verse is not
pure song, was most fatally evident in his attraction to the
metrical prose of Ossian. Here was his largest debt to
his age: it is a debt wholly deplorable. Blending in him
with the influence of Biblical prose, from which it was
itself derived and from which he had not the trained
literary sense to distinguish it, this manner of writing was
destined to be the pitfall of his maturer genius.

But when he is content to be the lyric poet, Blake is his
true self. Of his contemporaries Chatterton alone had
gained metrical effects comparable with his, and Blake,
when he wrote his *Poetical Sketches*, had read no Chatterton. And his achievement was finer than Chatterton's, in
that he committed no violence upon the language. Chatterton escaped from conventional poetic phrasing into a diction in its own way as unreal as that which he rejected.
Blake, with a finer artistic instinct, went back to the
elemental simplicities.

The *Poetical Sketches* is as remarkable for its pictorial
as for its musical attainment. Its very title suggests its
inherent character as the work of an imagination that as
readily expressed itself in line and colour as in words,

and when words were his medium, he had an equal power
to evoke a vivid picture. Personification in contemporary
verse had become a mere trick of style, so that, as Coleridge
pointed out, it 'depended wholly on the compositor's
putting, or not putting, a capital letter whether the
words should be personifications or mere abstractions'.
But Blake's art knows no abstractions. From the first his
vision was anthropomorphic. 'Think of a white cloud',
he said, 'as being holy, and you cannot love it: think of a
holy man within a white cloud and love springs in your
thought: to think of holiness as distinct from man is
impossible to the affections.' His sensitive response to
nature finds expression partly through pure description,
but partly through a power akin to that which he noted in
the ancient poets, 'of animating all sensible objects with
Gods or geniuses':

> O thou with dewy locks, who lookest down
> Thro' the clear windows of the morning, . . .
> .   .   .   .
> Come o'er the eastern hills, and let our winds
> Kiss thy perfumed garments.

So he addresses the spring: winter he sees as a 'direful
monster, whose skin clings to his strong bones', as he
'strides o'er the groaning rocks', and 'withers all in silence';
and thus he invokes the Evening Star:

> Thou fair-haired angel of the evening,
> Now, whilst the sun rests on the mountains, light
> Thy bright torch of love; thy radiant crown
> Put on, and smile upon our evening bed!
> Smile on our loves, and while thou drawest the
> Blue curtains of the sky, scatter thy silver dew
> On every flower that shuts its sweet eyes
> In timely sleep. Let thy west wind sleep on
> The lake; speak silence with thy glimmering eyes,
> And wash the dusk with silver.

And as he saw nature anthropomorphically, so his feeling
for nature gave a vividness to his grouping of human

figures. His dull Ossianic fragment, *Samson*, is redeemed from nullity by the superbly imaginative picture of Delilah at her husband's feet:

> He seemed a mountain, his brow among the clouds;
> She seemed a silver stream, his feet embracing.

These lines have the quality of some of Blake's own drawings.

Such is the character of the *Poetical Sketches*. We can as a rule be content to describe the effusions of authors in their teens as *Juvenilia*. Blake and Chatterton alone among our poets produced in boyhood verse which can be judged not merely on its promise but on its achievement. The best things in the *Poetical Sketches* bear no signs of immaturity; further advance was hardly possible in either musical or pictorial power; it was only left to him to put his art to a deeper purpose, and to become the poet of the human soul.

In 1789 Blake engraved the *Songs of Innocence*. If, as has been suggested, these lovely poems owe their origin to Dr. Watts's verses for children, we can only marvel at the transforming power of genius. Blake does not merely sing, however tenderly and intimately, of childhood: in him the spirit of childhood is vocal. Many poets have sought to recapture the radiance of that Heaven that lies about us at our infancy; and more than a century earlier Vaughan had lamented its loss with a passionate regret:

> I cannot reach it; and my striving eye
> Dazzles at it, as at eternity,

he cries; yet he can only

> see through a long night
> (its) edges, and (its) bordering light:

Blake lived at its 'centre and mid-day'. Nearer to him than Vaughan is Traherne's reminiscence of 'those sweet and glorious apprehensions of the world, when all things were spotless and pure and glorious', and 'everything was at rest, free, and immortal'. But Blake does not merely recall his childhood, he relives it; and utters it in song,

subtle and sweet beyond the reach of Traherne's somewhat limited and halting Muse. The child's first vision
of the world he renders with an art so fine that we are
conscious of no style, no metrical device, no effort of
thought. Yet the metres vary with a delicate aptness;
the language is as vital as it is transparent, the thought as
profound as it is simple. Here, indeed, he fulfils what he
felt to be the aim of poetry: he converses with Paradise—
with a Heaven on earth where Infant Joy finds immediate
response in the mother's ecstasy, and the green re-echoes
with merry laughter alike of young and old, and where,
if sorrow enters, it is but for a moment, to give a greater
reality to happiness. If the little boy is lost on a lonely
fen, God appears in his father's guise and brings him
back to his mother's arms, if even a tiny emmet misses its
way there is a glow-worm to guide it homewards. For to
the child the divine image of Mercy, Pity, Love, and Peace
lights up natural and human worlds alike. The spirit that
pervades these lovely songs is nowhere more fully expressed,
or rendered with a more delicate music, than in the poem
called *Night*.

> The sun descending in the west,
> The evening star does shine;
> The birds are silent in their nest,
> And I must seek for mine.
> The moon, like a flower,
> In heaven's high bower,
> With silent delight
> Sits and smiles on the night.
>
> Farewell, green fields and happy groves,
> Where flocks have took delight.
> Where lambs have nibbled, silent moves
> The feet of angels bright;
> Unseen they pour blessing,
> And joy without ceasing,
> On each bud and blossom,
> And each sleeping bosom.

. . . .

And there the lion's ruddy eyes
Shall flow with tears of gold,
And pitying the tender cries,
And walking round the fold,
Saying 'Wrath, by His meekness,
And, by His health, sickness
Is driven away
From our immortal day.

'And now beside thee, bleating lamb,
I can lie down and sleep;
Or think on Him who bore thy name,
Graze after thee and weep.
For, wash'd in life's river,
My bright mane for ever
Shall shine like the gold
As I guard o'er the fold.'

That same idealistic vision, which here anticipates the
day when the lion shall lie down with the lamb, can illumine
for him an incident from the present world of reality:

'Twas on a Holy Thursday, their innocent faces clean,
The children walking two and two, in red and blue and green,
Grey-headed beadles walk'd before, with wands as white as snow,
Till into the high dome of Paul's they like Thames' waters flow.

O what a multitude they seem'd, these flowers of London town!
Seated in companies they sit with radiance all their own.
The hum of multitudes was there, but multitudes of lambs,
Thousands of little boys and girls raising their innocent hands.

Now like a mighty wind they raise to Heaven the voice of song,
Or like harmonious thunderings the seats of Heaven among.
Beneath them sit the aged men, wise guardians of the poor;
Then cherish pity, lest you drive an angel from your door.

The strangely moving quality of these poems defies all
attempts at criticism. The first published account of them
tells us that *Holy Thursday* 'expresses with majesty and
pathos the feelings of a benevolent mind, on being present
at a sublime display of national munificence and charity'.

But how little does this well-meant comment enter into the spirit in which Blake conceived it! Of that, we may be sure, a part lay in the appeal to the artist of the beauty of form and colour, as the procession, flowing like Thames water, wound its way into the cathedral; part in its appeal to the musician within him. So Haydn, we are told, visiting St. Paul's on a Holy Thursday some years before Blake, spoke of the children's singing as the most divine music he had ever heard. And these impressions of eye and ear are fused in the poem in an exquisitely tender religious feeling, and are set down in language that seems inevitable.

Six years later Blake added to these *Songs of Innocence* his *Songs of Experience*, wherein the purer vision of childhood is crossed and shadowed by the darker realities of life. The more completely the imagination has made its home in the Eden of trustful happy infancy, the more keenly alive will it be to the perplexities, the sorrow, and the shame of the maturer outlook. The world was not to Blake a kindly foster-nurse, weaning him by imperceptible stages from the sweet pieties of boyhood, till he came to accept the sophistries and deceits of age without a consciousness of his loss: it burst upon an unclouded vision with all the force of contrast, and his exposure of it was all the more searching. In this 'contrary state of the soul', as he has called it, those very qualities of Mercy, Pity, Peace, and Love that gave beauty to the life of innocence are now seen to depend on their opposites:

> Pity would be no more
> If we did not make somebody poor;
> And Mercy no more could be
> If all were as happy as we.

If there is peace in this discordant world it is only because we are afraid of one another, and fear breeds cruelty and deceit. Sympathy, which had seemed to unite in one bond of fellowship old and young, rich and poor, is now replaced by apathy and hatred; and hatred has its ecstasies no less

than love. But in love itself the contraries are most be-
wildering:

> 'Love seeketh not itself to please,
> Nor for itself hath any care,
> But for another gives its ease,
> And builds a Heaven in Hell's despair.'

> So sung a little Clod of Clay,
> Trodden with the cattle's feet,
> But a Pebble of the brook
> Warbled out these metres meet:

> 'Love seeketh only Self to please,
> To bind another to its delight,
> Joys in another's loss of ease,
> And builds a Hell in Heaven's despite.'

Several of the *Songs of Experience* are expressly designed
as contrasts to poems in the earlier series. The nurse whose
heart filled with love and peace as she entered into the
children's play, thinks now only of her lost youth, and her
face turns green and pale. The song of praise raised in
St. Paul's on *Holy Thursday* is now a trembling cry:

> Is this a holy thing to see
> In a rich and fruitful land,
> Babes reduc'd to misery,
> Fed with cold and usurous hand?

The same contrast pervades the world of nature, where the
dark secret love of the invisible worm destroys the rose;
and in place of the lamb, symbol of divine love and tenderness, Blake sees the tiger, 'burning bright in the forests of
the night', emblem of mysterious terror, whose fearful symmetry was beaten out by strokes from immortal hammers:

> When the stars threw down their spears,
> And water'd heaven with their tears,
> Did he smile his work to see?
> Did he who made the Lamb make thee?

In such a world how will a man's fate differ from that of
the little fly whose summer play is brushed aside by a

thoughtless hand? Yet the bewilderment, the scorn, the
sense of shame with which he views the world about him
wrings from him a more varied and a deeper music. In
the earlier series there is nothing to match the solemnity
of the appeal to earth in the introductory poem, or the
pulsating splendour of the Tiger, or the poignant beauty
of the address to the Sunflower, wherein he hymns that
thwarted passion which must look for its fulfilment to
another world than ours:

> Ah, Sun-flower! weary of time,
> Who countest the steps of the sun;
> Seeking after that sweet golden clime,
> Where the traveller's journey is done;
>
> Where the Youth pined away with desire,
> And the pale Virgin shrouded in snow,
> Arise from their graves, and aspire
> Where my Sun-flower wishes to go.

The *Songs of Innocence* were engraved in the year of the
storming of the Bastille, and naturally enough Blake, the
rebel against all conventions, was among the most ardent
sympathizers with the early Revolutionists. He was a
frequent visitor at the house of Johnson the bookseller,
where the enthusiasts were wont to congregate—Godwin
and Mary Wollstonecraft, Price, Priestley, and Tom Paine.
He shared with them the passion for liberty, like them
attributed the world's miseries to the organized tyranny of
which kings and priests were the type, like them he looked
in the near future for a millennium, when all should be, in
simplicity and happiness at least, as little children. The
French Revolution became to Blake for a time the incarnation of an ideal which was an eternal reality to his imagination. But when news reached him of the Reign of Terror
he cast aside the *bonnet rouge* which he had donned as
a token of his sympathy; and even from the first the historical fact had been less to him than the ideal which it
had seemed to embody. Hence from its collapse he suffered
no spiritual crisis. The issues at stake were not to him

political. 'I am really sorry', he wrote later, 'to see my countrymen trouble themselves about politics. If men were wise the most arbitrary princes could not hurt them; if they are not wise the freest government is compelled to be a tyranny.' Moreover from men of Godwin's intellectual temper he had an instinctive shrinking. The materialism of the Revolutionaries revolted him; their deification of reason was in his eyes the very cause of the evils they sought to eradicate. His battle was against that God whom they had enthroned; and their arid philosophy which admitted no evidence that could not be apprehended by the physical senses, he met with a passionate faith in intuition as the only source of knowledge. 'Innate ideas', he insisted, 'are born in every man: the man who says that we have no innate ideas must be a fool or a knave.' To the question 'Does a firm persuasion that a thing is so, make it so?' he replies, 'All poets believe that it does, and in ages of imagination this firm persuasion removed mountains.' He was undisturbed by the dilemma that contrary notions held by different men, or by himself at different times, made truth purely relative. Scepticism, the distrust of intuition or of any tenet that cannot be established by the scientific reasoning, was death to the spirit:

> If the sun and moon should doubt,
> They'd immediately go out;

and the sterile cynicism of the materialist he meets with a triumphant confidence:

> Mock on, mock on, Voltaire, Rousseau;
> Mock on, mock on, 'tis all in vain!
> You throw the sand against the wind,
> And the wind blows it back again.

> And every sand becomes a gem
> Reflected in the beams divine;
> Blown back they blind the mocking eye,
> But still in Israel's paths they shine.

In this he was uttering his own deepest experience. When truth came to him it came, not at the end of a train of reasoning, but by a flash of inspiration, as it always comes to the poet. 'The spirit', he told Crabb Robinson, 'had said to him, Blake, be an artist and nothing else: in this there is felicity.' And where Blake the artist speaks his vision compels acceptance.

But unfortunately he was not content to 'be an artist and nothing else'; and in a series of *Prophetic Books* he subordinated his artistic impulse to the desire to expound an elaborate metaphysic:

'I must create a system', he says, 'or be enslav'd by another man's: I will not reason and compare: my business is to create;'

and he set himself to create a mythology through which to body forth his conception of the origin and progress of the world, the different states of the human soul, and the forces against which the soul must struggle in its passage through time and eternity. But he underrated the part that reason must play in any system. For how 'create a system', without reason or comparison? Moreover, his refusal, or rather his inability, to 'reason and compare', affects his *Prophetic Books* no less fatally when they are viewed as works of art. Despite his visionary power of seeing abstract ideas in human or superhuman form, he had not that constructive imagination which alone can develop them in their relation with one another, and make of their interaction of character a coherent and consecutive plot. The true myth-maker has a gift alike for narrative and for drama: Blake's artistic genius, like his thought, was lyrical and pictorial.

He was still further deluded by the crude naïvety with which he interpreted his doctrine of inspiration. The Muses, he maintained, were the daughters of Imagination, not of memory. But even Blake's Muses must be allowed two parents, and surely Memory is one, though they may take more after the other. He ignored the part played by Memory, and by tradition, handmaid of Memory, in a poet's acquisition of both form and imagery. Hence, consciously and with a lofty arrogance, he rejected the lessons he might have learned from Shakespeare or Milton, and when he fondly thought himself most original he fell into unconscious imitation of less happy models. If the Books of Ezekiel and the Revelation had been expurgated from his Bible, if he had never read the works of Swedenborg, or fallen beneath the spell of MacPherson's *Ossian*, his prophetic writings might have been spared some of their worst obscurities and excesses of cloudy rhetoric and vague symbolism. And further, convinced of the divine origin of any idea that presented itself to his mind, and persuaded that he was less its author than the secretary recording a truth transmitted to him, he accepted the first language which came into his head as the final and inevitable form of its expression. This fallacy of immediate verbal inspiration had not deluded him when he was writing his lyrics; many extant variants and alternative drafts go to prove how great the care he expended, before he was satisfied with them as the true verbal counterpart of his vision. But in the *Prophetic Books*, refusing to sift and weigh and correct language that came to him only too readily in the first excitement of his vision, he often failed in poetic creation. For art is not vision, but the communication of vision, and adequately to communicate it calls for a patient labour which is in itself a vital element in poetic inspiration; indeed, it is only in the effort to communicate it that the artist becomes fully and vividly aware of its real content and character. He was deluded, too, in his choice of medium; there is no doubt that the rhythmical prose form, which he adopted, if he had only known it, simply because it was easy to write, and the noisy rhetoric and exaggerated phrasing which characterize what he calls the 'terrific parts' of the *Prophetic Books*, dulled his once delicate ear to the subtler cadences of verse. The flute player who lays aside his instrument that he may blare away upon the trumpet inevitably loses something of his delicacy of tone and feeling. Blake's later poetry has little of the fine modulation and subtle music that charms us in the earlier.

Yet though the *Prophetic Books*, judged as a whole, are neither poetry nor philosophy, few of their darkest pages do not of a sudden light up with flashes of lyrical beauty, or radiate with noble and penetrating thought. Blake's reading of life is, in reality, fundamentally simple. His deepest intuition, and in this he may be compared with Walt Whitman, was of the essential divinity of man. 'We are all members of the Divine body, and partakers of the divine nature.' Asked if he believed in the divinity of Christ he replied, 'He is the only God,' but quickly added 'and so am I, and so are you'. Hence sprang his paradoxical attacks on humility, and his fierce antagonism to that element in orthodox faith which regards man as an abject being who must incessantly crave mercy from an outraged God. Though in one place he can pray 'O Saviour, pour on me thy spirit of meekness and love', in his *Everlasting Gospel* he insists not upon the meekness but on the pride of Jesus, and on his contempt for all conventional authority. Humility, he says, is only doubt, doubt, that is, of your own divine nature. Hence springs, too, his impassioned advocacy of natural instinct. 'Everything that lives is holy.' The ordinary distinctions between good and evil have to him no eternal validity, they are merely the self-imposed conditions of our temporal existence. Desire or energy is the one vital force: reason, the restraining or negative power. 'Energy is eternal delight.' 'Restraint breeds pestilence.' 'Act out your spiritual desires, whether the spirit or the body be the appointed medium of action.' 'Jesus was all virtue, and acted from impulse, not from rules.' Blake might have echoed the famous words of Rousseau, 'Man was born free, but everywhere he is in chains'; but to him the chains were self-imposed, by man's own restraining reason.

> I wander thro' each charter'd street,
> Near where the charter'd Thames does flow,
> And mark in every face I meet
> Marks of weakness, marks of woe.

> In every cry of every Man,
> In every Infant's cry of fear,
> In every voice, in every ban,
> The mind-forg'd manacles I hear.

These manacles cut deepest into humanity where they restrict the natural intercourse of the sexes, so that enforced chastity becomes to him the symbol of any baneful curb laid by legality upon natural impulse. In his mythological attempts to explain the temporal separation of man from the Godhead, he conceived of the division into male and female as the work of an evil demon, the most cruel disaster that had befallen him, the chief cause of the disharmony of earthly life:

> What may man be? Who can tell? But what may Woman be,
> To have power over man from cradle to corruptible grave?

Here, and most psychologists would agree with him, the problem culminates. Blake saw in their true colours the evils that beset sex-relationships in a convention-ridden world, with its false idea of love as a selfish proprietary passion, rather than as the spirit of selfless devotion; and he exposed, with an insight that any modern novelist might envy, its resultant vices—jealousy, secrecy, hypocrisy, harlotry; but the sovereign remedy that he would apply pays too little regard alike to the inherent frailty of human nature and to the complexity of the whole problem. So obsessed is he with a single aspect of it that he spoils one of his loveliest lyrics in order to press it home:

> I laid me down upon a bank,
> Where Love lay sleeping;
> I heard among the rushes dank
> Weeping, weeping.

But he loses this exquisite melody, as he deserves to lose it, when he appends to it a propagandist stanza which robs it of its full imaginative significance:

> Then I went to the heath and the wild,
> To the thistles and thorns of the waste;
> And they told me how they were beguil'd,
> Driven out, and compell'd to be chaste.

Yet the tedious reiteration with which Blake, a model and devoted husband, advocates free love, will not disturb those who bear in mind his total subordination of the body to the spirit. No one more beautifully than he has pierced the core of love and realized that its essence is not desire but sympathy:

> I thought Love lived in the hot sunshine,
> But O, he lives in the moony light!
> I thought to find Love in the heat of day,
> But sweet Love is the comforter of night.
>
> Seek Love in the pity of others' woe,
> In the gentle relief of another's care,
> In the darkness of night and the winter's snow,
> In the naked and outcast, seek Love there!

For all Blake's dogmatic assertiveness, the pervading element in his gospel is a tender sympathy. In the *Songs of Innocence* he had shown this to be the natural impulse of childhood:

> Can I see another's woe,
> And not be in sorrow too?
> Can I see another's grief,
> And not seek for kind relief?

and in a stanza which reveals a scrutiny of that dark world hidden from the child, he voices the same feeling with a deeper imaginative force:

> For the tear is an intellectual thing,
> And a sigh is the sword of an Angel King,
> And the bitter groan of the martyr's woe
> Is an arrow from the Almighty's bow.

The *Book of Thel* sets forth the tenet that 'everything that lives lives not alone nor for itself'. The *Auguries of Innocence*, a collection of poetic aphorisms, teach pity and love towards all creatures animal and human as the supreme law of life, and denounce all forms of cruelty, oppression, and war. Read consecutively as forming one poem these couplets tend by mere accumulation to lose their full effect: taken separately they haunt the memory, for each, in an arresting image, carries to the heart a deep spiritual truth:

> A robin redbreast in a cage
> Puts all Heaven in a rage.
>
> .   .   .   .   .   .
>
> He who mocks the infant's faith
> Shall be mock'd in Age and Death.
>
> .   .   .   .   .   .
>
> The beggar's rags, fluttering in air,
> Does to rags the heavens tear.
>
> .   .   .   .   .   .
>
> Nought can deform the human race
> Like to the armour's iron brace.

In this transitory world of ours, where

> Joy and woe are woven fine,
> A clothing for the soul divine;

and where no man is perfect, the one thing needful is love, with its essential corollaries, mutual charity, and forgiveness. Indeed, by one of Blake's boldest paradoxes, sin itself is justified in that it leaves something to forgive. 'It is not', he says, 'because angels are better than men or devils that they are angels, but because they do not expect holiness from one another, but from God only;' and of his picture of the *Last Judgment* he remarks, 'The ladies will be pleased to see that I have represented the Furies not by three women but by three men. The spectator may suppose them to be clergymen in the pulpit, scourging sin instead of forgiving it'. And whilst one of his chief quarrels with orthodoxy was the stress it laid upon punishment and retribution for sin, nothing stirred him more deeply than the moral beauty of forgiveness. Dwelling once on the parable of the Prodigal Son he began to repeat it, but at the words 'When he was yet a great way off his father saw him' he could go no farther, but burst into tears. Forgiveness is the central theme of his two most elaborate *Prophetic Books, Milton* and *Jerusalem*; and

in his last poem, written after a long interval which he had
devoted to painting rather than to verse, he returned to
the same point. Cain, even in murdering his brother, had
offended less heinously against divine law than the Ghost
of Abel, which cried aloud for vengeance—blood for blood.
For without forgiveness of sin life itself is eternal death:
in forgiveness lies the secret of immortality. And to Blake,
for whom this life was merely a passage from eternity to
eternity, immortality was the axiom of his whole faith.
Death was merely the emancipation of the spirit from the
bonds of the flesh. One of his most powerfully inspired
drawings, an illustration to that dreary poem, Blair's *Grave*,
depicts an old man tottering through the gates of Death,
and above the gates is his glorified youthful body entering
into the eternity of imagination:

For God himself enters Death's door always with those that enter,
And lays down in the Grave with them in Visions of Eternity,
Till they awake and see Jesus and the Linen Clothes lying
That the Females had Woven for them, and the Gates of their
    Father's House.

In all this Blake is the pioneer of that spiritual renaissance of which Wordsworth is the acknowledged leader.
Blake's poems were hard to come by in his own day, and
Wordsworth possessed no copy of them; but early in the
century some friend must have lent them to him, and they
impressed him so profoundly that he took the trouble to
copy four of them into a notebook; and the four that he
chose, 'I love the jocund dance' from the *Poetical Sketches*,
Holy Thursday and the *Laughing Song* from the *Songs of
Innocence*, and the *Tiger* from the *Songs of Experience* show
how clearly he recognized the essential characteristics of
Blake's genius: later, when some of Blake's perversities
were reported to him, he remarked that 'the insanity of this
man interests me more than the sanity of Byron and
Moore'. To Blake, Wordsworth was the greatest poet of
the age, and when the *Immortality Ode* was read to him
he was thrown into almost hysterical rapture. Each of

these poets was, indeed, conscious of his affinity with the
other. They were at one in their exaltation of the imagination as the only avenue to the highest truth, the sovereign
power which apprehends the world beyond the senses, as
opposed to the reason which murders to dissect, and each
denounced with equal fervour the deadening effects of
scepticism upon the spiritual life, preferring the most
primitive superstition to

> The repetitions wearisome of sense,
> Where soul is dead, and feeling hath no place;
> Where knowledge, ill begun in cold remark
> On outward things, with formal inference ends.

Both had turned from the delineation of man in society
to the elemental feelings, and had realized that to do this
effectively poetry must be shorn of all its conventional
trappings, and rely on the sheer force of simplicity and
truth. And as Wordsworth's theory of poetic diction was
Blake's practice, so Wordsworth's conception of the character of the poet found in Blake a living example. Com-
batting the popular notion of the inherent melancholy of
the poetic temper, Wordsworth conceived of joy as both
its creative impulse and its accompaniment. He was himself, he said, 'a happy man, and therefore bold to look on
painful things', and he insisted that only by 'the deep
power of joy' could we 'see into the life of things'. Blake
lived in the spirit of this creed.

> The Angel that presided o'er my birth
> Said 'Little creature, form'd of joy and mirth,
> Go, love without the help of anything on earth'.

'I am happy', he said, 'I want nothing', and his eyes
glistened while he spoke of the joy of devoting himself
solely to divine art. This joy for both of them had its
source in their faith in the divine element in human nature.
If the maturer Wordsworth allowed to law and duty a
validity which Blake would never have admitted, he too
had known the time when

> 'love is an unerring light, and joy its own security;'

and though as he grew older his essential faith was hidden
beneath too thick a cloak of orthodoxy, Blake's boldest
assertion of the divinity of man would not have troubled
the poet who speaks of

> A soul divine which we participate,
> A deathless spirit,

and who exalts that

> one interior life
> In which all beings live with God, themselves
> Are God, existing in the mighty whole,
> As indistinguishable as the cloudless east
> Is from the cloudless west, when all
> The hemisphere is one cerulean blue.

Strangely enough, it was Blake who was shocked at Wordsworth. For when Wordsworth, in the Preface to the *Excursion*, spoke of passing Jehovah unalarmed, and asserted
that nothing

> can breed such fear and awe
> As fall upon us often when we look
> Into our minds, into the mind of man—

'Does Mr. Wordsworth think he can surpass Jehovah?' he
asked in horror. Yet these lines, which, Blake protested,
had upset him so much as to bring on a bowel complaint
that nearly killed him, only give utterance to that exaltation in contemplating the divine nature of the human
mind which was the essence of Blake's own faith.

And further, to Wordsworth's attitude to Nature Blake
expressed a violent antagonism. Both poets prized the
visible as the symbol of the invisible:

> To see a World in a grain of sand,
> And a Heaven in a wild flower,
> Hold Infinity in the palm of your hand,
> And Eternity in an hour;

this was for both of them the supreme glory of the imaginative life. But whereas Wordsworth joyfully accepted the
Universe as the expression of divine will and purpose,

Blake professed the gnostic dogma that Nature was not the work of God but of an evil demon. Whoever believes in Nature, he said, disbelieves in God. He persuaded himself that the forms of Nature only served to obscure his vision of the eternal realities. 'Natural objects', he maintained, 'always did, and do now, weaken, deaden and obliterate imagination in me. Wordsworth must know that what he writes valuable is not to be found in nature. I assert for myself that I do not behold the outward creation and that it is to me hindrance and not action, it is the dirt of my feet, not part of me. I question not my corporeal eye, any more than I would question a window concerning a sight. I look through it, and not with it.'

But Blake's acceptance of the gnostic conception of Nature was not an imaginative intuition, it was merely an attempt of that reason, which he always distrusted in others, to account for his deep sense of the imperfections of the world of matter. Yet for all his strength of spiritual vision, the world of matter was its indispensable medium. Without it there would *be* no vision.

> Piping down the valleys wild,
> Piping songs of pleasant glee,
> On a cloud I saw a child:

the images in this delightful song, which Blake not merely engraved in words, but pictured in lovely outline and colour, were first seen with the corporeal eye. Nature had given him the laughing child, the cloud, the valley, as surely as the imagination had given him the vision of which they were the symbols. And to his triumphant attack on the limited scope of sensual perception:

> How do you know but ev'ry Bird that cuts the airy way,
> Is an immense World of Delight, clos'd by your senses five?

we answer that though our imagination may accept his vision of the bird, if it were not for one of the senses five, neither he nor we would know that there was a bird at all. The senses alone are, doubtless, inadequate; but, as human nature is constituted, they are the chief inlet to the soul,

and to reject as from the devil the only material on which
the senses can exercise their function is surely the wildest
of paradoxes. Blake writes more truly of what he calls,
with some scorn, 'this vegetable universe', when he regards
it as 'a faint shadow of the eternal world, in which we
shall live in our imaginative bodies, when these vegetable
bodies are no more'. But a shadow, however faint, can
only be thrown by the substance of which it is the shadow.
In this conception, which is quite inconsistent with his
gnosticism, Blake is at one with many poetic thinkers:

> What if Earth
> Be but the shadow of Heaven, and things therein
> Each to other like, more than on earth is thought?

So our earth always appears to the imaginative artist; for,
in truth, what the poet dreams of the infinite wonders of
eternity, he can only express in terms of that which he has
seen and loved.

But Blake's ingratitude to Nature is easily accounted for.
It springs from the conflict within him, a conflict that in
part he realized, of the artist and the mystic. He feared
to become a slave to his senses, so enthralled by his love
of beauty as to lose all hold of the supersensuous eternal
world. His immortal spirit chafes against the temporal
conditions of his earthly life; whilst the artist within him
rejoices in the beauty which Nature has lavished about
him ('may God', he once said to a child, 'make this world
as beautiful to you as it has been to me'), the mystic yearns
for that state wherein he can attain to a complete union
and absorption in the divine: when

> the breath of this corporeal frame
> And even the motion of our human blood
> Almost suspended, we are laid asleep
> In body, and become a living soul.

Blake, like Wordsworth, knew at times this mystical felicity: it is, indeed, the supreme spiritual state, entirely
beyond all consciousness of nature or of art; but nature
and art are the divine media through which the poet

attains it. And the aridity and incoherence that mar Blake's *Prophetic Books* spring, in some measure at least, from his vain attempt to give, to that lower spiritual state of artistic vision, the immediacy of the complete mystical experience. In pouring scorn on those

> Who pretend to poetry that they may destroy imagination
> By imitation of nature's images drawn from remembrance,

and striving, as he puts it, 'to cast off the rotten rags of memory', he repudiates the very medium by which he attains to the beatific vision. But his practice was often better than his theory. For when he comes to delineate the Land of Beulah, which lies on the borders of the Celestial City, he calls to his aid those very images of nature which he would fain reject:

> Thou hearest the nightingale begin the song of spring:
> The lark, sitting upon his earthy bed, just as the morn
> Appears, listens silent; then, springing from the waving cornfield, loud
> He leads the choir of day—trill! trill! trill! trill!
> Mounting upon the wings of light into the great expanse,
> Re-echoing against the lovely blue and shining heavenly shell:
> His little throat labours with inspiration; every feather
> On throat and breast and wings vibrates with the effluence divine:
> All nature listens silent to him, and the awful sun
> Stands still upon the mountain looking on this little bird
> With eyes of soft humility and wonder, love and awe.

It is in passages such as this, in his lyrics and in his lovely designs in line and colour, rather than when he is striving to 'create a system', that Blake realized his life's aim, 'the liberty both of body and mind to exercise the divine arts of imagination'. And if at times he mistook his path, few poets have gained that liberty as completely as he. Poverty and neglect had no power to turn him from his goal. Misunderstanding and ridicule only stiffened his resolve; and much that is perverse, extravagant, and grotesque in his work can be explained as the inevitable reaction of a fervid but undisciplined mind to the apathy and antagonism of his environment. His life has a beautiful unity of purpose. In early childhood he was both a draughtsman and a poet, and when at the age of threescore and ten he lay upon his deathbed, a pencil was still in his hand and a song of ecstasy upon his lips. The essential character of his intervening years, in their struggle and achievement, their persistent quest of truth and beauty, and the unwavering faith that sustained him in it, is distilled into one perfect song:

> To find the Western path,
> Right thro' the Gates of Wrath
> I urge my way;
> Sweet Mercy leads me on
> With soft repentant moan:
> I see the break of day.
>
> The war of swords and spears,
> Melted by dewy tears,
> Exhales on high;
> The Sun is freed from fears,
> And with soft grateful tears
> Ascends the sky.

VII

WORDSWORTH'S PREFACE TO 'THE BORDERERS'[1]

WORDSWORTH's one drama, *The Borderers*, has had a curious history. It was begun soon after he had settled, in September 1795, with his sister Dorothy at Racedown, and finished in the following year. In June 1797 Coleridge paid them his memorable visit. 'The first thing', writes Dorothy, 'that was read after he came was William's new poem *The Ruined Cottage*, with which he was delighted; and after tea he repeated to us two acts and a half of his tragedy *Osorio*. The next morning William read his tragedy.' Coleridge's enthusiasm knew no bounds. 'I speak with heart-felt sincerity', he wrote off to Cottle, 'and I think unblinded judgment, when I tell you that I feel a little man by his side. . . . His drama is absolutely wonderful. . . . There are in the piece those profound touches of the human heart which I find three or four times in *The Robbers* of Schiller, and often in Shakespeare; but in Wordsworth there are no inequalities.' In the lively intellectual circle which Coleridge had gathered round him at Nether Stowey the drama achieved immediate reputation, and through one of the Pooles was offered to Covent Garden Theatre. Wordsworth had not written it for the stage, and he 'had not the faintest expectation that it would be accepted'; yet in the following November he made some alterations in it with a view to its performance. But he was already emerging from that state of mind in which the play had been conceived, and when, before the close of the year, it was rejected by Covent Garden, he put it behind him. He still thought highly of it as a composition, for had it not won unqualified praise from the greatest of living critics? and a year later he wrote anxiously from Germany to learn what had become of the only extant copy; but, filled as he was with

[1] Reprinted from *The Nineteenth Century and After*, Nov. 1926.

the optimism of his newly-found faith, he was increasingly reluctant, not only to publish his gloomy drama, but even to circulate the manuscript among his friends. Josiah Wedgewood, probably through Coleridge's intervention, was allowed to read it, but Lamb could not get so much as a sight of it. 'I would pay five and forty thousand carriages', he wrote in 1800, 'to read W.'s tragedy, of which I have heard so much and seen so little.' During twenty years of intimate friendship that indefatigable literary enthusiast Crabb Robinson 'never heard Wordsworth allude to it', and when he came upon a reference to it in Cottle's *Recollections*, and wrote to make inquiries, Mrs. Wordsworth gave him little encouragement. 'The tragedy is in existence,' she replied; 'but say nothing about it, lest its destruction should follow.' But in 1842 Wordsworth found it among papers which had lain unregarded for nearly half a century. With that weakness for one's offspring natural to humanity, even when they are not all one might wish them to be, he could not bring himself to destroy it, and he rightly felt that he rather than his executors should decide its fate. He revised it with some care, making, however, no changes either in the conduct of the story or the composition of the characters, and published it in a volume entitled *Poems Chiefly of Early and Late Years*.

The days were long past when a volume from Wordsworth was greeted with shouts of derision. His fame was now assured. The reviewers as a whole treated *The Borderers* with respect, if not with enthusiasm. But it was little read. The mere lover of poetry was satisfied, as he will always be satisfied, with a greater or smaller selection from the poet's undoubted masterpieces. Pious Wordsworthians did not find in it the true milk of the word. Soothed by the moral edification of his later work, they read their poet backwards; and if they were puzzled and not a little distressed by his 'immortal' ode or the *Lines composed a few miles above Tintern Abbey*, they could hardly be expected to sift the grain from his still wilder oats.

The Borderers was almost ignored until M. Legouis, in his masterly *La Jeunesse de Wordsworth*, called attention to its value as illustrating a stage in the poet's spiritual evolution. Students of the poet to-day, though they vary both in their estimate of its intrinsic merits as poetry and in their interpretation of its significance, are fully agreed as to its importance as a document for his biography.

The general stages in the growth of the poet's soul, from uncritical enthusiasm for the French Revolution to reasoned conviction, from conviction to doubt and to renunciation, and from renunciation to the building up of a new faith upon the wreck of the old, can be traced with sufficient clearness in *The Prelude*: the detailed chronology of the later stages of that growth has been the subject of much conjecture. Wordsworth returned from France (December 1792) an ardent revolutionary. The first great shock to his moral nature came from the declaration of war between France and England (February 1793); but so deeply rooted was his devotion to the ideals of liberty that he could rejoice in the victory of France over his beloved country (September 1793), whilst at the celebration of English successes he 'fed on the day of vengeance yet to come'. The Reign of Terror (September 1793–July 1794) brought him many nights of anguish, and shook for the time his faith, but with the fall of Robespierre (July 1794) his hope revived; for his 'trust was in the people' and 'in those virtues which [his] eyes had seen'; and he once more looked to the future 'with unabated confidence'. But when the French 'became oppressors in their turn' he received a moral shock deeper than the first. In attacking the liberty and the property of other peoples France seemed to him to be a traitor to her own root principles. He had staked his all upon her faith, and he felt that she had betrayed him. In recoil from the Revolution he became a whole-hearted Godwinian. He had before accepted such of Godwin's tenets as were compatible with revolutionary ideal—his humanitarianism, his condemnation of war and of the criminal law, his

necessitarianism: now he embraced the creed in all its
implications, in its exaltation of reason at the expense of
the passions, and of the individual against the collective
will, in its insistence on the right of each man to reject
all general rules of conduct and act in each situation as his
independent reason prompted him. Under this tutelage
opinions took the place of faith, feelings, instincts,

> till round my mind
> They clung as if they were its life, nay more,
> The very being of the immortal soul.

It was a state of mind not without its value to him. He
now saw for the first time the real harm that can be done
in the name of custom and written law and moral sentiment, though conventional society is always blind to it;
and so, probing beneath the surface, he learnt much of
truth. But at the same time he fell into deadly errors.
His heart had been 'turned aside from Nature's way'. He
denied the fundamental natural instincts and passions,
and the obligations and sanctions which go with them;
and the Nature that he denied took her revenge. Reason
itself began to crumble before the restless analysis which
his mind applied to the whole moral problem. Reason,
he argued, may tell us the difference between good and
evil, but whence comes the moral obligation to choose one
rather than the other? A man 'rebellious to acknowledged
law,' because he sees through its evils and hypocrisies,
may ask and find no answer, and yet act himself 'as selfish
passion urged', so that he becomes, in fact, 'the dupe of
folly or the slave of crime'. Thus the way of reason led him
to an impasse, wherein 'sick, wearied out with contrarieties',
he 'yielded up moral questions in despair'. From this, 'the
last and lowest ebb' of his soul, his recovery was gradual.
He owed it partly to the return of happier circumstances,
partly to the companionship of his sister Dorothy, and,
later, to the guidance of Coleridge; it was not completed
till towards the close of the year 1797. So much we learn
from *The Prelude* and other sources. The question arises:

what stage in his development is represented by *The Borderers*? If we can form a firm opinion on this point, light may be thrown upon the actual processes of his mind, not only then, but also in the obscure preceding years.

Let us first take a rapid survey of its plot. The scene is laid on the English border in the reign of Henry III, a time analogous to the French Revolution, in that the absence of established law and government gave men liberty to act on their own impulses. Here a band of freebooters, formerly crusaders, are led by the young idealist Marmaduke to a life of active benevolence, so that

> aged men
> Have blessed their steps, the fatherless retire
> For shelter to their banners.

But they are filled with apprehension at the influence which Oswald, a late recruit to their band, has already gained over their 'confiding, open-hearted leader'. They recall Oswald's haughty bearing in Palestine, where ugly rumours were afloat of some dark deed he had committed in early life; they know, too, that he hates Marmaduke, for Marmaduke has saved his life, and 'Gratitude's a heavy burden to a proud spirit'; and they suspect that his 'perverted soul' is plotting against their 'much-loved captain'. Oswald has had a strange past. As a young man he had embarked for Syria under a captain to whom he was bound by close ties of intimacy, whose daughter[1] had exacted from him a promise never to desert her father; but, persuaded by the crew that his old friend has designs on his honour, he has left him on an island to starve, only to learn afterwards that his victim was innocent, and that the crew had tricked him into this crime in order to be rid of a master whom they hated. On hearing the news the captain's daughter goes mad and dies, and Oswald is beside himself with remorse, but at length he recovers his self-

---

[1] Allusion to the captain's daughter is only found in the early manuscript: it was omitted from the published text, probably to avoid too unnatural a symmetry in the stories of Oswald and Marmaduke.

possession in the acceptance of a philosophy that regards all human feelings as weakness, and recognizes no authority outside the promptings of his own reason. His pride and restless energy throw him once more into a world of adventure where he can act out his new philosophy.

Impelled by hatred and jealousy, Oswald conceives a plan for reproducing in Marmaduke his own history. Marmaduke loves the beautiful and innocent Idonea, sole prop of her aged father Herbert, who has returned from the Holy Land, blind and helpless, to find himself ousted from his barony. Oswald suborns a beggar woman to inform Marmaduke that Idonea is in reality her daughter, bought by Herbert from her to wait hand and foot on him, and that Herbert, despite his saintly show, is in reality an abandoned scoundrel, who now intends to sell Idonea to the old lecher Lord Clifford in exchange for supporting his claims on a barony to which he is merely a pretender. Oswald manages the interview with the beggar woman so skilfully that Marmaduke, who trusts him implicitly, sees no loophole for doubt; and when he brings forward other evidence to prove that Idonea is herself no unwilling agent in the filthy bargain, Marmaduke feels the foundations of his life sinking beneath him, and foresees his own ruin. At a time when Idonea is separated from her father, Oswald offers Herbert his guidance over the lonely moor, and there easily convinces Marmaduke that it is his moral duty to execute justice on so hardened a criminal. Again and again, under the alternate arguments and taunts of Oswald, Marmaduke attempts to kill Idonea's father; again and again, though he interprets Herbert's utterances of piety and devotion to his daughter as the rankest hypocrisy, and his own pity for Herbert's helplessness as mere weakness, he cannot bring his hand to the deed; at last he resolves to leave his victim to the ordeal of Heaven: if Herbert is innocent Heaven will guide him to safety. Then Oswald, under the impression that his purpose is now achieved, reveals his own past story. At first Marmaduke is all sympathy with him, and execrates the ship's crew who had gulled him into the murder of an innocent man: but when Oswald extols them for the service they have done him in freeing his soul from the conventional trammels of pity and remorse, it dawns upon him that he too has been entrapped. Finally Oswald openly avows Herbert's innocence, and calls upon Marmaduke to profit by his own unwitting action and become his fellow labourer in enlarging man's intellectual empire. Towards this great goal his present shock of revulsion from his crime was, says Oswald, a necessary but only a transient step:

> We need an inward sting to goad us on.

But Marmaduke's whole nature revolts against the hideous crime into which he has been led. Hoping against hope that Herbert may be yet alive, he rushes off to seek him, and when he learns the worst is for a time bereft of sense. But sanity returns to him, and he breaks to Idonea the news of the horrible part he has played in her father's tragedy. In the meantime the beggar woman, horror-stricken at the fatal results of her deceit, makes a full confession to the troop of Borderers, who seize Oswald and kill him, still unrepentant. Marmaduke, entrusting Idonea to the care of his friends, leaves their fellowship for a life of solitary expiation.

It is an ingenious, improbable story. But though Swinburne was shocked at its 'morbid and monstrous extravagance of horrible impossibility', it is no more horrible or impossible than many an Elizabethan tragedy of blood and vengeance before which he never quailed. The prime weakness of *The Borderers* as a drama lies, not in the plot viewed in itself, but rather in that plot's unsuitability for making clear the central idea on which the poet is working. Its chief incident, Oswald's desire to reproduce his own fate in that of Marmaduke, befogs rather than elucidates our understanding of his character. For, it might be argued, if Oswald's motive was hatred and a jealous love of power, he would never act in such a way as to lead the object of his hate to share with him his

intellectual supremacy and that freedom from all conventional codes of morality on which his supremacy is
based. The plot could easily enough have been fitted to
either of two widely divergent conceptions. Without any
moral casuistry Oswald could be presented, either as a
villain who, conscious of his own misery and the degrada-
tion that had followed on his crime, is led by hatred and
envy of one more fortunate than he to drag down his
rival to his own level, or, on the other hand, he could
be presented as a genuine but deluded enthusiast for the
intellectualism that he professes, who ruins a man he loves
by the desire to share with him his own vaunted freedom.
Wordsworth's conception was far subtler, and he had not
the dramatic genius necessary to convey it; hence an
ambiguity results such that even so acute a critic as Professor Garrod is 'not sure that the term villain' (as applied
to Oswald) 'does not beg the question'. That Coleridge,
in his admiration for the poetry with which the play is
full, and for those 'profound human touches' which are
certainly to be found in it, overlooked this flaw is easily
understood. He knew the circumstances which led Wordsworth to its composition—had in his own way passed
through something of the same mental experience; and
it would be natural for Wordsworth to preface his recital
of the play with a few sentences which would give a key
to its interpretation, even if he did not actually read to
him the explanatory essay which he had written at the
time of its composition.

This essay, which is referred to in the Fenwick note
dictated by Wordsworth in 1843, has long been regarded
as lost. It has lately been found in a manuscript volume
in Mary Hutchinson's (Mrs. Wordsworth's) handwriting,
prefixed to a copy of the play as it was revised for the stage
in 1797.[1] From the other contents of the volume—the

[1] The manuscript is in the possession of Mr. Gordon Wordsworth, to
whose generosity I am indebted for permission to make use of it for the
purposes of this article. That the version of the play preserved in it is
that which was prepared for dramatic representation is proved by the stage

bulk of *The Prelude,* Books i, ii, and *The Old Beggar* (published in 1800 as *The Old Cumberland Beggar*), it is clear that the copy was made at least not later than the summer of 1800, when Mary Hutchinson visited Dove Cottage. It contains some corrections in a darker ink, in Mrs. Wordsworth's later hand, which show it to be one of the copies used for revision in 1842; and a comparison of the text with the published version fully bears out the poet's statement that, though the drama was revised with some care for the press, no alteration was made in the conduct of the story or the composition of the characters. The essay, which is of deep interest, not only in its elucidation of the play but also for the acuteness and profundity of its psychology, runs as follows:

'Let us suppose a young man of great intellectual powers, yet without any solid principles of genuine benevolence. His master passions are pride and the love of distinction. He has deeply imbibed a spirit of enterprise in a tumultuous age. He goes into the world and is betrayed into a great crime.—That influence on which all his happiness is built immediately deserts him. His talents are robbed of their weight, his exertions are unavailing, and he quits the world in disgust, with strong misanthropic feelings. In his retirement, he is impelled to examine the unreasonableness of established opinions; and the force of his mind exhausts itself in constant efforts to separate the elements of virtue and vice. It is his pleasure and his consolation to hunt out whatever is bad in actions usually esteemed virtuous, and to detect the good in actions which the universal sense of mankind teaches us to reprobate. While the general exertion of his intellect seduces him from the remembrance of his own crime, the particular conclusions to which he is led have a tendency to reconcile him to himself. His feelings are interested in making him a moral sceptic, and as his scepticism increases he is raised in his own esteem. After this process has been continued some time his natural energy and restlessness impel

directions which it contains: e.g. Act iv, sc. 1, *a desolate prospect—a ridge of rocks rises at the bottom of the stage, an old chapel on the summit of one of them. . . . Herbert enters in the depth of the stage much exhausted; he crosses the stage with difficulty.* Like many of the Wordsworth manuscripts, the essay is very inadequately punctuated. I have added stops where they seem to be necessary.

him again into the world. In this state, pressed by the recollection of his guilt, he seeks relief from two sources, action and meditation. Of actions those are most attractive which best exhibit his own powers, partly from the original pride of his own character, and still more because the loss of authority and influence which followed upon his crime[1] brought along with it those tormenting sensations by which he is assailed. The recovery of his original importance and the exhibition of his own powers are, therefore, in his mind almost identified with the extinction of those powerful feelings which attend the recollection of his guilt. Perhaps there is no cause which has greater weight in preventing the return of bad men to virtue than that good actions being for the most part in their nature silent and regularly progressive, they do not present those sudden results which can afford sufficient stimulus to a troubled mind. In processes of vice the effects are more frequently immediate, palpable and extensive. Power is much more easily manifested in destroying than in creating. A child, Rousseau has observed, will tear in pieces fifty toys before he will think of making one. From these causes, assisted by disgust and misanthropic feeling, the character we are now contemplating will have a strong tendency to vice. His energies are most impressively manifest in works of devastation. He is the Orlando of Ariosto, the Cardenio of Cervantes, who lays waste the groves that should shelter him. He has rebelled against the world and the laws of the world, and he regards them as tyrannical masters; convinced that he is right in some of his conclusions, he nourishes a contempt for mankind the more dangerous because he has been led to it by reflexion. Being in the habit of considering the world as a body which is in some sort of war with him, he has a feeling borrowed from that habit which gives an additional zest to his hatred of those members of society whom he hates and to his own contempt of those whom he despises. Add to this, that a mind fond of nourishing sentiments of contempt will be prone to the admission of those feelings which are considered under any uncommon bond of relation (as must be the case with a man who has quarrelled with the world), and[2] the feelings will mutually strengthen each other. In this morbid state of mind he cannot exist without occupation, he requires constant provocations, all his pleasures are prospective, he is perpetually in(vok)ing[3] a phantom, he commits new crimes to

[1] Manuscript *reads* crime and.   [2] and *not in manuscript*.
[3] invoking: *a hole in the manuscript makes this word partly illegible*.

drive away the memory of the past. But the lenitives of his pain
are twofold, meditation as well as action. Accordingly, his reason
is almost exclusively employed in justifying his past enormities
and in enabling him to commit new ones. He is perpetually impos-
ing upon himself, he has a sophism for every crime. The *mild*
effusions of thought, the milk of human reason are unknown to
him. His imagination is powerful being strengthened by the habit
of picturing possible forms of society where his crimes would be
no longer crimes, and he would enjoy that estimation to which,
from his intellectual attainments, he deems himself entitled. The
nicer shades of manners he disregards; but whenever upon looking
back upon past ages, or in surveying the practices of different
countries in the age in which he lives, he finds such contrarieties
as seem to affect the principles of *morals*, he exults over his discovery,
and applies it to his heart as the dearest of consolations. Such a
mind cannot but discover some truths, but he is unable to profit
by them, and in his hands they become instruments of evil.

He presses truth and falsehood into the same service. He looks
at society through an optical glass of a peculiar tint; something of
the forms of objects he takes from objects, but their colour is
exclusively what he gives them; it is one, and it is his own. Having
indulged a habit, dangerous in a man who has fallen, of dallying
with moral calculations, he becomes an empiric, and a daring and
unfeeling empiric. He disguises from himself his own malignity
by assuming the character of a speculator in morals, and one who
has the hardihood to realize his speculations.

It will easily be perceived that to such a mind those enterprizes
which are most extraordinary will in time appear the most inviting.
His appetite from being exhausted becomes unnatural. Accordingly
he will struggle so[1] to characterize and to exalt actions little in
themselves by a forced greatness of manner, and will chequer and
degrade enterprizes great in their atrocity by grotesque littleness
of manner and fantastic obliquities. He is like a worn out volup-
tuary—he finds his temptation in strangeness, he is unable to
suppress a low hankering after the double entendre in vice; yet
his thirst after the extraordinary buoys him up, and supported by
a habit of constant reflexion he frequently breaks out into what has
the appearance of greatness; and in sudden emergencies, when he
is called upon by surprize and thrown out of the path of his regular
habits, or when dormant associations are awakened tracing the

[1] Manuscript *leaves blank space for a word here.*

revolutions through which his character has passed, in painting his former self he really *is* great.

Benefits conferred on a man like this will be the seeds of a worse feeling than ingratitude. They will give birth to positive hatred. Let him be deprived of power, though by means which he despises, and he will never forgive. It will scarcely be denied that such a mind, by very slight external motives, may be led to the commission of the greatest enormities. Let its malignant feelings be fixed on a particular object, and the rest follows of itself.

Having shaken off the obligations of religion and morality in a dark and tempestuous age, it is probable that such a character will be infected with a tinge of superstition. The period in which he lives teems with great events which he feels he cannot controul. That influence which his pride makes him unwilling to allow to his fellow-men he has no reluctance to ascribe to invisible agents: his pride impells him to superstition and shapes the nature of his belief: his creed is his own: it is made and not adopted.

A character like this, or some of its features at least, I have attempted to delineate in the following drama. I have introduced him deliberately prosecuting the destruction of an amiable young man by the most atrocious means, and with a pertinacity, as it should seem, not to be accounted for but on the supposition of the most malignant injuries. No such injuries, however, appear to have been sustained. What then are his motives? First it must be observed that to make the non-existence of a common motive itself a motive to action is a practice which we are never so prone to attribute exclusively to madmen as when we forget ourselves. Our love of the marvellous is not confined to external things. There is no object on which it settles with more delight than on our own minds. This habit is in the very essence of the habit which we are delineating.

But there are particles of that poisonous mineral of which Iago speaks gnawing his inwards; his malevolent feelings are excited, and he hates the more deeply because he feels he ought not to hate.

We all know that the dissatisfaction accompanying the first impulses towards a criminal action, where the mind is familiar with guilt, acts as a stimulus to proceed in that action. Uneasiness must be driven away by fresh uneasiness, obstinacy, waywardness and wilful blindness are alternatives resorted to, till there is an insurrection of every depraved feeling of the heart.

s, in a course of criminal conduct every fresh step that

we make appears a justification of the one that preceded it, it seems
to bring again the moment of liberty and choice; it banishes the
idea of repentance, and seems to set remorse at defiance. Every
time we plan a fresh accumulation of our guilt we have restored
to us something like that original state of mind, that perturbed
pleasure, which first made the crime attractive.

If after these general remarks (I am asked[1]) what are Rivers's[2]
motives to the atrocity detailed in the drama? I answer they are
founded chiefly on the very constitution of his character; in his
pride which borders even upon madness; in his restless disposition; in his disturbed mind; in his superstition; in irresistible pro-
pensities to embody in practical experiments his worst and most
extravagant speculations; in his thoughts and in his feelings; in his
perverted reason justifying his perverted instincts. The general
moral intended to be impressed by the delineation of such a
character is obvious—it is to shew the dangerous use which may
be made of reason when a man has committed a great crime.

There is a kind of superstition which makes us shudder, when we
find moral sentiments to which we attach a sacred importance
applied to vicious purposes. In real life this is done every day, and
we do not feel the disgust. The difference is here. In works of
imagination we see the motive and the end. In real life we rarely
see either the one or the other; and when the distress comes it
prevents us from attending to the cause. This superstition of which
I have spoken is not without its use; yet it appears to be one great
source of our vices; it is our constant engine in seducing each other.
We are lulled asleep by its agency, and betrayed before we know
that an attempt is made to betray us.

I have endeavoured to shake this prejudice, persuaded that in
so doing I was well employed. It has been a further object with
me to shew that from abuses interwoven with the texture of society
a bad man may be furnished with sophisms in support of his crimes
which it would be difficult to answer.

One word more upon the subject of motives. In private life
what is more common than when we hear of lawsuits prosecuted to
the utter ruin of the parties, and the most deadly feuds in families,

---

[1] I am asked: *I have supplied these words to fill a blank space in the manuscript.*

[2] Rivers. The names given to several of the leading characters were
altered in 1842: in the version that follows this *Essay* in the manuscript
Oswald is called Rivers, Marmaduke Mortimer, and Idonea Matilda.

to find them attributed to trifling and apparently inadequate sources? But when our malignant passions operate the original causes which called them forth are soon supplanted, yet when we account for the effect we forget the immediate impulse, and the whole is attributed to the force from which the first motion was received. The vessel keeps sailing on, and we attribute her progress in the voyage to the ropes which first towed her out of harbour.

To this must be added that we are too apt to apply our own moral sentiments as a measure of the conduct of others. We insensibly suppose that a criminal action assumes the same form to the agent as to ourselves. We forget that his feelings and his reason are equally busy in contracting its dimensions and pleading for its necessity.

A Tragedy

'Of human actions reason though you can,
It may be reason, but it is not man;
His principle of action once explore,
That instant 'tis his principle no more.'

Pope.

In 1843 Wordsworth stated that *The Borderers* was written to preserve in memory those transitions of character which he had witnessed during his residence in France; this essay fully corroborates the statement. He was impelled to write it by the desire to analyse, and if possible explain, by the light of his own experience, those types of character which had brought the Revolution to disaster —men who, like Oswald, used their power for the gratification of their own passionate hatred, and with a cynical contempt for conventional morality erected a philosophy of their own to justify their evil deeds, so that in their hands even truth became an instrument of evil; and, in a second degree, men like Marmaduke, who are led into crime abhorrent to their very natures by playing upon their sentiment of public duty. In the first dismay at the collapse of the Revolutionary ideal he had laid the blame solely upon man's passions, and had sought an escape in the pure intellectualism of Godwin: now it dawned upon him that the worst excesses of the Revolution were themselves justified at the time of their perpetration on Godwinian principles. 'Imagine', as M. Legouis has said, 'Godwin's arguments for the necessity of extirpating all the human feelings read in the light of '93; conceive his condemnation of all traditional rules of conduct interpreted by aid of the wholesale executions decreed by the *Mountain* in the name of public welfare, or, in other words, of the greatest amount of human happiness, and *The Borderers* acquires a meaning . . . it reflects a reality which it is only too impossible to deny.'

And so Oswald becomes at once a mouthpiece and an exposure of Godwinism. He is not, indeed, the perfect Godwinian, for he is using the doctrines of Godwin, not to promote the general good, but to justify his own evil passions. But that is just Wordsworth's difficulty. A philosophy of life which bears no relation with actual conditions has for him no real value. Human nature must be reckoned with, not as it might have been, but as it is. Man is not a mere machine whose reason can calculate a good which he will inevitably proceed to turn into action. His reason will always be in some measure affected by his passions, and passions are of widely different kinds. Hatred is innate in him as well as love. Oswald's lust for power is as natural as Marmaduke's pity and benevolence, and power is far more easily manifested in destroying than creating. 'A child will tear in pieces fifty toys before he will think of making one.' Thus reason, at the mercy of the passions, cannot fail to be put to dangerous uses, among the most dangerous of which will be that by its agency men of simple, unsuspicious character will become tools of the able but less scrupulous. In a state of society such as is depicted in the play, such as Wordsworth had himself witnessed in France, reason is the willing handmaiden of crime. While men like Oswald are at large, isolated acts of virtue, the redressing of a few obvious wrongs, avail us little; it is idle to lament open acts of violence; and the alacrity with which we rush to avenge them is a mere anodyne to thought. We are only scratching the surfaces of things:

> The deeper malady is better hid,
> The world is poisoned at the heart.

To this despairing cry from Marmaduke Wordsworth saw for the time no answer; but though he was soon to rise above the pessimism which is the dominating note of *The Borderers*, there was much in its teaching which remained for him permanently true. Professor Garrod thinks it odd that Wordsworth should enunciate, so late as 1842, 'the conception that "sin and crime are apt to spring from their very opposite qualities, and that, a crime once committed, there are no limits to the hardening of the heart"'. 'The first part of the thesis', he comments, 'is Godwinism . . . the second part is an addition of Wordsworth, and either part is wholly false.' But in the first part, though it might perhaps be better expressed, Wordsworth's meaning is surely both clear and unimpeachable, i.e. that a man may be led to commit a crime by a specious appeal to those instincts and feelings which are in general productive of the noblest actions, as Marmaduke was tricked into the murder of Herbert by an appeal to his sense of justice and the public good, as many a revolutionary was led to acts of violence at which he was afterwards appalled. The second part of the thesis is false enough, as Professor Garrod has abbreviated it. But to the categorical and obviously false statement that 'a crime once committed there are no limits to the hardening of the heart' Wordsworth added the words '*to which they may carry their slaves*'. The conception of Marmaduke, who revolts from his crime as soon as he realizes its enormity, and devotes the rest of his life to remorse and expiation, is answer enough to Garrod's misleading version of Wordsworth's statement. The conception of Oswald, who is the slave to his own passions, and bolsters himself up in crime with a perverted understanding, is Wordsworth's own illustration of his meaning, a meaning supported by the searching

analysis of Oswald's character which he has provided in
his prefatory *Essay*.

Critics of *The Borderers* have paid some attention to its
literary ancestry, and have pointed out its debt to the
romantic novels and plays of the period, to Schiller's
Robbers, the self-appointed scourges of tyranny, to casuisti-
cal villains like the Marquis in Mrs. Radcliffe's *Romance of
the Forest*, to Godwin's *Caleb Williams*, in which 'an
atrocious crime is committed by a man previously of the
most exemplary habits'. Professors Campbell and Mueschke,
in a careful and suggestive study, have recently developed
this relation still further, and shown that the aesthetic on
which the tragedy is based aims definitely at appealing
through the traditional modes of terror and sentimental
pity then in vogue: to terror, in the use of all that parapher-
nalia that is the property of Gothic romance—the lonely
storm-swept moor, the ruined castle with its dungeon, the
foaming torrent and howling tempest: to sentimental pity
for undeserved suffering in the stress laid on Idonea's
innocence and devotion, and Herbert's saintly old age.
The conformity of *The Borderers* with prevalent literary
taste explains, doubtless, how much that to us appears
forced and melodramatic seemed to Wordsworth and to
Coleridge no unfit background for a work of profound
spiritual import. But the prefatory *Essay* suggests, at
least, discipleship to a greater master. It should not be
forgotten that Wordsworth was already an eager student
of Shakespeare; and we can well believe that his special
devotion to *Othello*, which he recorded some years later,
went back to the time when he was writing *The Borderers*.
The reference to Iago, and the subtle analysis of Oswald's
Iago-like motives, which, as Wordsworth suggests, are 'unintelligible to all but careful observers', indicate clearly
enough that throughout the composition of his play *Othello*
was at the back of his mind. He was probably unconscious
of the extent to which he was drawing upon his great
forerunner. Like Iago, Oswald plots the ruin of a man of
free and open nature, who trusts him implicitly and has

every claim upon his gratitude and affection; and, like
Iago, he effects his ruin by undermining his faith in those
who are dearest to him, and by driving him to destroy
them; Oswald's real motives, like Iago's, are hatred of the
good, lust for power, a loathing engendered by envy that
one whom he feels to be his intellectual inferior holds a
higher place in the world's esteem than he; like Iago, he
bolsters himself up with a philosophy of his own, of which
the main features are a cynical contempt for all human
feeling and for the claims of conventional morality; like
Iago, he uses as his tool a woman who is ignorant of the
terrible part she is playing in the tragedy; and as in *Othello*,
the woman so employed is the main agent in his final
discomfiture. *The Borderers* owed far more to *Othello* than
to any other influence outside the poet's own experience.
The immeasurable distance which separates Wordsworth's
dramatic achievement from Shakespeare's is explained by
this crucial difference in their presentation of their subtle
villain. While neither Iago nor Oswald can be said fully
to understand himself, Shakespeare both understands Iago
and makes him alive and real to us; whereas Wordsworth,
for all his mastery of Oswald's complex psychology, is
unable to bring him to life in the play. Shakespeare has
no interest in Iago's philosophy, except in so far as it is
a part of Iago: Wordsworth is really more interested in
Oswald's philosophy than in Oswald; at one time intent
on his philosophy, at another on his character, he has not
the dramatic skill to fuse the two, and as a consequence
we are left uncertain how far Oswald really accepts his
philosophy himself, and how far he is actuated by motives
diametrically opposed to it. *Othello* needs no commentary:
Wordsworth's intention in *The Borderers* is not completely
understood till we have read his exposition of it in the
Essay.

Wordsworth seems himself to have realized that his
conception of Oswald was more complex than he could
handle dramatically: thus the element of superstition in
his mind, developed with penetration in the *Essay*, is only

perfunctorily suggested in the play; it is not made a vital part of him, or worked into the fabric of his being. The character of Oswald, as Wordsworth conceived it, was, indeed, subtler than Iago's; and if Iago is one of Shakespeare's most notable triumphs we can hardly be surprised that Wordsworth failed in his harder task. It was always his fate, in his more ambitious writings, to attempt something more difficult than his great models, and thereby to court artistic failure. In *The White Doe of Rylstone* his conception is more profoundly spiritual than Spenser's in *The Faerie Queene*; in his vast unfinished epic of the human mind he strives to overpass Milton. A mere comparison of *The Excursion* with *Paradise Lost* is from some points of view ludicrous enough, but Keats thought it worth making, and did not on all scores give the palm to Milton: *The Borderers* is dismissed by the majority of readers, and still more by students of Wordsworth who do not read it, as almost negligible, yet to Coleridge it seemed 'absolutely wonderful', and it was after listening to its recital that he recognized its author as dowered with one of the noblest attributes of poetic genius—a profound insight into the human heart. To the penetrating critic there is, in truth, something more impressive in the very failures of a great poet than in all the easy successes of smaller fry.

In the light of this *Essay*, corroborated by Wordsworth's Preface to the published edition of the drama, it is difficult to accept the theory advanced by Professors Campbell and Mueschke, that 'its initial aesthetic impulse was the remorse that his abandonment of Annette Vallon had aroused in him'. For in the first place we have no direct evidence as to the state of Wordsworth's feelings towards Annette at the time he wrote *The Borderers*. He had been separated from her three years before by the force of circumstances, and not by his own will. Letters written by Annette to him and to Dorothy some months after his return to England take for granted that their separation is only temporary; and it is at least probable that in September

1794 he went as far as Paris in an attempt to reach Orleans, and was only turned back by realizing that his presence there would be a danger not only to himself but also to her and to her whole family; in September 1795 he was still in correspondence with her, and there is no reason for believing that he had given up the idea of rejoining her as soon as the end of the war made it feasible. The fact that Godwinian philosophy, to which he became a convert early in 1795, rejected marriage proves nothing. Godwin was himself married twice. Moreover, Godwin had repudiated all human affections as unreasonable, so that we have no more justification for supposing that Wordsworth as a Godwinian ceased to care for Annette than that he had ceased to care for his sister Dorothy. Professor Campbell calls attention to the stress laid in the play upon the sanctity of the paternal tie, but surely it is somewhat fanciful to find in the aged Herbert's relations with his daughter, who was the sole prop of his helpless old age, a reflection of Wordsworth's feelings for the baby he had never seen; whilst remorse, if it were his dominant mood at the time, would more naturally be associated with thoughts of the mother than of their infant, and he would have been led to a plot which gave him some scope for expressing it. In the statement that *The Borderers* is 'the result of a clash between Godwin's philosophy and his own bitter and searching personal experience' Professors Campbell and Mueschke are undoubtedly correct: in their limitation of that experience to one element in it they throw over all the evidence in favour of pure hypothesis.

The whirligig of time brings in his revenges, and after years in which Wordsworth's poetry has been mocked for its lack of passion his whole development is now explained by the psychology of sex. Critics will always differ in the stress they put on the influence over his mind of his love for Annette, and in the view they take of his omission of all but covert allusion to the episode when he came to record his soul's evolution in *The Prelude*. It may well be that that experience had a far deeper influence upon him than he himself realized when he looked back upon it ten years later. But it should not be forgotten that he wrote *The Prelude* expressly for Coleridge, from whom he had no secrets: and it is certain that a distorted account of the most critical period of his life would have been neither acceptable to Coleridge nor worthy of the confidence of their friendship. Despite the new psychology, man is an infinitely complex being, and is capable of being stirred to the depths by other impulses than those of sex. Other men than Wordsworth have been devoted to public causes whose triumph or disaster has affected them personally as profoundly as the most intimate occurrences in the narrower circle of their homes. Wordsworth had given his heart to the Revolution—he was ready to give his life for it—and its tragic failure was a blow beneath which he almost sank.

This *Preface* to *The Borderers* throws a valuable light on that obscure period, the first stage in his recovery. It should also settle for us, once for all, his prime intention in composing his tragedy, and so enable us to date more accurately those stages in the evolution of his mind which immediately preceded it. For it is not only clear that his complete subservience to Godwin was over, but also that he was already emerging from that moral apathy which followed his renunciation of Godwinism. In the drama itself the outlook is still gloomy enough: the *Essay* is the work of a man who has recovered his interest in moral questions, and is at least striving to reach the light. All this points to the conclusion that his renunciation of France in favour of Godwinism must be dated early in 1795, and his renunciation of Godwinism, with its consequent despair, some time during the same summer. His sister tells us that his life in London during the months preceding his settlement at Racedown had been 'altogether unfavourable to mental exertion'; and exertion was needed to rouse him from his moral apathy. But the return to a simple country life, with frugal fare and plenty of outdoor exercise and large spaces of undisturbed leisure, was the best means to revive his spiritual energy. His love of Nature was reawakened; it quickened his emotions and brought him moods of calmness; though still 'dead to deeper hope' he yet 'had joy in her', and joy, as he was later to recognize, both heals the spirit and gives it vision. At the same time reunion with his beloved sister renewed his confidence in those simple natural affections whose value Godwin had discounted. But though, in such conditions, the cold Godwinistic creed had no hold over his heart, he was still unable to cast it entirely from his mind. Acute memories of the pains and miseries that he had suffered, when his 'strong disease' was at its height, flooded in upon him. He realized that he had himself but lately passed through that mental state which made colossal criminals of some of the revolutionary leaders. Had fate been less kind to him, he might himself have become a Marmaduke, if not an Oswald. The psychology of crime acquired a morbid hold over his imagination. He had watched it at work in that hotbed of theory and action created by the Revolution, where, in the name of reason, all natural human feelings were violated, so that blasts

From Hell came sanctified like airs from Heaven,

and where, in reality, the forces that found outlet were not set in motion by this much vaunted reason, but by the most violent of human passions,—a region, indeed,

Where passions had the privilege to work
And never hear the sounds of their own names.

Wordsworth now realized the moral casuistry that lay at the root of all this; but he could not as yet see his way clear of it. He re-read Godwin in a more critical spirit, 'hoping though not expecting to find the work much improved in the second edition'; but, though his attitude to it was widely different now from his former acceptance, there was much of its argument that he could not controvert. It is true, he saw, that reason may be abused by evil and misguided men, but that does not impugn its right to ascendancy. It is true that emotion cannot be

eliminated from human nature, and is, indeed, the main
source of our strength and happiness, but that does not
give it rights against the reason. And what is the moral
sanction which justifies us in applying our own moral
sentiments as a measure to the conduct of others? For
in different individuals the forces of reason and emotion
combine or react one against the other in widely different
ways. Between those two forces, antagonistic, often mutually destructive, in society as he had seen it about him,
some reconciliation must be effected. But how? To this
tormenting problem he could find, as yet, no satisfying
solution.

But the cloud that darkened his intellect and depressed
his heart was soon to lift. After that notable morning in
June 1797, when he read *The Borderers* aloud at Racedown,
his friendship with Coleridge ripened apace; and in almost
daily intercourse with that

> capacious soul
> Placed in this world to love and understand,

he learned how to resolve the discord. A year later he
gave triumphant expression to his new faith in the *Lines
composed a few miles above Tintern Abbey*.

VIII

KEATS[1]

FOR the study of no English poet have we ampler material than for the life and art of John Keats. Of all his chief and many of his minor poems we have manuscripts recording not merely their final form, but earlier drafts or readings which enable us to see the poet at his work and watch the ripening of his inspiration. Keats wrote rapidly, but whilst many of his happiest phrases came to him in the first flush of imaginative vision, others came more gradually as he reviewed his work and realized that the words before him were inadequate to express the conception he had desired to shape. Lamb might regret that he had seen the manuscripts of Milton's early poems, and like to think of *Lycidas* as a full-grown beauty 'springing up with all its parts absolute, wishing never to go into the workshop of any great artist again'. But few students of the poetic art will share these scruples. The visit to the workshop may explain nothing of the mystery of artistic genius, but it throws floods of light upon its methods, and we learn from it as a student of painting might learn as he stood by the easel of Leonardo or Turner. Keats's sureness of touch in the correction of his verse reveals a rare sense of the consummate artist.

In this we owe a profound debt to Richard Woodhouse, who treated the work of his friend with all the reverence that is accorded to an established classic. The manner in which Woodhouse noted, as far as he could, every variant reading in the poems, the date of their composition, their sources of inspiration, gives him the right to be regarded, though he printed nothing himself, as Keats's first editor, and to his labours all later editors have owed their greatest debt.

The material for the study of Keats's biography is no

[1] The Warton Lecture on English Poetry, read before the British Academy on the occasion of the Centenary of the death of Keats. Feb. 23, 1921.

less complete. The society in which he passed his brief but crowded days is among the most vivid in our literary history. It was a company of alert and striking personalities, keenly interested in the world about them—men who loved to talk and write of themselves and one another. Keats, with his genius for friendship, seldom failed to make a deep and lasting impression upon those with whom he came into close contact, and some of them for years after his death spent their best hours with his memory. Lastly, we have his correspondence. In his letters to all who had won his confidence he gave himself without reserve or pose. If in casual society and among acquaintance it is a man's duty to present only the more presentable side of himself, love demands a less guarded surrender; and in what Keats wrote to his brothers, to his little sister, to Fanny Brawne, and to his friends, his character and opinions are revealed to us with a touching intimacy. In the portrait that he draws thus unconsciously of himself, a strongly emotional nature, at once generous and tender-hearted, but disturbed by a strain of morbidity and some of the faults attendant on it, is hardly more evident than manliness and courage, keen self-knowledge, and piercing common sense in the judgement of men and things. The letters of Keats would be precious to us solely for their charm of style and for the beauty of the character they reveal. But they have a further value; for in them we can study the growth of a poet's mind even more minutely than in Wordsworth's *Prelude*; and their evidence is more authentic, in that they are less conscious, and are a spontaneous record of the present rather than a careful recollection of the past.

We like to think that great poetry needs no external commentary, and that its appeal is immediate to all who have ears to hear. The story of the tardy growth of Keats's fame is a sufficient answer to this delusion. Keats was never, indeed, without warm admirers even beyond the circle of his friends; and, as we should expect, they were those whose homage has the highest worth. From Shelley

he won the noblest tribute ever laid by one genius at the
feet of another. Even Byron recognized in *Hyperion* 'a
monument that will keep his name'. Landor and Lamb
were alike eloquent in his praise. He inspired the youthful
genius of two poets so widely divergent in ideal and
method as Browning and Tennyson, and later still became
the god of Pre-Raphaelite idolatry. Yet to the general
reader Keats remained no more than a name. Not one of
his three slender volumes was reprinted. The first English
collected edition of his poetry, reproduced from a volume
published at Paris in 1829 for the continental public, did
not appear till nearly twenty years after his death, and its
sale was so slight that some time later it came into the
market as a remainder. It was only with the appearance
in 1848 of the *Life, Letters, and Literary Remains of John
Keats*, by Monckton Milnes, afterwards Lord Houghton,
that he assumed his place among the accepted masters of
English song. Lord Houghton's fine literary instinct and
his grace of style have made his book one of our classics of
biography. Since its publication the study of Keats has
steadily progressed; new poems and letters have come to
light and many additions have been made to our knowledge
of the sources of the poet's inspiration, and of his methods
as an artist; and now we have a full and definitive biography by Sir Sidney Colvin. In his pages the art of Keats
is examined with the fine taste and the acute judgement
of a ripe scholar, and the poet's life and character stand
out in all their subtle and tragic beauty. It is a book
worthy of its noble subject.

In a sense there is no more to be said. Yet the lover of
poetry will not cease to pay his willing tribute, and though
he add nothing that is new, his time may not be ill-spent.
Re-reading what I wrote of Keats some sixteen years ago,
I have thought that I might bring out more clearly what I
conceive to have been the reaction of his life and character
upon his art. If I fail in this, I shall at least record once
more a personal homage that the passage of years has only
served to deepen.

Every age has the poetry it deserves, and Keats was born into a great age. The French Revolution had shaken the foundations of society; it had liberated thought and widened speculation; and poetry had turned from the ephemeral interests of man to voice his nobler aspirations. To Wordsworth, as to Milton before him, poetry was not merely an accomplishment, it was a divine vocation, and the poetic imagination was man's highest faculty, by means of which he communed with the infinite. With Coleridge he had destroyed the barrier set up by a blind convention between the wonderful and the familiar, the supernatural and the natural; and with Coleridge, too, he had directed attention to the spiritual adventures recorded by the poets of bygone days. The *Prefaces* of Wordsworth are often spoken of as though they were merely a perverse discussion of the technique of poetic style: far more significant is their conception of the character of the true poet, and their review of earlier poetry to prove its validity, with the constant appeal to Milton and to Shakespeare, the beauty of whose sonnets Wordsworth was the first to proclaim. But here the inspired eloquence of Coleridge diffused the wider influence. As Coleridge expounded the eternal principles of art and shed light upon the masterpieces of Greece and of the Elizabethans from his own radiant spirit, his words worked like leaven upon the rising generation. Lamb was his disciple from boyhood: Hazlitt's eager youth submitted to his spell. Leigh Hunt followed in their steps. Hunt published in his *Reflector* and *Examiner* their first critical essays, and with a ready pen gave cheaper currency to the same tastes and enthusiasms, whilst their friend Haydon applied the same principles to painting and sculpture, and pointed to the Elgin marbles and the cartoons of Raphael as they to the greater Elizabethans.

In this atmosphere Keats grew to be a poet. Small wonder that he cried in the fervour of awakening genius: 'Great spirits now on earth are sojourning.' Young as he was, he felt his kinship with them.

Of them all he was the most richly endowed with the nature and temperament of the artist. Never was poet more alert to detect beauty nor more quickly responsive to its apparition. 'Nothing', we are told, 'escaped him. The humming of a bee, the sight of a flower, the glitter of the sun seemed to make his nature tremble: then his eye flashed, his cheek glowed, his mouth quivered.' His response to the beauty of literature and art was as immediate. He 'looked upon fine phrases like a lover'. At the first perusal of a masterpiece he felt

> like some watcher in the skies
> When a new planet swims into his ken;

all that he saw or read became at once part of his imaginative experience, a 'sensation', as he somewhat misleadingly termed it, and he identified himself with its spirit. 'If a sparrow come before my window,' he writes, 'I take part in its existence, and peck about the gravel.' 'According to my state, I am with Achilles in the trenches, or with Theocritus in the vales of Sicily. Or I throw my whole being into Troilus, and repeating those lines "I wander like a lost soul upon the Stygian bank staying for waftage", I melt into the air with a voluptuousness so delicate that I am content to be alone.' And when, after his first incoherences, his passion for the beautiful, like all true passion, became creative, his instinct took him to the great tradition, and he found voice in a magical felicity of phrase that none but Shakespeare or Milton has equalled.

But these gifts alone would not have made Keats the poet that he became. We are all familiar with the vulgar conception of him as a man entirely absorbed in the sensuous side of experience. But a man is known by his works. The sensuous weakling of the Keats legend might, indeed, have written much of *Endymion* and part even of the *Eve of St. Agnes*, but would have been no more capable of attaining to the majesty of *Hyperion* or the serenity of the *Ode to Autumn*, than the stiff-necked and strait-laced clergyman who still masquerades in the popular mind as

Wordsworth could have written *Ruth*, or *Beggars*, or the
Ode: Intimations of Immortality. In truth, Keats is the
most striking example of a poet self-educated and disci-
plined by his own severe and strenuous mental effort. His
artistic evolution can be traced step by step, for he continually reviewed his art in the light of his ideas which
grew in acuteness, and of his experience which grew in
depth and bitterness. As an artist he tends naturally to
think in images rather than in abstract terms; hence the
careless reader may often miss his meaning in the beauty
of the picture; but his mind is continually reacting upon
his art, diagnosing its weaknesses, probing its unhealthy
parts, and strengthening its natural growth. Keats is a
poet, first of all because he had the supreme sensitiveness of a poet's imagination, and caught up the beauty
about him as a lake takes colour and shadow from the sky,
partly because he was a born artist and studied with constant devotion the technique of his art, but also because
he had a mind and spirit bent on applying to his art the
searching test of hard thought and vital experience. We
only read Keats aright when we learn from his own lips
that he wrote, not for art's sake only, but for the sake of
truth and for the sake of life. He did not throw up the
study of medicine in order to become a minor poet. When
he took the fateful resolve to devote his life to poetry he
determined to be satisfied with nothing short of supremacy.
'I would sooner fail', he said, 'than not be amongst the
greatest,' and he knew instinctively what that resolve
entailed. If he was ambitious he had the humility of all
worthy ambition. To him there was 'no greater sin than
to flatter oneself into the idea of being a great poet'. His
devotion to the principle of beauty was associated with
the memory of great men—Spenser, Shakespeare, Milton,
Wordsworth—who in his eyes illustrated that principle,
and in the light of their achievement he was intolerant
of any false pretensions either in himself or in others.
The three short years of his poetic life show an astonishing
growth, but they were only a fraction of the time which

from the first he regarded as indispensable for his apprenticeship:

> O for ten years, that I may overwhelm
> Myself in poesy; so I may do the deed
> That my own soul has to itself decreed.

This is his prayer in *Sleep and Poetry*, and it is no mere phrase. At the end of two of these years he still finds himself 'very young-minded' even in that quality in which to us he stands pre-eminent, 'the perceptive power of beauty', and when the third was drawing to its close he was still looking forward to six more years of labour before he could hope to satisfy his own idea. 'I have left no immortal work behind me,' he said, 'but if I had had time I should have made myself remembered.' In his own eyes the achievement that we celebrate to-day was merely the fruit of an early stage in his education, the uncertain prelude to a loftier strain.

His development as an artist, dimly foreshadowed in *Sleep and Poetry*, went hand in hand with a growing realization of his goal. He found the clue in Wordsworth's *Tintern Abbey*, but the difference between the two poems is at least as instructive as their likeness. For whereas Wordsworth records the stages of an intense spiritual experience through which he has already passed to a maturer vision, Keats as yet can only voice an aspiration. Despite the call of his ambition, his joy in the Beauty that he knows makes him for the time almost content to rest,

> in the bosom of a leafy world,

and though he is aware that he must bid these joys farewell, and pass them for a nobler life

> Where I may find the agonies, the strife
> Of human hearts,

he is not ready to take the arduous journey.

But as soon as his first volume was published he girded his loins for the high enterprise. *Endymion* was to be his *Excursion* into the innermost recesses of that Beauty which

is coextensive with the reach of man's thought and passion;
yet he lost his way in the pleasant wilderness that was about
their outskirts, and his vision of what is at their centre
was fitful and blurred. The poem is lit up throughout by
gleams of exquisite poetry, revealing that 'joy for ever'
which is in the beauty of nature and of art, for this joy
was his poet's birthright; but it becomes inarticulate and
breaks down both in style and sentiment whenever it
attempts to go farther. In 'the realm of Flora and old
Pan' Keats was still delightfully at home; of all else he
had no vital experience.

But when he had finished this 'great trial of his invention', and looking back upon his six months' labour saw
that it had failed, his intellectual life awakened. While he
was writing it the fever of composition had absorbed his
energies, and though, as always, he was reading with
avidity, in particular Shakespeare and Wordsworth, he
was not conscious of his growth. But now he could take
stock of himself. 'I think a little change has taken place in
my intellect lately,' he writes. 'I cannot bear to be unin-
terested or unemployed, I who for so long have been
addicted to passiveness.' The remark is strange from one
who has been busily engaged upon a poem of over 4,000
lines. Yet its meaning is obvious. In *Endymion*, despite
his intention of working out a problem, the oneness of
Beauty in all the relations of life, his intellect was passive,
and his senses followed the lure of those delights with
which his memory was crowded. He had not grappled
with his theme, and the beauty he delineated was no
more than a fine luxury. But now on picking up *King
Lear* it dawns upon him that 'the excellence of a very art
is its intensity, capable of making all disagreeables evapo-
rate from their being in close relation with Beauty and
Truth'. And such is the power of Beauty 'to obliterate all
other considerations', that 'the man of achievement' pursues it in those paths of life where the ground seems most
stubborn and unyielding. Keats had believed this before,
he was now to act upon it. With the sonnet written *On*

sitting down to read 'King Lear' once again, his poetry and his thought alike enter upon a new stage.

> O golden-tongued Romance with serene lute!
> Fair plumed Syren! Queen of far away!
> Leave melodizing on this wintry day,
> Shut up thine olden pages, and be mute:
> Adieu! for once again the fierce dispute
> Betwixt damnation and impassion'd clay
> Must I burn through; once more humbly assay
> The bitter-sweet of this Shakespearian fruit.
> Chief Poet! and ye clouds of Albion,
> Begetters of our deep eternal theme,
> When through the old oak forest I am gone,
> Let me not wander in a barren dream,
> But when I am consumed in the fire,
> Give me new Phœnix wings to fly at my desire.

The significance of this appeal to Shakespeare is clear enough. As he faces, in *King Lear*, a pitiless reality, he sees that he has unwittingly belittled even that golden-tongued romance which had first awakened his poetic life, but which now he lays aside. For 'in the old oak forest' our dreams need not be barren: Spenser's world may be far away, but he took there a mind and a heart stored with memories of his own experience. Keats realizes that if he, too, is to be a 'man of achievement', he must learn to think and feel.

'And so you see', adds Keats, after copying out this sonnet for his brothers, 'I am getting at it with a sort of determination and strength.' Yes, he was 'getting at it'.

He showed it in the first place by his severity on his own past achievement. As he revised *Endymion* its crudities offended him far more acutely than they have hurt his most fastidious critic. He saw in it every error denoting a feverish attempt rather than a deed accomplished, and in one cruel word, 'mawkishness', he laid bare its worst defect. But he had the wisdom not to regret its composition. He felt that in writing it he had worked through a morbid state of mind. It was as good as he could make it at the

time, and it gave him material on which he could judge
himself. 'The genius of Poetry', he says, 'must work out
its own salvation in a man. In *Endymion* I leaped headlong
into the sea and thereby became better acquainted with
the soundings, the quicksands, and the rocks than if I had
stayed on the green shore and took tea and comfortable
advice.' Had he rewritten it now, he could have made it
a far better thing; he preferred to be 'plotting and fitting
himself for verses fit to live'. As he saw it through the
press, he was already at work upon *Isabella*, in which he
made his first sustained effort to wring beauty out of pain
and ugliness. On the 24th of April 1818 he sent his last
corrections to the publishers, and *Endymion* was cast behind
him. Within a week he wrote the *Ode to Maia*.

> Mother of Hermes! and still youthful Maia!
>   May I sing to thee
> As thou wast hymned on the shores of Baiæ?
>   Or may I woo thee
> In earlier Sicilian? or thy smiles
> Seek as they once were sought, in Grecian isles,
> By bards who died content on pleasant sward,
> Leaving great verse unto a little clan?
> O, give me their old vigour, and unheard
> Save of the quiet primrose, and the span
>   Of heaven and few ears,
> Rounded by thee, my song should die away
>   Content as theirs,
> Rich in the simple worship of a day.

Here, as in *Endymion*, Greek legend and the English
countryside are the blended sources of his inspiration,
but it is the 'old vigour', the 'content' of the one, the
'quiet' of the other, to which he now surrenders his spirit.
In this classic simplicity and restraint we are far from the
restless exuberance of *Endymion*.

Keats included the *Ode to Maia* in that famous letter to
his friend Reynolds which sums up the state of mind
through which for the last six months he had been passing.
Though poetry is his first passion, he now classes himself

definitely with 'thinking people', and feels his need for a wider knowledge 'to take away the heat and fever, and by widening speculation to ease the burden of the mystery'. For this burden has begun to weigh upon him. And then, reviewing his own mental growth, he compares human life to a mansion of many apartments. 'The first we step into we call the infant, or thoughtless chamber, in which we remain as long as we do not think' . . . from which 'we are at length imperceptibly impelled . . . into the chamber of Maiden thought'. Here at first we 'become intoxicated with the light and the atmosphere, we see nothing but pleasant wonders, and think of delaying there ever in delight. However, among the effects this breathing is father of is that tremendous one of sharpening one's vision into the heart and nature of man—of convincing one's nerves that the world is full of misery and heartbreak, pain, sickness, and oppression—whereby this chamber of maiden thought becomes gradually darkened, and at the same time, on all sides of it, many doors are set open—but all dark—all leading to dark passages. We see not the balance of good and evil; we are in a mist, *we* are now in that state, we feel the "burden of the mystery". To this point was Wordsworth come when he wrote *Tintern Abbey*, and it seems to me that his genius is explorative of those dark passages. Now if we live and go on thinking we too shall explore them.'

Life was soon enough to play a remorseless part in his poetic equipment; meanwhile he saw clearly that the road he must pursue lay 'through study, application, and thought'. He was steeped already in our earlier poetry and claimed 'to know, perhaps, Shakespeare to his very depths'. Now he became absorbed in *Paradise Lost*, and a little later studied Dante in Cary's translation. But poetry was not enough. 'Every department of knowledge', he says, 'we see excellent and calculated towards a great whole.' So he keeps his medical books by him, renews his study of history and French, turns to his friends for instruction in the social and political problems of the hour, and proposes to 'take up Greek and Italian and in other ways prepare myself to ask Hazlitt in about a year's time the best metaphysical road I can take'.

Yet he has the wisdom not to force the pace of his education. The eager impetuosity of youth, impatient of delays, is often anxious to anticipate its own future achievement. The failure of *Endymion* had warned Keats from this danger. 'Nothing is finer', he wrote, 'for the purpose of great production than the very gradual ripening of the intellectual powers.' 'If poetry comes not as naturally as leaves to a tree it had better not come at all,' and these leaves must not be the premature sickly growth of a forcing house, but should spring from branches that have stood the winter storms and the blight of the east wind. He perceived that an ill-digested learning has no intellectual value. 'Memory', he remarked profoundly, 'is not knowledge.'

This belief had its roots in his conviction of the need for unfettered independence of judgement. Born into an age of theorists, surrounded by men who were doctrinaires in art, in politics, in religion, he resolved to accept nothing at second hand, but rather to lie open to all impressions, till the truth dawned upon him of itself. He was particularly intolerant of those who lived in a world of their own fancy, either ignoring inconvenient facts or bending them to fit the Procrustean bed of theory. Here his instinct as an artist steadied and guided his intellectual growth. If he spoke of the 'principle of abstract beauty' it was a principle which he sought in beautiful things. Even in his earliest poetry looseness of description was a fault of borrowed style rather than of blurred vision. His eye was always on the object. Thus the vague emotionalism of his

> posy
> Of luxuries bright, milky, soft and rosy,

is followed at once by that vividly accurate picture of the

> sweet peas on tiptoe for a flight:
> With wings of gentle flush o'er delicate white,
> And taper fingers catching at all things,
> To bind them all about with tiny rings.

And just as his conception of beauty had grown from what his own eyes had recognized as beautiful, so his mind could only accept as truth ideas which had stood the test of his own experience. 'Axioms of philosophy', he said, 'are not axioms until they are proved on our pulses.' 'I have made up my mind to take nothing for granted.' Despite his genuine affection for Leigh Hunt, and his gratitude for generous encouragement given when needed most, it galled him to learn that he was taken for 'Hunt's *élève*', and it is significant that the alterations he made in his revision of *Endymion* were all in the opposite direction to the advice that Hunt had tendered him. He was conscious of the debt he owed to Hazlitt's 'depth of taste'; but when Hazlitt seems to belittle Chatterton he is ready with an eager protest. The impassioned reflections of Wordsworth were the starting-point of many of his deepest cogitations, and nothing could show more conclusively the receptivity of his mind than his readiness to learn from a genius so widely different from his own. But what was true for Wordsworth was not necessarily true for him, and he resented the manner in which Wordsworth seemed to force his theories of life upon a reluctant world. 'For the sake of a few fine passages,' he exclaims, 'are we to be bullied into a certain philosophy engendered in the brain of an egoist? Every man has his speculations, but every man does not brood and peacock over them till he makes a false coinage and deceives himself. Many a man can travel to the very bourn of heaven, and yet want confidence to put down his half-seeing.' Keats will be no man's disciple, but rather keep his mind fluid, receptive, not like the bee that seeks honey from the flower, but like the flower that is fertilized by the bee. Often this lack of a fixed philosophy of life troubled him. He knew how much more comfortable are those who reside within the four walls of a strictly defined creed. 'What a happy thing it would be', he writes, 'if we could settle our thoughts and make up our minds on any matter in five minutes, and remain content, that is, build a sort of mental cottage of feelings,

quiet and pleasant, to have a sort of philosophical back-
garden, and cheerful holiday-keeping front one—but alas,
this can never be.' He charged himself with an unsteady
and vagarish disposition. Horrid moods would break in
upon his calm joy in nature, obstinate questionings that
he could not lay by. But amid all his 'half-seeings', as he
calls them, he never lost hold on the two cardinal points of
his faith—'the holiness of the heart's affections and the
truth of the imagination'—and from such a starting-point
he could safely explore all avenues of mental experience,
awaiting the hour of clearer vision.

Thus he prepared himself for his next great flight of
song. Throughout twelve months of strenuous intellectual effort *Hyperion* was seldom from his mind, and his
education was all directed to fit him for its execution.
The choice of subject was itself an inspiration. Its remote
heroic theme gave little scope to the weaker side of his
genius which had luxuriated in the mazes of *Endymion*,
and took him to the more arduous heights of song. The
sublimity of *Paradise Lost*, distasteful to him before, now
appealed to his sterner mood, and he caught from its full
harmonies and majestic language something of that diction
fit for 'the large utterance of those early gods'. At home
in the rural beauties of the country around London, and
the richer scenery of Devon, he had as yet no acquaintance
with a landscape suited to be the stage of his Titanic
action, and he undertook a journey through the English
Lakes and Scotland 'to give me more experience, rub off
more prejudice, use to more hardship, identify finer scenes,
load me with grander mountains, and strengthen more
my reach in Poetry'. He gained what he sought. For himself he heard

> the solid roar
> Of thunderous waterfalls and torrents hoarse;

in the mist of dawn he saw

> rocks that seemed
> Ever as if just rising from a sleep;

a stroll upon a grey evening revealed to him the Titans of
his imagination

> like a dismal cirque
> Of Druid stones, upon a forlorn moor,
> When the chill rain begins at shut of eve,
> In dull November, and their chancel vault,
> The heaven itself, is blinded throughout night.

Thus from his own experience he drew the atmosphere for
a poem that since Milton has had no rival in sublimity.
And this surer mastery of his art went hand in hand with
a profounder conception of the principle of beauty, no
longer to him a luxury, but a power:

> 'tis the eternal law
> That first in beauty should be first in might.

This power can only spring from knowledge, from the
widening of the mind till it comprehends all intellectual
and spiritual experience, and such knowledge is won
through struggle and through pain. 'Until we are sick we
understand not.' Apollo attains to godhead through an
anguish keener than any felt by the Titans in their over-
throw. Moreover this eternal law is a law of progress:

> So on our heels a fresh perfection treads,
> A power more strong in beauty, born of us,
> And fated to excel us.

Beauty is a greater thing than any of her worshippers.
They are outstripped in the race, and the supreme test of
their faith lies in their acceptance of defeat. The religion
of beauty is no comfortable doctrine. To their suffering
the only balm, and it is a stern medicine, is to see things
as they are, and to acquiesce in the divine order:

> to bear all naked truths,
> And to envisage circumstance, all calm,
> This is the top of Sovereignty.

Few have the heroic temper to endure. Some, like Saturn,
are too stunned by their own desolation; others, like
Enceladus, reject the truth in wrath; some, like Clymene,

flee from it, too weak to endure the thought of a joy that
she cannot share. Oceanus alone can confront his destiny
with 'severe content'; and the power comes to him simply
through his finer perception of beauty:

> Have ye beheld the young god of the seas,
> My dispossessor? Have ye seen his face?
> Have ye beheld his chariot, foam'd along
> By noble winged creatures he hath made?
> I saw him on the calmed waters scud,
> With such a glow of beauty in his eyes,
> That it enforc'd me to bid sad farewell
> To all my empire; farewell sad I took.

This maturer conception of Beauty had not come to
Keats from intellectual travail alone, it was the fruit also
of the relentless discipline of outward circumstance. The
year through which he had passed was one of growing trial.
His sharpened intellect penetrated into the failings of
friends whom the eager enthusiasm of youth had accepted
at their own valuation; his belief in 'the holiness of the
heart's affection' held through a growing disillusionment,
and he did not love them less; but their self-assertion,
vanity, and petty quarrels opened his eyes to that human
frailty which contributes no less than crime to the misery
of the world. Meanwhile his own troubles thickened.
The financial anxieties which had been a bed of nettles to
him during the composition of *Endymion* pressed closer
upon him, and were increased by a generosity which could
never deny another's importunity. And his heart was
stricken in its tenderest place. His deepest love was given
to his two brothers, George and Tom. 'My love for my
brothers,' he wrote, 'from the early loss of our parents,
and even from earlier misfortunes, has grown into an affection passing the love of women.' But from both he was to
be separated. The one was 'driven by the burden of
society to America' and the other 'with an exquisite love
of life [was] in a lingering state'. In the December of 1818
he began to write *Hyperion* as he watched by the bedside

of the dying Tom; and when he told of the anguish of
Apollo which

> made flush
> All the immortal fairness of his limbs;
> Most like the struggle at the gate of death;
> Or liker still to one who should take leave
> Of pale immortal death, and with a pang
> As hot as death's is chill, with fierce convulse
> Die into life,

he recorded a vivid reminiscence of what his eyes had
witnessed. Then, when this agony was over, and with a
heart made more susceptible from what it had just endured,
he fell deeply in love with Fanny Brawne, the love that
might have healed him was poisoned by the growing
consciousness that his own days were numbered:

> In his heart is a blind desire,
> In his eyes foreknowledge of death.

Love and death; from the clash of these two supreme
experiences the genius of Keats reached its brief but
splendid consummation.

Keats's relations with Fanny Brawne have been the
subject of much comment, some of it from persons of
impeccable breeding and of a sound physical constitution
which precludes them from understanding the humiliating
influence which a weakened body may exercise over the
strongest mind. But no one could be severer upon Keats
than he was upon himself. He had never understood
women, nor felt at ease in their society, and the chivalric
ideal of his youth was continually belied by the triviality
of his daily experience. The egoistical absorption of the
lover in his own emotions had often been the butt of his
good-natured scorn, and now that he was in like case, he
turned his keenly critical mind upon himself, and let his
intellect prey upon his heart. 'Love,' he said, 'was a
cloying treacle to the wings of independence'; he felt it to
be wasting a nervous energy that he could ill spare, and he
wore himself out 'in vain reasonings against the reasons of

love'. There is as much of pathos as of wisdom in the words that he wrote to his little sister, 'Do not suffer your mind to dwell upon unpleasant reflections—that sort of thing has been the destruction of my health.' He lacked the physical constitution to react healthily against the strain of his experience. How far under happier circumstances this love would have satisfied him is another matter. But the greatest poetry is not necessarily that of satisfied desire; the despair of Leopardi is as poetical as the triumph of an *Epithalamion*. Yet to suppose that with a body unsapped by disease he would not have been able to turn his emotion to noble account is to be blind to his true character. His pathetic remark to Charles Brown, 'I should have had her when I was in health and I should have remained well', sums up the whole truth. As it was, the measure of his suffering was, in fact, the measure of his greatness of soul. When his passion was at its height he could still write 'Poetry is all I care for, all I live for'. True to his constant conception that poetry should 'soothe the cares and lift the thoughts of man', he longed to write a poem 'to be a consolation for people in such a situation as mine'. His greatest torture was that his emotion was too fevered to be transmuted into art, and it is no idle fancy to imagine that he was drawn to his renewed study of the *Divine Comedy* in the summer of 1819 by Dante's spiritualization of earthly passion. For his own bitter experience had awakened in him the longing to conceive a love

> All breathing human passion far above,
> That leaves a heart high-sorrowful and cloy'd,
> A burning forehead, and a parching tongue.

This tragic passion, though it wrought havoc with his body, deepened his emotional power, and made him realize more profoundly that beauty which is born of pain. It opened up fresh vistas to his imagination and raised his art to heights that he had not yet scaled.

Yet 'at tender eye-dawn of aurorean love' the gathering clouds lifted for a moment, and he could give flawless utterance to the ecstasy of a triumphant heart. The *Eve of St. Agnes* is the eager tribute lavished at the shrine of Venus Victrix by the artist lover, who attests his utter sincerity by his readiness to 'load every rift with ore'. To view the poem merely as a finely decorated but slender narrative is surely to misread its intention. Its impulse is purely lyrical. All its lovely imagery, all its magic atmosphere, every superb touch of colour, every haunting cadence of its music, are the clear expression of a poet's heart. For Keats, as indeed for all men, such emotion is transient, but the knowledge of its transience only serves for the time to intensify its beauty and its joy, just as the storm that rages about the castle, and the withered, tottering forms of Angela and the bedesman, intensify our sense of the calm within the bedchamber, and of the warm desire of young Porphyro,

> And Madeline laid asleep in lap of legends old.

The *Eve of St. Agnes* is as true and as vital an experience as its companion picture, that masterpiece of tragic concentration wrung from a spirit already disillusioned with itself, *La Belle Dame Sans Merci*.

But more characteristic of Keats's prevailing state of mind at this period is *Lamia*, wherein those two aspects of love which had inspired the *Eve of St. Agnes* and *La Belle Dame Sans Merci* are presented in bitter conflict. Modest as Keats was about his art, *Lamia* is the one poem of which he speaks with praise. 'I am certain', he says, 'that there is a fire in it, which must take hold of people in some way.' True, and the fire that burns through it leapt from his own distracted heart. As a work of art *Lamia* has not the completely satisfying beauty of the two earlier poems; for the cheap cynicism that here and there disfigures it and the divided sympathy which mars its unity of feeling betray a mind at war with itself. There is, in fact, as much of Keats in the stern sage Apollonius as in Lycius the credulous lover, and he could not rise above his own experience so as to harmonize the dissonance. In this his

chief enemy was Time, for already he was preoccupied
with thoughts of death. A full year earlier, even at the
moment when his mind had awakened to the significance
of beauty, he had a premonition that he would die

> Before high-piled books, in charact'ry,
> Held like rich garners the full-ripen'd grain;

and now his sense of fate's tightening grip gave an added
depth and poignancy to his meditations. At times he
would exult in the dream of a love indestructible by death,
immortal even in its sorrow, as in company with Dante he
fled away

> to that second circle of sad Hell,
> Where in the gust, the whirlwind, and the flaw
> Of rain and hail-stones, lovers need not tell
> Their sorrows;

at times he is bewildered by the mystery of death, its irony
overwhelms him. And he writes a sonnet in what he calls
'the agony of ignorance'. What is this Death, that mocks
with its relentless power the vain desires of the human
heart?

> Verse, Fame, and Beauty are intense indeed,
> But Death intenser—Death is life's high meed.

At other times he would avert his eyes from its attendant
decay and ugliness, wooing it in some happy moment, such
as that in which all sensibility to human suffering is lost in
the joy with which his spirit enters into the song of the
nightingale:

> Now more than ever seems it rich to die,
> To cease upon the midnight with no pain,
> While thou art pouring forth thy soul abroad
>   In such an ecstasy!
> Still would'st thou sing, and I have ears in vain—
> To thy high requiem become a sod.

If Death be the end of all, at least it will bring peace. Yet
out of his very pain comes the triumph of that faith which

he had set forth in *Hyperion*. Man passes, but beauty is immortal. When he is most conscious of decay and sorrow as man's lot on earth, he is most conscious too of the victory of beauty over death and time:

> Thou wast not born for death, immortal bird!
> No hungry generations tread thee down,
> The voice I hear this passing night was heard
> In ancient days by emperor and clown:
> Perhaps the selfsame song that found a path
> Though the sad heart of Ruth, when, sick for home,
> She stood in tears amid the alien corn:
>   The same that oft-times hath
> Charm'd magic casements, opening on the foam
> Of perilous seas, in faery lands forlorn.

And what nature does in the eternal resurrection of her loveliness man can achieve by the creative energy of art. Such is the thought which inspires the *Ode to a Grecian Urn*. 'The form remains, the function never dies.' Art distils the beauty from a fleeting moment and gives it immortality:

> When old age shall this generation waste,
> Thou shalt remain, in midst of other woe
> Than ours, a friend of man, to whom thou say'st,
> 'Beauty is truth, truth beauty.'

'Poetry', as Bacon said, 'submits the shows of things to the desires of the soul.'

The *Odes* of Keats, like all great poetry, reveal to us no striking novelty of thought. The emotions that pulse through them are as old as man's aspirations and man's aching heart. But nowhere in our literature, save in some of Shakespeare's Sonnets, do those emotions affect us with the same haunting pathos, for nowhere else do they find such intensely imaginative expression. And this faith in the principle of beauty, held through all pain and disillusionment, brought to Keats its own reward. Blessed moods came to him, when his heart was so filled with the beauty

of the moment that it had no place for sorrow, no place
for other desires. Thus in the *Eve of St. Agnes* he had
entered into the spirit of young love: thus he could enter
into the spirit of Autumn; and as in the *Eve of St. Agnes*,
so now, the completeness of his possession by the theme is
attested by the rich perfection of his art:

> Who hath not seen thee oft amid thy store?
> Sometimes whoever seeks abroad may find
> Thee sitting careless on a granary floor,
> Thy hair soft-lifted by the winnowing wind:
> Or on a half-reap'd furrow sound asleep,
> Drows'd with the fume of poppies, while thy hook
> Spares the next swath and all its twined flowers:
> And sometimes like a gleaner thou dost keep
> Steady thy laden head across a brook;
> Or by a cyder-press, with patient look,
> Thou watchest the last oozings hours by hours.
>
> Where are the songs of Spring? Ay, where are they?
> Think not of them, thou hast thy music too—
> While barred clouds bloom the soft-dying day,
> And touch the stubble-plains with rosy hue;
> Then in a wailful choir the small gnats mourn
> Among the river sallows, borne aloft
> Or sinking as the light wind lives or dies:
> And full-grown lambs loud bleat from hilly bourn;
> Hedge-crickets sing; and now with treble soft
> The red-breast whistles from a garden-croft;
> And gathering swallows twitter in the skies.

The serenity of the *Ode to Autumn* was Keats's prevailing
temper in the last few weeks of his sojourn at Winchester
in September 1819. In that critical mood which never
slept in him for long he reviewed his mental state, and
once more was conscious of a change. His friends think
that he has 'lost his old poetic ardour'; he hopes 'to substi-
tute for it a more quiet and thoughtful power'. For he is
now content to read and think. The growth of this 'quiet
and thoughtful power' can, indeed, be traced all through
the letters he had written in the previous months of

storm and stress. His trials instead of making him an egoist had deepened his sympathetic understanding of men and things. He showed a wider interest than before in the spectacle of life, and saw farther into its spiritual meaning. The 'burden of the mystery' was already less unintelligible to one who, like him, could view 'a world of pains and troubles as the vale of soul-making, necessary to school an intelligence and make it a soul, a place where the heart must feel and suffer in a thousand diverse ways'. And now, alone with his books and his meditations, as he drank in the spirit of town quietude and the tranquillity of the season, it seemed as though he was gathering strength for a further flight towards his goal. But with his return to London in October this peace of mind forsook him, and he became the prey of torments too powerful for his weakening health to withstand. In the despair of genius thwarted by circumstance he turned once more upon himself, to subject his life's work to the 'fierce hell of self-criticism'.

There is a strange similarity in the spirit and purpose of those two poems which Shelley and Keats left as fragments—the *Triumph of Life* and the *Fall of Hyperion*. Each is a vision inspired by Dante and owes much both in idea and temper to the great master. Each, like the *Divine Comedy*, is a poem of self-purgation, recording a bitter confession of its author's failure to shape his life according to the light that was in him; in each case the poet is helped to see the truth about himself by an admonitory guide. And different as they were in character and genius the faults with which each poet charges himself are much the same. Shelley's guiding star had been love, and yet, 'love more than hate had been the source of all sorts of mischief' to him, he was 'a love in desolation masked, a power girt round with weakness'. In the *Triumph of Life* he probed into the reason of his failure. Among the victims chained to the car of Life, or driven before it, are not merely those who have fallen a prey to vulgar passions, but those, too, whose thirst for the ideal, however noble, has warped them from a full understanding of the common relations of life. Complete mastery Shelley assigns to those only who knew both themselves and the world, and despising the common allurement of the wayside, were true to their immortal destiny—

> [They were] the sacred few who could not tame
> Their spirits to the conqueror's.

Shelley sees how far he fell short of their attainment, and his poem is a passionate exposure of his own weakness. In the *Fall of Hyperion* Keats passes a like judgement upon himself. His ideal had been the principle of Beauty. At first he had identified it with pure sensation, and later, when he saw its all-embracing power, and realized that extreme sensitiveness to suffering was the price paid for poetic vision, the knowledge had come to him as a fever: he had felt the pain without the power to allay it; he had never boldly confronted the realities of life, but sought to escape from them into a world of his own creation. He had been a dreamer of dreams, which only vexed himself and the world into whose ears he poured them. Better than this was the unimaginative life of simple men and women, who without vain questionings accept the common lot:

> They seek no wonder but the human face,
> No music but the happy-noted voice.

He is less even than they; above, on the heights of poetry, are only the sacred few who have pierced the darkest reality with their imaginative vision, and subduing their own emotions to a sublimer purpose have 'envisaged circumstance all calm'. Thus Keats weighs himself in the balance and is found wanting.

How far do we endorse this bitter self-condemnation? Assuredly Keats had neither the range of thought nor the wealth of insight of the world-poets, nor had he learnt, as they, to rise above his own experience. But the serene heights of song are not scaleable by a youth of twenty-four. Already in *Endymion* he had set his foot upon the lowest stair, and in the two years that followed he had mounted with a swiftness and energy that has no parallel. His passion for beauty, as Arnold said, was no mere sensuous passion, it was an intellectual and spiritual passion. But when death cut short his labours he was still 'straining at particles of light in a great darkness'. His keen self-criticism, at least as much as the strength of his emotions, was a disturbing factor in his life. His mind criticized the slightness of his themes, the want of profound thought in his poetry, as surely as his instincts as an artist checked his thought from premature crystallization. The process was entirely salutary, it was a necessary stage in his growth to full poetic stature. But that stature he did not live to gain; and lovely as is much that he has left us, we know that his greatest poetry was still unwritten at his death.

Whether he would have achieved his last ambition, 'the writing of a few fine plays', is less certain. The strongest evidence in its favour is that he believed himself to be capable of it. For he was always his own best critic. It is true that no poet ever had a more magical power of projecting himself into remote and varied worlds. But this power over atmosphere is only faintly allied to the dramatic gift. For wherever his imagination took him, Keats never lost himself and his own personal emotions; the exultation or the sorrow is always his own. Even in *Hyperion*, the most objective of his poems, the effect is epic rather than dramatic, plastic rather than psychological, and when he remoulded it in an intensely personal vision, though he marred a phrase or two in the carriage, he was really following his natural bent.

But whatever form of art he might have practised, it is clear that his poetry, whilst losing nothing of its unique loveliness of phrase and imagery, would have gained an ever firmer hold upon the realities of human experience. For already, in two short years, he had shown a development in this direction at least as striking as his advance in sheer artistry. Listen to the lines from *Endymion* which present to us the mother of the gods:

> Forth from a rugged arch, in the dusk below,
> Came mother Cybele, alone, alone—
> In sombre chariot; dark foldings thrown
> About her majesty, and front death-pale,
> With turrets crown'd.

It is a superb picture; but sublimer is the art which could portray the fallen majesty of Saturn:

>   upon the sodden ground
> His old right hand lay nerveless, listless, dead,
> Unsceptred; and his realmless eyes were closed;
> While his bow'd head seem'd list'ning to the earth,
> His ancient mother, for some comfort yet.

The growth is not so much in power over the pictorial or the statuesque, as in depth of human feeling. So in *Endymion* there is a tender pathos in the picture of

> Dryope's lone lulling of her child;

but how much farther are we taken into

> the sad heart of Ruth, when, sick for home,
> She stood in tears amid the alien corn.

Even more notable is Keats's growth in penetrative insight into the mysterious response of nature to man's aspiring heart. The moon as she appears to her impassioned lover in *Endymion* is a vision of pure delight:

> She dies at the thinnest cloud; her loveliness
> Is wan on Neptune's blue; yet there's a stress
> Of love-spangles, just off yon cape of trees,
> Dancing upon the waves, as if to please
> The curly foam with amorous influence:

and yet, more moving is the benignant light from the eyes of Moneta, that

> in blank splendour beamed, like the mild moon,
> Who comforts those she sees not, who knows not
> What eyes are upward cast.

The same difference in feeling separates the 'sweet-peas on tiptoe for a flight' from the 'hush'd, cool-rooted flowers, fragrant-eyed' of the *Ode to Psyche*.

Lastly, recall those lines upon the sea in *Endymion*:

> Old ocean rolls a lengthened wave to the shore,
> Down whose green back the short-liv'd foam, all hoar,
> Bursts gradual, with a wayward indolence. . . .

It is perfect as a picture, perfect in cadence, perfect in the delineation of a careless human mood, the mood in which, despite its ambitious design, *Endymion* had been written. And yet, before Keats could watch

> The moving waters at their priest-like task
> Of pure ablution round earth's human shores,

he had to travel far through a soiled and stricken world. Even then his range might be limited compared with Milton's, or Shakespeare's, but he had at least learnt to 'think into the human heart'.

What he has revealed in lines such as these, is, in fact, just that power which in the bitterness of his spirit he had denied himself, the power 'to soothe the cares and lift the thoughts of man', that gift of healing which is the supreme quality of perfect beauty. Like Keats himself, we turn to poetry, as we turn to nature, that our infinite desire may be satisfied:

> Since every man whose soul is not a clod
> Hath visions and would speak, if he had loved,
> And been well nurtured in his mother tongue.

But alas! to speak is not so easy. For though we all have our visions only genius can utter them. We are for the most part silent poets. Yet with Keats we can pay homage to the 'principle of beauty in all things'. In the eager perception and the careless rapture of his early verse there is a joy and freshness in which the oldest heart regains its youth: in his later poems there is that noble melancholy which has her sovran shrine 'even in the Temple of Delight'. The emotion that they evoke is a spiritual triumph won from that very pain and passion which their beauty lays to rest. Are we wholly mistaken if, with Keats, we call that beauty, truth?

IX
ROBERT BRIDGES

ONLY a few months before his death Mr. Bridges bequeathed to us his *Testament of Beauty*. That great poem was, as he said, 'the intimate echo' of his life; it reflected his alert interest in the intellectual movement of his time, his deep knowledge and love of nature and the arts, his lyrical ecstasy, his pregnant humour, his fastidious taste—all that went to make up his lofty, distinguished personality. No revelation of the poetic mind, so complete and so illuminating, had appeared since Wordsworth's *Prelude*. The warmth of its reception surprised no less than delighted him, for he had never been widely popular. Though he had written a sonnet sequence, a long narrative poem, a series of masques, a sheaf of lyrics, matched by no living poet, the number of his readers had borne no relation to the value of his achievement. *The Testament of Beauty* won him many fresh admirers, and the reading of it sent them back to those earlier poems of his which they had neglected; they found in them the same genius for the creation of beauty, the same unswerving faith in its power 'to soothe the cares and lift the thoughts of man'. More than forty years before he made his Testament, Mr. Bridges had given clear expression to that faith:

> For beauty being the best of all we know
> Sums up the unsearchable and secret aims
> Of nature, and on joys whose earthly names
> Were never told can form and sense bestow;
> And man hath sped his instinct to outgo
> The step of science; and against her shames
> Imagination stakes out heavenly claims,
> Building a tower above the head of woe.

The spirit which prompted these lines was with him from the beginning. From infancy he was 'a nursling of great Nature's beauty'. As a child, though he loved companionship, his most memorable hours were passed alone

in his father's garden and orchard, in the cornfields and
on the downs beyond, and on the sea-shore at their feet.
They were hours of unclouded happiness. He seems never
to have known that discipline of fear which was so potent
an influence on Wordsworth's education. The Kentish
sea can be tempestuous enough, yet to this light-hearted
boy 'his wrath was mirth, his wail was glee':

> He from his dim enchanted caves
> With shuddering roar and onrush wild
> Fell down in sacrificial waves
> At feet of his exulting child.

With an early glad response to nature went that instinctive
feeling for the beauty of language which marks the poet,
a feeling which affects a sensitive child quite apart from
any intellectual understanding of the words, and springs
rather from a love of rhythm and cadence for their own
sakes, the sense of music in perhaps its subtlest form. At
the age of eleven his eyes were opened to poetry by the
reading of Ovid's *Elegiacs*; and soon afterwards he began
to write verse himself. But a passion for poetry, not
uncommon in boyhood, went in him with an abnormally
keen critical sense, and a sturdy independence of judgement. He was scornful of facile or sloppy sentiment, or of
phrasing either uncouth or merely elegant. In his last
year at Eton, whilst he had already acquired a love of the
great Greek poets, he was reading Shakespeare for the first
time, was deep in Milton and Shelley, and carried a copy
of Keats in his pocket. Nothing would satisfy him but the
best. A young enthusiast for letters generally likes to swim
on the crest of current fashion. But though Tennyson
was the rage, and Browning had already won the suffrages
of superior persons, the young Bridges was repelled by the
Idylls of the King, and Browning, save in *Saul*, left him
cold.[1] And this same severity with which he viewed the

[1] Robert Bridges's incapacity to warm to Browning's poetry was lifelong,
as the following incident, reported to me by Dr. F. Madan, puts beyond
all doubt. 'A few weeks after the publication of *The Spirit of Man*, an
anthology, I happened to meet him just between the South Gate of the

masters of his day made him dissatisfied with his own crude attempts at verse, so that for the time he almost gave up writing. He demanded from poetry, whether his own or another's, not merely the overflow of emotion, still less moral edification, but a flawless beauty of form and language.

This attitude was confirmed by his eager discussions on poetic first principles with his school friend Dolben, a boy who though some three years younger than himself was already marked by his fellows as a poet with a future. Dolben held uncompromisingly to the doctrine of poetic inspiration; he only wrote when he had some deeply felt emotion to express, and he could appreciate no poem, however perfect its artistry, unless it voiced his own emotions. 'What led *me* to poetry', Mr. Bridges tells us, 'was the inexhaustible satisfaction of form, the magic of speech, lying, as it seemed to me, in the masterly control of the material; it was an art which I hoped to learn. An instinctive rightness is essential, but, given that, I did not suppose that the poet's emotions were in any way better than mine, nor mine than another's: there is a point in art where these two ways merge and unite, but in apprenticehood they are the opposite approaches.' And, indeed, we may add that *until* they have merged there is no poetry, but merely formless or inarticulate emotion on the one hand, and poetic exercises on the other. But of the two approaches Dolben's was unquestionably the more fraught with peril. Every one admits that to become a painter, a sculptor, a musician, a man must live laborious days; for each of these artists works in a medium whose technical difficulties are obvious enough. But because the medium of poetry is

Bodleian Quadrangle and the North Gate of the Radcliffe Camera enclosure, and ventured to ask him why he had not included a single line of Browning in his book. He replied that several friends had been "at him" about it, and some had pressed him at least to include *Rabbi Ben Ezra*, if nothing else. To account for his refusal he told me that it always seemed to him that one line was wanting in most of his poems, namely

"With one hand slap his thigh, with one *pat God*".'

language, with which we all, from childhood, have some rough and ready acquaintance, there is a common tendency to ignore the technique in a poet's art, and to succumb to the fallacy that from a true poetic feeling poetry must result. But the gift of poetic vision is distinct from that difficult art by which alone it can be communicated. Poetry can only spring from what has been called 'the magical interaction of technical effort with imaginative insight'. And all technique, though it comes to one man more easily than to another, has to be acquired. Bridges resolved to acquire it. In his youth, doubtless, he under-rated both the rarity and the intensity of true poetic experience; yet he was only over-emphasizing a truth often lost sight of, viz. that the poet's power to move us lies primarily not in his depth of thought or feeling, but in his command over a language which compels us to enter into his experience, whatever it may be, and make it our own. And if there was a touch of boyish arrogance in his opinion that the poet's emotions were no better than his, Bridges did not fall into the kindred error of regarding poetry merely in the light of musical expression, which demands a beauty of form and sound, but regards as irrelevant the quality of the experience recorded in it. 'An instinctive rightness was essential': in this phrase spoke the relentless critic of all that loose thinking, vague observation, unreal sentimentality, which have often passed for poetry. His study of the great masters, with their 'instinctive right-ness', had saved him from that.

Approaching poetry, then, as an art which must be learned, and conscious of his own immaturity, Bridges did not grudge a long apprenticehood. He inflicted no *Juve-nilia* upon the world. He was nearly thirty when he pub-lished, in 1873, his first slender volume, and almost all its contents belonged to the previous year. It was followed, three years later, by a sheaf of twenty-four sonnets, and in 1879, after another three years, by a second slim book of lyrics.

He was now thirty-five years of age. Since leaving Eton

he had spent four crowded, deeply formative years at
Oxford, whence he took with him

> Bright memories of young poetic pleasure
> In free companionship, the loving stress
> Of all life beauty lull'd in studious leisure.

After Oxford he had widened his outlook by continental
travel, then settled down to undergo a medical training
at St. Bartholomew's, where he acted as casualty surgeon,
and later served as assistant physician at the Great Northern
and Children's Hospitals. There is plenty of evidence that
he threw himself with energy into his work as a doctor,
and he never lost his keen interest in the development
of medical science; but poetry, then as ever, was his
chief solace and delight. Among the earliest lines that
he thought worthy of preservation is a lovely little poem
wherein he tells how, after a day's toil, he returned home
to commune with his divine mistress:

> Long are the hours the sun is above,
> But when evening comes I go home to my love.
>
> .   .   .   .
>
> Aching and hot as my tired eyes be,
> She is all that I wish to see.
> And in my wearied and toil-dinned ear,
> She says all things that I wish to hear.
>
> .   .   .   .
>
> And so I sit here night by night,
> In rest and enjoyment of love's delight.
> But a knock at the door, a step on the stair
> Will startle, alas, my love from her chair.
>
> .   .   .   .
>
> And he wonders, my guest, usurping her throne,
> That I sit so much by myself alone.

As his mind slowly matured in rich contact with the world
of men and books, and his mastery of the technique of his
art came more nearly to satisfy his own scrupulous taste,
the call of the Muse grew ever more insistent. The publication, in 1880, of his third volume of Lyrics, only a year

after the second, is proof of the rapidity with which poetry was gaining its hold upon him; the nature of its contents show that claim to have become irresistible. This was his *annus mirabilis*. Delicately phrased expression of poetic moods, both light and solemn, are to be found throughout the first two volumes, but they impress us more often with their exquisite craftsmanship than with their imaginative intensity: in the third volume, whilst the art is brought to an even finer distinction, there is a new spirit, the ecstasy of passion, the vital experience of poetry as not merely a loved pastime, but a terrible joy, an uncontrollable force within, driving he knew not whither.

> O my vague desires!
> Ye lambent flames of the soul, her offspring fires:
> That are my soul herself in pangs sublime
> Rising and flying to heaven before her time.

So opens the volume, and there follow deeply felt responses of the soul to nature in her different moods, *To a Dead Child*, that most poignant of all his lyrics,

> Perfect little body, without fault or stain on thee,

and also the most thrilling of his love poems:

> Awake, my heart, to be loved, awake, awake!
> The darkness silvers away, the morn doth break,
> It leaps in the sky: unrisen lustres slake
> The o'ertaken moon. Awake, O heart, awake!

But most significant of all is his address to 'sweetest life-born Joy', a poem which, like Shelley's *Hymn to Intellectual Beauty*, is at once a confession of his faith, a record of his own experience in the quest of his ideal, and a solemn dedication of his powers to its pursuit.

Pondering on the elusiveness of true joy in the life of man, he is overcome by the contrast between that joy in beauty which finds an abiding home in the creations of man's art, and the lot of the artist who creates it. For those only are capable of creating beauty who are themselves most susceptible to pain. The very loftiness of their aim brings sorrow upon them, their acute sensitiveness makes them intolerant of what most men account pleasure; the ideal joy for which they hunger seems destined for higher beings than they, and for a world far different from that in which it is their fate to labour: and even when they are rewarded with a fitful glimpse of it there is always something that they cannot capture: it vanishes, and they are left with a sense of irrecoverable loss:

> For who so well hath wooed the maiden hours
> As quite to have won the worth of their rich show,
> To rob the night of mystery, or the flowers
> Of their sweet delicacy ere they go?
> Nay, even the dear occasion when we know,
> We miss the joy, and on the gliding day
> The special glories float and pass away.

> Only life's common plod: still to repair
> The body and the thing which perisheth:
> The soil, the smutch, the toil and ache and wear,
> The grinding enginry of blood and breath,
> Pain's random darts, the heartless spade of death;
> All is but grief, and heavily we call
> On the last terror for the end of all.

Yet, in this veritable Slough of Despond, comes, as it were by miracle, the sudden vision, and he vows a lifelong surrender to its service:

> Then comes the happy moment: not a stir
> In any tree, no portent in the sky:
> The morn doth neither hasten nor defer,
> The morrow hath no name to call it by,
> But life and joy are one,—we know not why,—
> As though our very blood long breathless lain
> Had tasted of the breath of God again.

> And having tasted it I speak of it,
> And praise him thinking how I trembled then
> When his touch strengthened me, as now I sit
> In wonder, reaching out beyond my ken,
> Reaching to turn the day back, and my pen
> Urging to tell a tale which told would seem
> The witless phantasy of them that dream.

But O most blessèd truth, for truth thou art,
Abide thou with me till my life shall end.
Divinity hath surely touched my heart;
I have possessed more joy than earth can lend:
I may attain what time shall never spend.
Only let not my duller days destroy
The memory of thy witness and my joy.

Bridges was not unfaithful to the heavenly vision. Two years after writing this poem he left London, and gave up medical practice that he might devote himself wholly to his art. He had found his vocation.

I will be what God made me, nor protest
Against the bent of genius in my time,
That science of my friends robs all the best,
While I love beauty, and was born to rhyme.
    Be they our mighty men, and let me dwell
In shadow among the mighty shades of old,
With love's forsaken palace for my cell;
Whence I look forth and all the world behold,
And say, These better days, in best things worse,
This bastardy of time's magnificence,
Will mend in fashion and throw off the curse,
To crown new love with higher excellence.
    Curs'd tho' I be to live my life alone,
My toil is for man's joy, his joy my own.

For the rest of his life his 'toil is for man's joy'. The next volume of lyrics opens with a fresh resolve to live and work in the spirit of his creed:

I love all beauteous things,
I seek and adore them;
God hath no better praise,
And man in his hasty days
Is honoured for them.

I too will something make
And joy in the making;
Altho' to-morrow it seem
Like the empty words of a dream
Remembered on waking.

The songs that follow are all triumphant variations on the theme of the joy that lives in beauty—in the beauty of nature, and of each season as it passes, in the beauty of love satisfied, in the consciousness of experience daily enriched. No book of poems so entirely happy in tone had appeared since Blake's *Songs of Innocence*, and not a few of their number are touched with something of Blake's own moving simplicity:

> The idle life I lead
> Is like a pleasant sleep,
> Wherein I rest and heed
> The dreams that by me sweep.
>
> And still of all my dreams
> In turn so swiftly past,
> Each in its fancy seems
> A nobler than the last.
>
> And every eve I say,
> Noting my step in bliss,
> That I have known no day
> In all my life like this.

Henceforth he will so order his life that he 'may walk with the feet of joy in idleness'. But this term 'idleness', so often a reproach, in Bridges barely conceals a protest against what is commonly called business, 'with its sick hurry, its divided aims'; it denotes, indeed, a high virtue; it is but another name for a glad unity of purpose, and an unflagging devotion to that Muse who

> In nuptial sacrament of thought and sense
> Hallowest for toil the hours of indolence.

In point of fact, the ten years 1881–90, of which these 'idle' songs are the scant but precious gleaning, produced a rich harvest, and were, except perhaps for those last years which gave us *The Testament of Beauty*, the most strenuous in Bridges's whole career. Freed from the claims of an exacting profession he now turned to the composition of longer works: *Prometheus*, a masque, appeared in 1883,

Eros and Psyche in 1885, and before the end of the decade some half-dozen plays.

Prometheus must have been conceived and in part written in the previous year; for that exultant ode, *O my vague desires*, which had come first in the lyrical volume of 1880, was clearly written for its place in *Prometheus*, and voices the inspiration of the one book no less than of the other. The 'heavenly flame' which *Prometheus* brought for the comfort of man was no mere alleviation of physical distress: it betokens the emancipation of his whole being from that crushing tyranny of circumstance which checks the soul's flight:

> My heart, my heart is freed.
> Now can I sing: I loose a shaft from my bow,
> A song from my heart to heaven, and watch it speed.
> It revels in the air, and straight to its goal doth go.

If *Prometheus* can thus be associated in spirit with the third volume of lyrics, as clearly does *Eros and Psyche* breathe the atmosphere of the fourth. That 'loveliest vision far of all Olympus' faded hierarchy', which shadows forth the fortunes of the soul in her quest for love, and the glad issue of their union in the birth to Psyche of a daughter Hedone,

> whom in our noble English Joy we call,

had a significance to Bridges that I need not labour. Nor did Bridges labour it. Telling the story for its own sweet sake, he is content to follow the original prose version of Apuleius, but, as he justly says, with a gentler handling of motive and a substitution of Hellenic feeling for Latin vulgarity. There is no more delightful long narrative poem in our language. Morris had included the tale of Psyche in his *Earthly Paradise*; but Morris's rendering, fine as it is, seems heavy and mannered beside the swift movement and exquisite grace of Bridges. The metre he uses is his own development from the rhyme royal, and he handles it through all its 365 stanzas with a delicacy and lightness that never fails. The natural ease with which the poem flows on its course seems all the more remarkable when we note its elaborately careful structure, with its division into twelve books apportioned to the twelve months of the year, and one stanza allotted to each day of the month. Yet his story fits into the scheme as though no other had been possible. If the young Keats could rejoice in the story of Psyche as a 'blessing melodiously given' him by the sententious Mrs. Tighe, we can well imagine with what ecstasy he would have 'ramped' through Bridges's poem. For another such narrative as the *Eros and Psyche* one would gladly sacrifice some of the dramas. For Bridges had little of the dramatic gift, and though all his plays have a high distinction of style and diction, in them alone he fell below himself. But without dramatic genius a poet may excel in the masque, if only he have the lyric and narrative gifts, a true sense of decorative design, and an instinctive sympathy with the spirit of the 'lovely mythology of Greece'. Here, indeed, Bridges was at home, and in *Achilles in Scyros* and still more in his later masque *Demeter* he achieves a beauty which only *Comus* has surpassed. And to *Demeter* indeed, one might apply not inaptly the words in which Wootton praised *Comus*: 'wherein I should much commend the tragical part, if the lyrical did not ravish me with a certain Doric delicacy in your songs and odes: *ipsa mollities*'.

It is on his lyrics, along with *Eros and Psyche* and *The Testament of Beauty*, that Bridges's fame rests secure. Other lyrists may have reached greater imaginative heights, or struck a more ardent note of passion: none has produced a large body of verse more varied in music and design and yet so faultless in taste and workmanship. There is nothing freakish or mannered about his language; in poetry as in music Bridges 'loved the purer style', and his diction has the limpidity and ease of the best classical writing. In their form, too, and their melody they are in the line of that great tradition, to which, as he thought, his contemporaries had shown too scant respect. 'At the present', he wrote in the preface to his first volume, 'men seem to affect to have outgrown the rules of art'; such merit as his own poems might possess he attributed to the fact that he 'turned to the great masters, and attempted to work in their manner'. It was probably his love for old music that led him for many of his models to that purest period of English song, when 'music and sweet poesy agreed, as sister with the brother'. The delicately cadenced Elizabethan and Carolingian rhythms he has made his own:

> Haste on, my joys! your treasure lies
> In swift, unceasing flight.
> O haste: for while your beauty flies
> I seize your full delight:

this might have been set to an air by Dowland, or Byrd, or Campion. In others, such as *O Love, my muse*, or *Love on my heart from heaven fell*, or *Vivamus*, he has caught the triumphant lilt of the seventeenth century. Like so many of his great predecessors, Milton, Shelley, Keats, he sat early at the feet of Spenser, that master of dreamy processional music:

> Let the priests go before, arrayed in white,
> And let the dark-stoled minstrels follow slow,
> Next they that bear her, honoured on this night,
> And then the maidens, in a double row,
> 　　Each singing soft and low,
> And each on high a torch upstaying:
> Unto her lover lead her forth with light,
> With music, and with singing, and with praying.

In the sonnets there is often an unmistakeable echo of Shakespeare:

> They that in play can do the thing they would,
> Having an instinct throned in reason's place,—
> And every perfect action hath the grace
> Of indolence or thoughtless hardihood—
> These are the best:

at times there is a touch of Milton:

> Is old forgot? or do ye count for nought
> What the Greek did and what the Florentine?

and the debt to Milton, though seldom more than an undercurrent in his verse, grew in depth and strength as Bridges developed his own individual harmonies. His music does not hark back only to the sixteenth and seventeenth centuries. In that late elegy *Recollections of Solitude*, as he calls to mind his own early love for Keats, his impassioned address to the muse recalls the tones in which Keats in *Endymion* had invoked his beloved moon-goddess:

> O mighty Muse, wooer of virgin thought,
> Beside thy charm all else counteth as nought;
> The revelation of thy smile doth make
> Him whom thou lovest reckless for thy sake;
> Earthborn of suffering, thou knowest well
> To call thine own, and with enamouring spell
> Feedest the stolen powers of godlike youth
> On dear imagination's only truth,
>
> .   .   .   .
>
> The only enchantress of the earth that art
> To cheer his day and staunch man's bleeding heart.

In all this there is no imitation: the singing robes of his great forebears have fallen to him as his lawful heritage, and he wears them with a dignity and grace that is his own.

Yet though Bridges could often thus express himself within the limits of the great tradition, he loved, almost from the first, to explore the possibilities of new rhythms, whenever the subtleties of his own thought and feeling called for a more individual music.

The rhythmical beauty of verse lies in its subtle variation from a strict metrical basis, in its avoidance, by the shifting or resolution of its normal stresses, of a regularity which would soon become intolerably monotonous. Its aim is thus to achieve the greatest elasticity of movement compatible with a strict sense of form. The art of the poet consists in his power to do this, and to do it in such a way as to create a music not only beautiful in itself, but peculiarly expressive of the emotion he has to convey, just as the musical composer may take a melody and express his moods in the variations he plays upon it. But the poet's difficulty is greater than the musician's, in that the syllables of his words, which are the equivalent in poetry of the musician's notes, are not mere notes in a scale, but are essential parts of the intellectual symbols which convey his thought. In the desire to develop as far as possible this affinity of the music of verse to its intellectual and emotional content, Gerard Manley Hopkins, an Oxford friend of Bridges, started, about the year 1877, on a series of experiments in what he called counterpointed rhythms, and in the imposition of one rhythm upon another. Bridges, for all his deep-rooted sense of tradition, saw his art as a living thing with infinite capacity for growth, and he followed these experiments with an eager interest. Hopkins aimed, said Bridges, 'at an unattainable perfection, as if words, each with its two-fold value in sense and sound, could be arranged like so many gems, so as to compose a whole expression of thought in which the force of grammar and the beauty of rhythm absolutely correspond'. But like many another pioneer, Hopkins had not patience or judgement equal to his adventurous spirit. By eccentricity and extravagance he wrecked both his meaning and his music. His rhythmical variations are often so bold that his whole metrical scheme is lost in chaos; more often still, in forcing his language to fit his rhythmical purpose, his meaning becomes impenetrably obscure. Intermittent flashes of real beauty light up his poetry, but it lacks that lucidity and perfect sense of form which the true lyric demands. Yet it was, undoubtedly, the admiring but critical study of Hopkins's brilliant, wayward verse that gave Bridges the initial stimulus towards metrical adventure; and where Hopkins failed, he, with his finer ear and infallible taste, achieved some of his most signal successes.

The first triumphant example of his variation of rhythm to suggest the dominant emotion is to be found in an early sonnet. The effect of occasional anapaests to give lightness to lines whose predominant movement is iambic, was, of course, no new discovery. So Florizel to Perdita:

> when you do dance, I wish you
> A wave o' the sea, that you might ever do
> Nothing but that.

Bridges carries this suggestion to its farthest limits, and by the introduction of anapaests in the proportion of one in four into an iambic groundwork gives to his poem the soaring flight of a bird:

> I would be a bird, and straight on wings I arise,
> And carry purpose up to the ends of the air:
> In calm and storm my sails I feather, and where
> By freezing cliffs the unransom'd wreckage lies:
> Or, strutting on hot meridian banks, surprise
> The silence: over plains in the moonlight bare
> I chase my shadow, and perch where no bird dare
> In tree-tops torn by fiercest winds of the skies.
>
> Poor simple birds, foolish birds! then I cry,
> Ye pretty pictures of delight, unstir'd
> By the only joy of *knowing* that ye fly;
> Ye are not what ye are, but rather, sum'd in a word,
> The alphabet of a God's idea, and *I*
> Who master it, *I* am the only bird.

In his later poetry Bridges developed, with even greater skill and subtlety, this correspondence of rhythmical suggestion with sense. But rhythm cannot be isolated from other metrical values. To a fundamental sense of rhythm the true artist must add a nice feeling for the musical quality of separate vowels and consonants and of their combinations, for alliteration, assonance and rhyme, and for the infinitely variable quantity of different syllables; and he must have the gift of subordinating such technical minutiae to one emotional purpose. In all this Bridges was a master. It would be hard to rival the exquisite effect with which in this perfect lyric internal rhymes are introduced, and the various vowel sounds manipulated:

> Wanton with long delay the gay spring leaping cometh;
> The blackthorn starreth now his bough on the eve of May:
> All day in the sweet box-tree the bee for pleasure hummeth:
> The cuckoo sends afloat his note on the air all day.
>
> Now dewy nights again and rain in gentle shower
> At root of tree and flower have quenched the winter's drouth:
> On high the hot sun smiles, and banks of cloud uptower
> In bulging heads that crowd for miles the dazzling south.

Browning, too, a master of facile rhyming, loved to introduce quickly recurrent internal rhymes, but their effect on his verse has been justly, if somewhat profanely, compared to a hiccough. In Bridges they add a tender sweetness to the melody. Swinburne was a master of all metrical devices, but he so rioted in his own facility that he never knew when to stop; and as a consequence, what delights us for a stanza or two becomes, before his poem is out, a merely tedious *tour de force*. In Bridges there is always a consummate control of the material; there is never a line too much, nor a note that cloys. Thus you will have observed in this lyric that the same scheme of internal rhyming is not carried uniformly through the poem. After its regular recurrence in the first five lines there comes a change, and in the last three, extra rhymes are still thrown in, but upon another plan, the middle of the sixth line echoing the end-rhyme of the fifth and seventh, whilst the seventh and eighth lines are given the cross rhymes—smiles cloud, crowd miles. This is the finest artistry; but it is not merely artistry—it is expression: it is like the spirit of April set to its own enchanting tune.

In his poems of nature Bridges brought to perfection his characteristic beauties of rhythm and melody. The 'landscape lure of rural England' was irresistible to him. He is among the finest poet-painters of our lovely varied countryside, making it live to the eye by his exact images and at the same time to our emotions by his delicately modulated music. How inevitably, in these two stanzas, is the contrast felt between the moods evoked by the melancholy English Channel as he knew it at the home of his childhood, and by the river which haunted his dreams at Eton and at Oxford.

> I stand on the cliff and watch the veiled sun paling
> A silver field afar in the mournful sea,
> The scourge of the surf, and plaintive gulls sailing
> At ease on the gale that smites the shuddering lea:
> Whose smile severe and chaste
> June never hath stirred to vanity, nor age defaced.
> In lofty thought strive, O spirit, for ever:
> In courage and strength pursue thine own endeavour.
>
> . . . .
>
> But far away, I think, in the Thames valley,
> The silent river glides by flowery banks:
> And birds sing sweetly in branches that arch an alley
> Of cloistered trees, moss-grown in their ancient ranks:
> Where if a light air stray,
> 'Tis laden with hum of bees and scent of may.
> Love and peace be thine, O spirit, for ever:
> Serve thy sweet desire: despise endeavour.

A still finer example of musical invention is his rendering of the spirit of the wide wind-swept downs, achieved by a deft use of rhythms of his own devising, enforced by subtle melodic effects of vowel and consonant, such as the reiteration of the broad *o* sound at the beginning of the poem:

> O bold majestic downs, smooth, fair and lonely;
> O still solitude, only matched in the skies:
> Perilous in steep places,
> Soft in the level races,
> Where sweeping in phantom silence the cloudland flies;
> With lovely undulation of fall and rise;
> Entrenched with thickets thorned,
> By delicate miniature dainty flowers adorned!

Perhaps the masterpiece in this kind is *London Snow*. The whole landscape is painted in language which might have

been chosen simply for its exact portrayal of the scene to
the mind's eye, yet it has throughout a haunting music
which, as exactly, conveys the emotional atmosphere. The
slow movement of the verse, with its double endings and
reiterated present participles, renders unerringly the slow,
ceaseless, wavering fall of heavy snow-flakes, whilst everywhere the poet fits rhythm and melody to the thought and
feeling of the moment, whether he is recalling the silence,
the mystery, or the muffled sounds; the fresh excited
delight of the schoolboy, or the more sober joy that lifts
the jaded toiler above his cares, to drink in the strange
beauty that is about him:

When men were all asleep the snow came flying,
In large white flakes falling on the city brown,
Stealthily and perpetually settling and loosely lying,
 Hushing the latest traffic of the drowsy town;
Deadening, muffling, stifling its murmurs failing;
Lazily and incessantly floating down and down:
 Silently sifting and veiling road, roof and railing;
Hiding difference, making unevenness even,
Into angles and crevices softly drifting and sailing.
 All night it fell, and when full inches seven
It lay in the depth of its uncompacted lightness,
The clouds blew off from a high and frosty heaven;
 And all woke earlier for the unaccustomed brightness
Of the winter dawning, the strange unheavenly glare:
The eye marvelled—marvelled at the dazzling whiteness;
 The ear hearkened to the stillness of the solemn air;
No sound of wheel rumbling nor of foot falling,
And the busy morning cries came thin and spare.
 Then boys I heard, as they went to school, calling,
They gathered up the crystal manna to freeze
Their tongues with tasting, their hands with snowballing;
 Or rioted in a drift, plunging up to the knees;
Or peering up from under the white-mossed wonder,
'O look at the trees!' they cried, 'O look at the trees!'
 With lessened load a few carts creak and blunder,
Following along the white deserted way,
A country company long dispersed asunder:
 When now already the sun, in pale display

Standing by Paul's high dome, spread forth below
His sparkling beams, and awoke the stir of the day.
    For now doors open, and war is waged with the snow;
And trains of sombre men, past tale of number,
Tread long brown paths, as toward their toil they go:
    But even for them awhile no cares encumber
Their minds diverted; the daily word is unspoken,
The daily thoughts of labour and sorrow slumber
At the sight of the beauty that greets them, for the charm they
        have broken.

It is worth noting that one of the happiest effects in the
poem, the break in the rhythm to express the school-boys'
delight, was clearly suggested by a line from Hopkins—
'Look at the stars! Look, look up at the skies!'

It was inevitable that Bridges, who in such verses had
added new rhythms to English poetry, should wish to
discover how far the prosody of those Greeks, whom he
loved so deeply, could be applied to our verse; and under
the influence of his friend Stone he spent some years in
the attempt to naturalize the classical hexameter and pentameter. This attempt was, perhaps, his only metrical failure,
and it had, I believe, a really unfortunate effect on his
reputation. For it has led a large public, ignoring both
his former triumphs and his latest developments, to speak
of him as though he were a metrical crank rather than a
true poet with the lively and proper interest of an artist
in his art. To me these experiments are proof enough
that the hexameter, as a medium for wholly serious thought
and feeling, is not suited to the English tongue, for where
Bridges failed who will succeed? In our language the
accent is fixed by our natural speech, whilst quantity,
though some syllables are clearly short and others as clearly
long, is as a whole infinitely variable: hence, in our verse,
accent must always take precedence of quantity. The
hexameter and pentameter, on the other hand, are essentially metres in which quantity takes precedence of accent;
with the result that in English you only get the true feeling
of the hexameter when accent and quantity coincide.

Now though one or two such lines may produce a pleasing effect, a succession of them produces a rhythm so marked as to become a monotonous sing-song; whereas in lines in which accent and quantity fall apart, the result is either a loss of rhythm altogether, or the substitution of another rhythm which bears no relation with the normal line, so that the rhythmical structure falls to pieces. The infallible test of good verse is to read it without thinking of its rhythm, simply with the object of giving the fullest force to its meaning. If it is good verse the rhythm will take care of itself, and the better you read it with a view to the sense, the more beautiful will be the rhythmical effect. Everywhere is this true, say, of Shakespeare or of Milton, everywhere of Bridges, except in his hexameters and pentameters. In these, if you read to bring out the metre you have often to violate not only the meaning but even the natural English accentuation; if you read for the meaning you often lose all sense of the metre, and though the line may have a beautiful rhythm of its own it is not the rhythm which we expect and which he has aimed at producing.

But if he was unsuccessful with the hexameter and pentameter, in certain of the more lyrical Greek measures he combined accent and quantity with entrancing effect. For sheer melody it would be hard to excel the song of the oceanides in *Demeter*:

> Gay and lovely is earth, man's decorate dwelling;
> With fresh beauty ever varying hour to hour;

and only a little less delightful is the ode in the last act,

> O that the earth, or only this fair isle wer' ours.

In his later years Bridges gave up direct classical experiment, a proof that he was dissatisfied with the result, and turning back for metrical inspiration to Milton, greatest of all English metrists, evolved that lovely measure which will always be associated with his name—a measure not perhaps primarily lyrical, though capable of voicing the choicest lyrical feeling. But if Milton was here his master, no one

can read *The Testament of Beauty* and earlier poems written
in the same metre, without realizing that some of the
many rhythms that find a home in it owe their presence
to what Bridges had learnt from his experiments in classical
prosody:

> Thus ever at every season in every hour and place
> visions await the soul on wide ocean or shore
> mountain forest or garden in wind and floating cloud
> in busy murmur of bees or blithe carol of birds:
> nor is it memoried thought only nor pleasured sense
> that holds us, nor whate'er Reason sits puzzling out
> of light or atom, as if—say, the Rainbow's beauty
> lay in our skill to fray the Sun's white-tissued ray
> to unravel and measure off the gaudy threads thereof:
> It is a deeper thrill, the joy that lovers learn
> taking divine instruction from each other's eyes,
> the Truth that all men feel gazing upon the skies
> in constellated night—O God the Father of Heaven!
> 'when I arose and saw the dawn, I sighed for thee'.

And what is the content of these lyrics? They are, at
their best, simply a record of the richest moments of one
to whom life, no less than poetry, was a fine art. When
they stray from his intimate experience they are seldom
happy. Bridges's one attempt at the idyll of humble life
is as feeble as any of Tennyson's, his few incursions into
the weird or the romantic are hardly more successful. He
had little of that dramatic sympathy which enables a man
to project himself into moods and conditions of life other
than his own. Still less is he one of those world-poets who
descend into the arena of blood and tears and snatch a
victory for their mistress Beauty out of the agony of human
conflict, or draw inspiration even from the chaffering of
the market place. Browning, for all his idealism, found

> Somehow the proper goal for wisdom was the ground
> And not the sky—so slid sagaciously betimes
> Down heaven's baluster ropes, to reach the mob of mimes
> And mummers:

Bridges slid down no baluster ropes; his graceful, retired muse
> will not leave her love
> to mix with men: her art
> is all to strive above
> the crowd, or stand apart;

and though he, too, sought wisdom on the ground of solid
earth, for there is nothing of 'the ineffectual angel' about
him, it was on a plot of his own careful choosing, where he
could 'build a heaven in hell's despite'. This limitation of
his range he frankly admits. To those masters of song whose
flight is more daring than his own he has paid glowing
tribute:
> Thrice happy he the rare
> Prometheus, who can play
> With hidden things, and lay
> New realms of nature bare;
> Whose venturous step has trod
> Hell underfoot, and won
> A crown from man and God
> For all that he has done.

To this, the highest gift of all, he lays no claims, but he is
'content, denied the best, in choosing right'. He 'will be
what God made' him, the ardent votary of beauty, the
perfect revealer of English landscape in her most delicate
moods, as he has felt them, of human love as he has
known it, at its rarest and most refined, of the sober joys
of wrapt contemplation.

His poems of love are eminently characteristic of his
art. By reason alike of depth and sincerity of feeling and of
flawless execution he is among the finest of our love poets;
but here again his range is strictly confined. There is
nothing in him of the cross currents of love, of impossible
longings, of tragic despair, of the pangs of mad desire,
'enjoyed no sooner but despised straight'. The physical
basis of all love is not slighted, but the love he pictures is
not Eros, the merely physical, with his soft unchristened
smile, and with his
> shameless will and power immense,
> In secret sensuous innocence.

How is it, he asks Eros, that for all your beauty of limb your face is wholly expressionless, so that none cares to look upon it? The countenance into which he loves to gaze reflects the mind and heart; it is at once 'a mark and a lodestar'. A more perfect sequence of lyrics hymning the course of a true love that runs smooth could nowhere be found than in Bridges's shorter poems. They range from early trifles wherein the young man, fancy-free, sports with an emotion he has not yet experienced, through *Wooing*, where first the emotion has become serious, to the bright dawn of passion in *Awake, my heart, to be loved*, and to love's triumphant fulfilment in *O my joy*; and so, through many a poem which marks an anniversary, or some special stage in love's progress, such as that exquisite mature reflection upon the days of early love:

> His little spring, that sweet we found,
> So deep in summer floods is drowned,
> I wonder, bathed in joy complete,
> How love so young could be so sweet;

on to *Vivamus*:

> When thou didst give thy love to me,
>   Asking no more of gods or men
> I vow'd I would contented be,
>   If Fate should grant us summers ten.
>
> But now that twice the term is sped,
>   And ever young my heart and gay,
> I fear the words that then I said,
>   And turn my face from Fate away.
>
> To bid thee happily good-bye
>   I have no hope that I can see,
> No way that I shall bravely die,
>   Unless I give my life for thee.

And from *Vivamus* it is but a step to that last spiritual *Vision* when, at the close of more than forty years, he finds that

> time has cleared
> Not dulled my loving: I can see
> Love's passing ecstacies endeared
> In aspects of Eternity.

The poems of Bridges have been criticized as lacking passion, and if by passion is meant uncontrolled excitement, the charge is just enough. But 'the gods approve the depth and not the tumult of the soul', and among the gods is Apollo, the god of song. The love which Bridges hymns is that

> Whereby the lips in wonder reconcile
> Passion with peace, and show desire at rest.

And this is, on the whole, typical of his attitude to life. Clear vision seemed to him to call for calm. There is nothing revolutionary about him; the noisy and the blustering repel him: beauty to him lies in order and discipline. In life, as in his art, he is the true aristocrat. He knew that moral sanity, though it may not inspire poetry, is yet an indispensable element in it. In an age which, revolting from the complacent righteousness of the Victorian, affected to extol incontinent freedom, he pays tribute to the 'duteous heart'. But convinced no less than Wordsworth that it is by the deep power of joy that we see into the life of things, he conceives of joy itself as a duty, no less than of duty as a joy. To experience this joy is to fulfil our destiny; to reveal it is the prime glory of the artist. Bridges is not blind to the darker elements in life, and in his poem *Nightingales* has re-echoed, in music as immortal as Shelley's, the cry that 'our sweetest songs are those that tell of saddest thought'; yet, he holds that the very act of turning sorrow into song is itself an act of joy, and hence that the true artist must perforce know happiness.

Bridges is the aristocrat also in his lofty gift of selection. He is the victim of no optimistic delusions. He has studied nature and human life too closely not to admit their 'mean ugly brutish obscene clumsy irrelevances'; but man, the highest product of nature, is endowed with consciousness and judgement, and of what good is judgement if it does not choose the best? Nowadays, it seems, to revel in the ugly is accounted to a man for strength and realism. But beauty is as real as ugliness, and to Bridges more noteworthy. And so, where he 'holds up the mirror to Nature, She, seeing her face therein, shall not be ashamed'. And of his own moods those which he chiefly delights to celebrate are the most worthy, i.e. the happiest. Only seldom does his song re-echo the plangent notes of his *Nightingales*; he is for the most part content to lead, in accents of a hardly less piercing sweetness, 'the innumerable choir of day', who 'welcome the dawn'. He is essentially the poet of joy, rather than of sorrow, of attainment rather than of unsatisfied longing. He has himself, indeed, felt the growing-pains of melancholy, but he declines to make easy poetic capital out of them. That *Dejection* which is, after all, a mere dip in the buoyant flight of youth, he sees in its true perspective:

> Wherefore to-night so full of care,
> My soul, revolving hopeless strife,
> Pointing at hindrance, and the bare
> Painful escapes of fitful life?
>
> .   .   .   .   .   .
>
> O soul, be patient: thou shalt find
> A little matter mend all this;
> Some strain of music to thy mind,
> Some praise for skill not spent amiss.

He has known too that deeper self-wrought distress of manhood, to which of all men the poet, with his high hopes and keen sensibilities, is most subject; but this he repudiates as a form of morbid egoism, a denial of his whole creed:

> Fool, thou that hast impossibly desired
> And now impatiently despairest, see
> How nought is changed; Joy's wisdom is attired
> Splendid for others' eyes if not for thee:
> Not love or beauty or youth from earth is fled:
> If they delite thee not, 'tis thou art dead.

'Not love or beauty or youth from earth is fled'; in the poetry of Robert Bridges they find immortal voice. And

we in this place can hardly forget how increasingly throughout his life he sought and found them in Oxford:

> The lovely city, thronging tower and spire,
> The mind of the wide landscape, dreaming deep,
> Grey-silvery in the vale; a shrine where keep
> Memorial hopes their pale celestial fire:
> Like man's immortal conscience of desire,
> The spirit that watcheth in me ev'n in my sleep.

He is in a special sense Oxford's poet, both in what he
owed her and what, so richly, he repaid. None better than
he has expressed the quiet charm of her countryside, none
has distilled into a finer fragrance her essential spirit. And
like a true son, the praise he most coveted was that which
might fall from the lips of those who acknowledge the
same loving allegiance. In one of his sonnets, addressing
his own poems, he asks them, in the humility of genius,
how they can ever hope to win a general welcome, and
then he adds:

> Should others ask you this, say then I yearn'd
> To write you such as once, when I was young,
> Finding I should have loved and thereto turn'd.
> 'Twere something yet to live again among
> The gentle youth beloved, and where I learn'd
> My art, be there remember'd for my song.

May we not affirm, to-day, that that 'something' has been
granted him?

X

THE TESTAMENT OF BEAUTY

ROBERT BRIDGES, in happy phrase, has spoken of that 'birthday of surprisal' which is ours when for the first time we light upon some masterwork of art: the pleasure and surprise are all the greater when the masterwork is a creation of our own time. Matthew Arnold has assured us that the future of poetry is immense; but it is always easier to believe in the future than in the present; and though much verse of real poetic quality had been written in our century, there was little of sustained power or wide sweep of thought. But now we have *The Testament of Beauty*. I would not suggest that the excellence of a poem depends upon its length; all we ask of any work of art is that it should approach perfection in its kind; yet surely scale has something to do with greatness, and the measure of a poet is to be gauged not only by the grace and energy of his flight, but also by his power of keeping on the wing. I am aware that another view is current. Some eighty years back, Edgar Allan Poe asserted that poetry is the language of excitement, and that as excitement must necessarily be brief the phrase 'long poem' was a flat contradiction in terms; and thus putting *Paradise Lost* in its place he proceeded to enlarge on the merits of *The Raven*. And Croce has lately shown Poe's view to be eminently reasonable. But, as Bridges reminds us,

> How in its naked self
> Reason were powerless showeth when philosophers
> wil treat of Art, the which they are full ready to do;
> . . . but since they must lack vision of Art
> (for elsewise they had been artists, not philosophers)
> they miss the way.

Perhaps, after all, Dante and Milton and Wordsworth knew their own business. Naturally enough, the long poem has not, throughout, the intensity demanded of the lyric; but its great moments are the more telling in that they are set in a wider context of thought and feeling. In the lyric we must supply this context for ourselves, and often fail adequately to supply it: in the longer poem we reach the heights step by step with the poet, following the same path as he had traversed; and his poem is far greater in its total effect upon us either than the mere sum of its finest parts or than a sheaf of separate lyrics. The argument against the long poem implies a simple antithesis between pure poetry and bald prose, whereas prose and poetry shade imperceptibly into one another; and the poet's aim is accomplished if his less inspired passages are lifted by style and metre so securely above the level of prose that the poetic impression is not disturbed. That all poets have not achieved this is true enough. To maintain a mastery of form when the emotional pitch is low needs a finer technical skill than to write well under the compelling influence of strong emotion. But Bridges, at least, never forgets that he is an artist, or rather he does not need to remember it; his innate distinction of style and deft handling of metre preserve from bathos his least poetic line.

This prejudice against the long poem tends to become more acute when its theme is philosophic. I suspect that the prejudice is not wholly modern, and that Rome had more than one Jeffreys to register his 'This will never do' against the *De rerum natura*. Poetry is to many an escape from the perplexities of thought to the luxuries of feeling, and they resent what they regard as the indecorous spectacle of philosophy masquerading in fancy dress. Yet, despite such protests, the poet will always write upon those themes that most firmly possess him; and if he is a comprehensive thinker as well as a poet, he will be impelled to express in verse an explicit philosophy of life. It is a difficult task; for abstract thought is recalcitrant to poetic handling. Coleridge complained that 'whatever in Lucretius is poetry is not philosophical and whatever is philosophical is not poetry', and he looked to Wordsworth to write 'the first and only philosophical poem in existence'.

He was disappointed. 'I expected', he said, 'the colours, music, imaginative life and passion of poetry, but the matter and *arrangement* of philosophy.' Yet, in truth, Wordsworth's failure does not lie where Coleridge placed it. *The Excursion* fails because, though it contains much superb philosophic poetry, it contains also too much that is neither philosophy nor poetry. In expecting the *arrangement* of philosophy Coleridge asks for something which the independent life of a poem cannot give. 'The fair train of imagery', that rises before the poet as he muses

On Man, on Nature, and on Human Life,

is likely enough to disturb the logical sequence of the thought, and where imagination leads the poet must follow; it is left for us to arrange his ideas as logically as we choose. For the philosophic poem is not a philosophic treatise in verse. It is, primarily, like any other poem, an impassioned personal experience. It is the work of a poet recalling in tranquillity the diverse emotional experiences that have kindled him into thought, and correlating them into a harmonious conception of life; but when he comes to record that conception, the emotions from which it arose once more regain their vividness, and in large measure direct the progress of the poem, substituting for the logic of prose argument the logic of the passions. Pope's *Essay on Man* fails as a poem because it is too much of a treatise and too little of a personal experience: it is the skilful versification of a train of thought which was not his own and which he only partially understood; and the reader is aware throughout of a definite prose argument distinct from its poetical embellishment. Lucretius, Dante, Milton, expressed ideas in which they lived and moved and had their being, and the work of each, despite some passages which, in isolation, may be prosaic, leaves the impression of great poetry, because it is the impassioned utterance of a great poetic personality. A poem, as Bridges says, is 'the intimat echo' of the poet's life.

And however much critics may cavil at the philosophical

poem, poetic readers have always welcomed it. *The Excursion*, with all its faults, was to Keats one of 'the wonders of the age'; and though it did not reach Coleridge's impossible ideal, its *Prelude*, at least, was to him 'an Orphic song', raising him to that mood of mystic rapture which great art induces in all who are worthy to receive it. What Wordsworth did for the choicer spirits of his own time, Bridges has done for ours. His poem is

> the bounteous gift
> of one whom time and nature have made wise,
> gracing his doctrine with authority.

The Testament of Beauty is an imaginative exposition of the spiritual origin and destiny of man. The world is conceived as the emanation of the Divine Mind:

> Reality appeareth in forms to man's thought
> as several links interdependent of a chain
> that circling returneth upon itself, as doth
> the coil'd snake that in art figureth eternity.
> From Universal Mind the first-born atoms draw
> their function, whose rich chemistry the plants transmute
> to make organic life, whereon animals feed
> to fashion sight and sense and give service to man,
> who sprung from them is conscient in his last degree
> of ministry unto God, the Universal Mind,
> whither all effect returneth whence it first began.

The general affinity of this to many theories of life, to Aristotle's conception of the Final Cause or to St. John's of the Logos, is clear enough; among our own poets it may be closely paralleled in Raphael's speech to Adam in *Paradise Lost*, whilst a kindred thought inspired Wordsworth with

> a sense sublime
> Of something far more deeply interfused,
> Whose dwelling is the light of setting suns,
> And the round ocean and the living air,
> And the blue sky, and in the mind of man;

and led him to speak of that 'Soul of all the worlds' which 'circulates from link to link', and has in the mind of man its most apparent home, i.e. that home where it is recognized for what it is.

For man's distinction as a link in this chain of being is his self-conscient mind; and with conscience comes reason, the incipient faculty of judgement; by his reason man endeavours to comprehend and harmonize the intuitions which spring from his sense-experience; and thus he learns to interpret the world about him, so that what in nature is mere innate propensity becomes in him spiritual aspiration, and he realizes the true purpose of his being, a conscious reunion with Universal Mind.

Now the Universal Mind, to Bridges as to Plato, is compact of different qualities or essences which are reproduced in the world, and act as vital controlling forces in its evolution. To the mind of man, these essences appear as ideas, and these ideas are the supreme efficient causes of his thoughts. He does not owe them to his reason, though it is through his reason that he is able to apprehend them; science cannot explain them; and if Aristotle and other philosophers have boggled at them, they yet cannot disprove them; they are the ultimate entities of Being, transmitted to us from the Universal Mind by the way of our animal senses. If man's mind held all ideas in due proportion and in their purity, it would be a perfect microcosm of the Divine Mind; but in man nothing is wholly pure; and individual differs from individual in the manner in which these ideas are co-ordinated in his mind, and in the strength and worth in him of that reason whose task it is to co-ordinate them. For consciousness implies a measure of freedom. The power of reflecting on things carries with it the power of getting outside them, and judging them, and consequently implies an infinite number of attitudes towards them and an infinite number of possible actions determined by those attitudes. But his mind is only an infinitesimal part of the Universal Mind, most of which lies below consciousness, and is expressed in those instincts which lie deeply imbedded in animal life. Reason has in itself no power to initiate; for the material on which it works it lies in deep insolvency to sense, and in its task of co-ordinating that material it is still a novice. It is often baulked by self-puzzledom and doubt, and in arrogant ignorance often goes astray, misreading the intentions of Nature, thwarting them, ordering human activities for ravage rather than defence. Thus we are confronted with the paradox that though without reason man would not be conscious of his spiritual destiny, nor could achieve it, yet his reason may often pervert those very instincts through which Nature has designed his spiritual ascent. For the reason only fulfils her true function when she subserves the soul. Hence the essential defining term of man as distinct from brutes is not reason but spirit:

> In truth 'spiritual animal' wer a term for man
> nearer than 'rational' to define his genus.

Here again we are reminded of the central thought of Wordsworth—his insistence on the prime importance of the experience of eye and ear as the only avenue to truth, and on the inferiority of reason, in itself a mere calculating process, to that higher Reason, or 'Reason in her most exalted mood', which is imagination, which enables its possessor to see the world of sense-experience in its real spiritual significance. With this conception the Greek idea that God is pure reason and that man can only attain to communion with him by θεωρία, or pure speculation, from which all emotion has been purged away, is inevitably superseded by the conception that God is essentially love, and that man's communion with Him is only attainable through the exercise of his whole being, in which, if reason directs, yet the emotions supply the energizing force:

> the arch-thinker's heav'n cannot move my desire,
> nor doth his pensiv Deity make call on my love.
> I see the emotion of saints, lovers and poets all
> to be the kindling of some Personality
> by an eternizing passion.

The higher function of reason, therefore, is to interpret in the light of spiritual intuition ideas which come to it

through the senses; and chief of these ideas in its spiritual
potency is the idea of Beauty.

> As some perfected flower, Iris or Lily, is born
> patterning heav'nly beauty, a pictur'd idea
> that hath no other expression for us, nor coud hav:
> for thatt which Lily or Iris tell cannot be told
> by poetry or by music in their secret tongues,
> nor is discerptible in logic, but is itself
> an absolute piece of Being, and we know not,
> nay, nor search not by what creativ miracle
> the soul's language is writ in perishable forms—
> yet are we aware of such existences crowding,
> mysterious beauties unexpanded, unreveal'd,
> phantasies intangible investing us closely,
> hid only from our eyes by skies that wil not clear;
> activ presences, striving to force an entrance,
> like bodiless exiled souls in dumb urgence pleading
> to be brought to birth in our conscient existence,
> as if our troubled lot wer the life they long'd for;
> even as poor mortals thirst for immortality:—
> And every divination of Natur or reach of Art
> is nearer attainment to the divine plenitude
> of understanding, and in moments of Vision
> their unseen company is the breath of Life.

Thus Bridges's song, like Wordsworth's, proclaims

> How exquisitely the individual mind
> . . . to the external world
> Is fitted, and how exquisitely too
> The external world is fitted to the mind.

For man is so framed that he recognizes beauty in the
world about him, and recognizing it, desires it. To see
beauty and to love it are one and the same thing. *The
Testament of Beauty* reveals the manner in which by the
influence of beauty man may rise to a consciousness of his
spiritual heritage.

The urge of the life-force within him finds elementary
expression in the two root instincts of Selfhood and Breed.
Bridges pictures them, after the manner of Plato's vision
in the *Phaedrus*, as two steeds driven by the charioteer

Reason; but he makes a significant change in the Platonic allegory. To Plato one steed figured the unruly passions of man, the other his nobler instincts; and the task of the charioteer was to force the unruly steed into accord with the heavenward path sought by his nobler fellow: to Bridges both steeds, though wilful and restive, are potentially good, and their course is determined for better or worse according as their charioteer, the Reason, is inspired by the idea of beauty or swayed by lower impulses. For both these instincts of selfhood and breed have within them a faint adumbration of soul. Selfhood is primarily a remorseless fight for existence, yet even in the animal kingdom Nature has placed the germs of a higher development. The wolves that hunt in packs, the flocks that herd together for mutual protection, show signs of escape from a blind idea of self; whilst motherhood, which is ready to jeopardize its own life to ensure the safety of its offspring, is an instinct which, becoming conscious in the human mind, rises to the noblest altruism. And the passion for life, without which life could not be, is everywhere associated with the idea of beauty.

> But since ther is beauty in nature, mankind's love of life
> apart from love of beauty is a tale of no count;
> and tho' he linger'd long in his forest of fear,
> or e'er his apprehensiv wonder at unknown power
> threw off the first night-terrors of his infant mind,
> the vision of beauty awaited him, and step by step
> led him in joy of spirit to full fruition.

So Breed, originally nature's provision for the continuance of the species, develops by association with the idea of beauty into the love of a Dante. For sensuous Beauty is the mother of heavenly Love. In so far as reason, the controlling force of these two animal instincts, is possessed of the true idea of beauty, man's spiritual destiny is achieved; but when reason is blind to its true purpose, these animal instincts are perverted, so that man sinks lower than the beasts, his selfhood degenerating into such vices as gluttony or cruelty, and breed into degrading lust.

As fundamental in man as selfhood and breed is his artistic instinct, which, like them, he owes to his animal nature. The beauty by which the animal—in song, in dance, in grace of movement—expresses his joy in life is recognized consciently by man's reason and exploited in his art, which thus becomes

> that ladder of joy whereon
> slowly climbing at heaven he shall find peace with God.

There is thus no contrast between art and Nature, for man's inborn passion for art is but Nature herself,

> who danceth in her garden at the blossoming-time
> 'mong the flowers of her setting.

But though in every man this instinct is innate, the genius for artistic creation is rare and not at his command. It is largely an unconscious process. Here, as with the other instincts, reason does not supply the impulse; it is the mere servant and drudge whose task it is to order what the creative impulse supplies. All excellence in art springs from a divine inspiration under whose influence man shows himself most clearly a partaker in the Divine Mind which, in its wisdom delighting in Beauty, created the world after Beauty's image. Hence just as Milton, with unerring vision, invokes his heavenly Muse:

> Thou with eternal Wisdom didst converse,
> Wisdom thy sister, and with her didst play
> In presence of th' Almighty Father, pleas'd
> With thy celestial song,

so to Bridges the wisdom of God granted this gift to man that she may

> take back from his hand her Adoration robes
> and royal crown of his Imagination and Love.

Even as all spiritual growth has its roots in the animal passions of selfhood and breed, and finds its true expression through the creative instinct of art, so our moral conceptions have developed from animal instinct awakened to consciousness of itself. Out of natural necessity arose the idea of obligation:

> Ther is a young black ouzel, now building her nest
> under the Rosemary on the wall, suspiciously
> shunning my observation as I sit in the porch,
> intentiv with my pencil as she with her beak:
> Coud we discourse together, and wer I to ask her for-why
> she is making such pother with thatt rubbishy straw,
> her answer would be surely: 'I know not, but I MUST.'
> Then coud she take persuasion of Reason to desist
> from a purposeless action, in but a few days hence
> when her eggs wer to hatch, she would look for her nest;
> and if another springtide found us here again,
> with memory of her fault, she would know a new word,
> having made conscient passage from the MUST to the OUGHT.

Thus Duty is not a law arbitrarily imposed by some external power: it is the conscious fulfilment of that law which nature follows by instinct. Wordsworth's sublime apostrophe to Duty,

> Thou dost preserve the stars from wrong;
> And the most ancient heavens, through Thee, are fresh and strong,

is no fanciful extravagance; it is a profound imaginative truth. The first rudimentary conception of morals sprang from the customs adopted by primitive man in order to safeguard for himself what he most valued in life; as his reason grew his sense of morality grew also, and was codified in laws. But such codification, though continually modified with man's moral growth, must always lag behind his spiritual capacity; true progress is only achieved by those great teachers who transcend established morality, and rise to heights as yet unscaled by the common herd, whom by precept and example they beckon to follow whither they

> with beauty [have] made escape, soaring away to where
> the Ring of Being closeth in the Vision of God.

And to Bridges, as to Wordsworth, the path of duty is essentially the path of joy. Pleasure, the intrinsic joy of life, is in itself an absolute good; for it is man's natural response to beauty. That there are bad pleasures as well as good is simply due to the weakness of man's reason, which has diverted joy from its natural function as the ally of spirit. Hence moralists, who from fear of bad pleasures repudiate all pleasure, are guilty of a reasoned folly. The pleasure of life attendant on all its activities is not to be denied the soul; rather is it true that the quality and value of man's pleasure rise with the growth of his spirit. The animal joy persists, but is transformed by the influence of Beauty into something greater than itself, till vision is gained of that omnificent Creator whose beauty and wisdom are only approached, and only apprehended, through a joyful understanding of his creation.

This approach of man to his Creator is what we call religion. That blind fear felt by the savage mind in the presence of incomprehensible power is gradually transmuted by the influence of Beauty into Love. The religious instinct, when not rightly ordered by reason, will, like man's other instincts, go astray, and thus often degenerates into superstition,

> with creeds and precise focusings of the unsearchable,

bringing religion into disrepute and provoking that scepticism which denies the spiritual claims of man. And scepticism, in revulsion, breeds new superstitions such as are rife to-day. For scepticism starves the soul; and the soul, bereft of its true nutriment, will 'ravin gall'. But man ever craves for beauty, and this hankering after a beauty, denied or lost, 'is the remnant grace of nature's covenant, the starved germ athirst for God'. Rightly directed it finds its consummation in a vision of love as of the essence of the divine nature.

God's love is, indeed, beyond the reach of man's comprehension. Our finite minds can only grasp it from its prefigurings in our earthly relationships; but even as the idea of the divine essence of beauty is derived from our intuitive recognition of beautiful things, so in the passion of motherhood, in the ecstatic dawn of man's love for woman, in the ideal of earthly friendship, we get a glimpse of Love's Infinity. Nor does the disparity between man with his finite imperfections and divine perfection cut him off from a real friendship with God:

> From this dilemma of pagan thought, this poison of faith,
> Man-soul made glad escape in the worship of Christ;
> for his humanity is God's Personality,
> and communion with him is the life of the soul.

Such, as I understand it, is our poem's main trend of thought. It offers, inevitably, many occasions for sceptical assault. To the question why this universe, if its source is divine, presents such a confusion of evil with good and ugly with beautiful Bridges replies that to ask *why* is fruitless; for the imperfect human mind the only profitable inquiry is to ask *what is*, not *why it is*. *What is*, at least, suggests to him that ideas have no significance without their opposites; the beautiful implies by contrast the ugly, joy implies sorrow, and morality vice. If he has not Browning's almost truculent combativeness in the presence of evil he yet holds that all hindrance to good

> maketh occasion for it, by contrast heightening,
> by challenge and revelly arousing Virtue to act;
>
> .   .   .   .
>
> rather 'tis as with Art, wherein special beauty
> springeth of obstacles that hav been overcome
> and to graces transform'd; so the lover in life
> will make obstructions serve, and from all resistance
> gain strength.

But this would not explain the presence of evil and ugliness in the natural world. How far, it might be objected, can the poets who expatiate upon the beauty and significance of Nature be acquitted of ignorance of half the facts, or of a sentimental blindness to them? Mr. Aldous Huxley has assured us that had Wordsworth visited the tropics, and seen what *he* has seen, he could never have written so complacently of nature; and, similarly, Keats might be set down as callous, in that he admits 'the fierce destruction of Nature's core', and yet averts his gaze from 'the hawk at pounce', and 'the gentle robin ravening the worm', to lay his head

> Mid hush'd, cool-rooted flowers, fragrant-eyed.

Bridges has met this objection with an argument which his predecessors would have accepted. In a beautiful allegory, published some years before *The Testament of Beauty*, he pictures the world as a room adorned with fair arras hangings,

> wherein my spirit hath dwelt
> from infancy a nursling of great Nature's beauty
> which keepeth fresh my wonder as when I was a child.

The modern young heir who inherits the estate orders his steward to turn this tapestry with its face to the wall, 'so we shall have more colour and less solemnity'. But though he would do well to take down the tapestry and examine it thoroughly, back as well as front, to look for ever on its back is to misconceive its artist's purpose:

> But as a man, owning a fine cloth of Arras,
> in reverence for his heirloom will examine it all
> inside and out, and learn whether of white wool or silk
> the high-warp, what of silver and gold, how fine the thread,
> what number of graded tints in hatching of the woof;
> so we study Nature, wrong side as well as right
> and in the eternal mystery of God's working find
> full many unsightly a token of beauty's trouble;
> and gain knowledge of Nature and much wisdom thereby;
> but these, making no part of beauty's welcome face,
> these we turn to the wall, hiding away the mean
> ugly brutish obscene clumsy irrelevances
> which Honesty will own to with baffling humour
> and in heightening the paradox will find pleasure.

And if to this the clever young man replies that he prefers the wrong side, or goes still further, and asks who are we to dictate to him which *is* the wrong side and which the right, that side which is a mere tangle of threads or that other which has a significant design, then the answer is only faith:

> The wise will live by Faith,
> faith in the order of Nature and that her order is good.

Of these two fundamental articles of faith, the first, faith in the order of nature, is itself a postulate of science; but science, that activity of man's reason which for its own specialized purposes rules out of count the things of the spirit, has no concern with the second. Bridges admits no quarrel between science and poetry. None of our poets, indeed, save Shelley, has shown so deep an interest in science, nor kept in closer touch with its advance. He delights in recording how

> comforting man's animal poverty
> and leisuring his toil, [she] hath humanized manners
> and social temper;

nor has more lovely tribute ever been paid to her than is found in his commemoration of her latest achievement:

> and now above her globe-spredd net
> of speeded intercourse hath outrun all magic,
> and disclosing the secrecy of the reticent air
> hath woven a seamless web of invisible strands
> spiriting the dumb inane with the quick matter of life:
> Now music's prison'd raptur and the drown'd voice of truth
> mantled in light's velocity, over land and sea
> are omnipresent, speaking aloud to every ear,
> into every heart and home their unhinder'd message,
> the body and soul of Universal Brotherhood.

Here, indeed, is the 'impassioned expression which is in the countenance of all science'. It calls to mind Shelley's prophetic ecstasy at man's conquest of the air, which he saw, not as we have seen it, as an instrument of ruthless destruction, but as a compelling influence to draw the world into closer bonds of peace and friendship. Yet Science does not satisfy the spirit. After her greatest triumphs we are no nearer to the First Cause of all than

a child who 'thinketh he is nearer to the Pole-star when he
is put to bed'. For Science knows nothing of Beauty:

> what kenneth she
> of color or sound? Nothing: tho' science measure true
> every wave-length of ether or air that reacheth sense,
> there the hunt checketh, and her keen hounds are at fault;
> for when the waves hav pass'd the gates of ear and eye
> all scent is lost: suddenly escaped the visibles
> are changed to invisible; the fine-measured motions
> to immeasurable emotion; the cypher'd fractions
> to a living joy that man feeleth to shrive his soul.

Hence to those who do not realize her limitations, Science
may prove a curse. The very benefits she has conferred on
man's animal life may lead him into a gross materialism,

> whence now whole nations, by their treasure-trove enrich'd,
> crawl greedily on their knees nosing the soil like swine,
> and any, if they can twist their stiffen'd necks about,
> see the stars but as stones;

whilst some of her nobler votaries, concentrating their
attention on the remorseless forces of nature, and those
cruelties that rend the heart, in a love of truth which
refuses 'to blink dishonestly the tribulation of man', deem
that tribulation to be 'final truth, and see no clue thereof'.
The only clue is found in that second faith, which is the
faith of the poet. To the man of science, indeed, such
faith is often granted, as when he is drawn by a spirit of
wonder before nature's immensity into a mystic rapture,
and himself becomes a poet; which thing happened to
Ptolemy the astronomer who

> gazing with naked eye into the starry night
> forgat his science and, in transport of spirit,
> his mortal lot. Then seem'd it to him as if his feet
> touch'd earth no longer.

By such faith alone a man can save his soul; and it is the
sense of beauty innate in all men that prompts and justifies
that faith. How far each man may attain it depends, in the
last resort, upon his native disposition; but to those who

have it the experience is as real as their experience of
scientific fact. Between pessimism and optimism there is a
great gulf; and yet the optimistic view finds some support
in man's innate passion for life, and this even the pessimist
cannot deny, or he would not himself be alive:

> for howso deliberatly a man may wish for death
> still wil he instinctivly fight to the last for life.

> .   .   .   .

> Verily indeed if hope wer not itself a happiness,
> Sorrow would far outweigh our mortal joy;

but our nature is so framed that

> our hope is ever livelier than despair, our joy
> livelier and more abiding than our sorrows are,
> which leak away until no taint remain; their seeds
> shriveling too thin to lodge in Memory's hustled sieve.

From the central ideas of the poem, the poet's quicken-
ing thought radiates over a wide and varied field. Most
memorable are those passages which illumine the life of
the child. The child, as father to the man, that human
being that is nearest to animal nature in impulse and
desires, in whom for good and ill reason has barely begun
its work, might be said to hold the key to the whole
position; and Bridges speaks with the freedom that is born
of imaginative insight when he expounds Plato's doctrine
of anamnesis in terms of heredity, or the significance of
our conception of Godhead as shadowed in the infant
Christ; or when he sets forth the child's instinctive response to beauty, and deduces from it the vital influence
of environment upon his spiritual health. Hardly less
suggestive are thoughts casually let fall on the love of man
and woman both in its ideal and its failures, and the
profound criticism of some of the diseases of our modern
body politic. The democratic idealist might, perhaps, be
inclined to protest against Bridges's truly Miltonic contempt for the herd. He might urge that he himself, no
less than our poet, recognizes 'spiritual attainment, individual worth' to be the true goal of our endeavour, and,

further, that his aim was not to reduce life to the lowest common level, but rather to open to all those chances for spiritual attainment which are, even to-day, the lot of but a favoured few; yet, even so, he could not deny the evils on which Bridges has thrown his searching light.

In prosaically laying bare the skeleton of the poem's thought I have hardly suggested the nature of that living organism which *is* the poem. Only, perhaps, for a few hundred lines in the centre of the last book does the argument get the better of the poetry. Taken as a whole *The Testament of Beauty* is imaginative rather than didactic. And the field of experience over which it ranges is astonishingly wide. It is the 'intimat echo' of the life of one whose home has always been in the land of the Muses, yet who has been a tireless adventurer in many countries, and from them all has brought back with him treasures with which to adorn the shrine of his divine mistress. In reaching his conclusions he has tested against his own experience the findings of many philosophers. Different facets of his thought sparkle in analogies drawn from physics or chemistry or medicine; others are expressed in vivid episodes from ancient or medieval history, or the achievements of the sister arts of painting and music, or the conditions of modern life. The dawn of wisdom in Hellas, the birth of modern poetry at the court of Raymond of Toulouse, the lives of St. Francis and St. Thomas and Henry VIII, the Crusades and the Albigensian war, Raphael's Madonnas and Titian's *L'Amor sacro e profano*, the feasts of city aldermen, and the latest discovery of prehistoric tombs in Mesopotamia—these are but a few of the scenes in which the thought of the poem takes life. The logical argument, indeed, sits lightly upon it; pedants might complain that it sits too lightly, and that some of the incidents are developed out of all proportion to their weight in the argument. But this charge could be met as another poet met it, with the plea that 'his course is often stay'd, yet never is astray'. For in whatever by-paths he wanders, Bridges finds beauty on the road. Beauty is all his argument; and even where poetic inspiration flags there is always the beauty of accomplished art.

Of versification Bridges is a master. If we have had greater poets than he, we have had few artists as impeccable. A classical scholar, who has made a life-long study of the technique of English verse and has probed, as far as they can be probed, the secrets of Milton's incomparable music, he has been also a bold experimenter; and if some of his classical adventures have not proved happy to an English ear, they have doubtless contributed to his own final facility. The new metre which he has evolved, in which our poem is written, loose Alexandrines, or neo-Miltonic syllabics, as he calls them, was suggested by the choruses of *Samson Agonistes*, with as generous a licence in the positions of stress, and the use of elision, substitution and extra-metrical syllables as is compatible with the rhythmical integrity of the line. This metre is a triumph of art. It is capable of infinite variety, as is proved by the ease with which quotations from poets writing in different languages and different metres can be fitted into its mould; and according as it is loosely or strictly handled it is adaptable to any mood and any subject. It can move with the sweet regularity of a softly gliding stream, or dance with the sparkling gaiety of a mountain torrent: it is equally successful in light familiar discourse or pithy reflection; it can assume a dignity consonant with high prophetic utterance. If it cannot rise to the majesty of blank verse, it is much happier than that measure upon the lower poetic levels. In range it can, perhaps, only be equalled by the metre of Byron's *Don Juan*, and in Bridges's hands it is capable of a delicate and subtle music quite out of Byron's reach. By its invention Bridges has definitely extended the musical capacities of our language; whether future poets will be able to develop it still further, or to handle it with his skill, I am not rash enough to prophesy.

With this metrical dexterity goes an exquisite sureness in the use of language, the gift only of those artists who are

also scholars, and those scholars who are also artists. Again
and again we meet that perfect union of sound and sense,
that effect of the unexpected that is yet inevitable, which
awakens the true poetic thrill. Sometimes we owe it to
single words, as of the baby who '*clarioneth* for food', or of
the historians who '*jaunt* on their *prancing* pens after their
man of war'; more often it comes to us from that magic
moulding of the right words into phrases at once melodious
and significant. What could be more lovely, and at the
same time more finally expressive, than the few lines that
speak of the voice of Duty?

> whereby the creature kenneth the creator's Will,
> that, in stillness of sound speaking to gentle souls,
> dowereth all silence with the joy of his presence.

Bridges has no cramping theory of diction, he uses those
words and forms of words in which lucidity is joined with
melodic grace: where he is slightly archaic, as in his use of
verb-forms in -*eth*, or such forms as birdës, it is not mere
caprice, but to gain a definite metrical effect. He is indeed
an aristocrat in his use of language, delighting in words
that have a noble association, so that his true savour can
only be tasted by those who have feasted at the same high
tables. Only at his peril will a minor poet recall to our
minds his great predecessors; Bridges in doing so both
honours them and enriches himself. In that lovely description of the bees in autumn he has blended reminis-
cences of Keats and Shelley into a picture that is all his
own:

> when, tho' *summer hath o'er-brim'd their clammy cells*
> the shorten'd days are shadow'd with dark fears of dearth,
> bees ply the more, issuing on sultry noons to throng
> *in the ivy-blooms*—what time October's flaming hues
> surcharge the brooding hours, till passionat soul and sense
> blend in a rich reverie with the dying year.

And like the true aristocrat he can be boldly familiar
without sinking to the vulgar or commonplace, using with
gallant light-heartedness phrases of everyday life; as of the

little chorister who, while 'the parson's mild discourse
pass'd o'er his head unheard', read his Bible with unassumed
devotion:

> What was it *fetch'd him?*
> Matthew Mark Luke and John *was it?* . . .
> . . . Nay 'twas the bloody books
> Of Jewish war.

Like Chaucer and like Byron, but like how few of our
poets, Bridges has a fine humour which he can use without
ceasing to be a poet; his witty mockery is a weapon of
attack far more effective than satire or denunciation. Thus
he can laugh even at his master Plato for bolstering up an
advocacy of the community of wives and children with the
assumption that

> a bastard nursed in a bureau
> must love and reverence all women for its mothers,

or he will contrast with those magi who follow'd the star
in the East to Bethlehem their descendants of to-day,
who

> hav seen
> the electric light i' the West, and come to worship,

or with light touch he will expose the psycho-analysts
who

> impute precocious puberty
> to new-born babes, and all their after trouble in life
> to shamefast thwarting of inveterat lust.

And since this same humour is the humour of a poet, it
can blend in a scene of real romantic beauty, heightening
by contrast its final effect. The story of the deluge has for
me a more lively charm since I read of

> old Methusalah
> who when the flood rose higher swam from peak to peak
> til, with the last wild beasts tamed in their fear, he sat
> watching the whelm of water on topmost Everest,
> as thatt too was submerged; while in his crowded ark
> Noah rode safely by.

The situation is irresistibly comic; but listen to the sequel:

> and sailors caught by storm
> on the wide Indian Ocean at shift of the monsoon,
> hav seen in the dark night a giant swimmer's head
> that on the sequent billows trailing silvery hair
> at every lightning flash reappeareth in place,
> out-riding the tempest, as a weather-bound barque
> anchor'd in open roadstead lifteth at the seas.

For the impression which the poem leaves upon us, which returns most often to the memory, is its pervading beauty, a beauty which at the flood-tide of its inspiration has power to recall to us and charge with deeper significance those moments of our own lives when we too have felt within us something of a poet's heart:

> As when a high moon thru' the rifted wrack
> gleameth upon the random of the windswept night;
> or as a sunbeam softly, on early worshippers
> at some rich shrine kneeling, stealeth thru' the eastern apse
> and on the clouded incense and the fresco'd walls
> mantleth the hush of prayer with a vaster silence,
> laden as 'twer with the unheard music of the spheres;
> —nay, incommunicable and beyond all compare
> are the rich influences of those moments of bliss,
> mocking imagination or pictured remembrance,
> as a divine dream in the vaulted slumber of life.

To such heights as these does the poem rise whether its theme be the loveliness of nature, or the glories of art, or the intimate simplicities of human experience. Where is the 'spiritual elation and response to nature' which is 'man's generic mark' brought home to us more vividly than in these faultless lines, in which a series of cloud-scapes such as Shelley alone could rival, is followed by a loving rehearsal of those features of an English countryside which have touched to fine issues all true poets from Chaucer and Shakespeare to the present day?

> The sky's unresting cloudland, that with varying play
> sifteth the sunlight thru' its figured shades, that now

stand in massiv range, cumulated stupendous
mountainous snowbillowy up-piled in dazzling sheen,
Now like sailing ships on a calm ocean drifting,
Now scatter'd wispy waifs, that neath the eager blaze
disperse in air; Or now parcelling the icy inane
highspredd in fine diaper of silver and mother-of-pearl
freaking the intense azure; Now scurrying close o'erhead,
wild ink-hued random racers that fling sheeted rain
gustily, and with garish bows laughing o'erarch the land:
Or, if the spirit of storm be abroad, huge molten glooms
mount on the horizon stealthily, and gathering as they climb
deep-freighted with live lightning, thunder and drenching flood
rebuff the winds, and with black-purpling terror impend
til they be driven away, when grave Night peacefully
clearing her heav'nly rondure of its turbid veils
layeth bare the playthings of Creation's babyhood;
and the immortal fireballs of her uttermost space
twinkle like friendly rushlights on the countryside.
       Them soon the jealous Day o'errideth to display
Earth's green robe, which the sun fostereth for shelter and shower;
The dance of young trees that in a wild birch-spinney
toss to and fro the cluster of their flickering crests,
as rye curtseying in array to the breeze of May;
The ancestral trunks that mightily in the forest choirs
rear stedfast colonnade, or imperceptibly
sway in tall pinewoods to their whispering spires;
The woodland's alternating hues, the vaporous bloom
of the first blushings and tender flushings of spring;
The slumbrous foliage of high midsummer's wealth;
Rich Autumn's golden quittance, to the bankruptcy
of the black shapely skeletons standing in snow:
Or, in gay months of swelling pomp, the luxury
of leisur'd gardens teeming with affection'd thought;
the heartfelt secrecy of rustic nooks, and valleys
vocal with angelic rilling of rocky streams,
by rambling country-lanes, with hazel and thorn embower'd
woodbine, bryony and wild roses; the landscape lure
of rural England;

or who has entered more profoundly into the spirit of
great art where 'man's pensiv play' outdoes nature, or

summed up for us with more imaginative penetration the
undying appeal of Homer and the tragic writers of Hellas?

> But these and all old tales of far-off things, bygones
> of long-ago whereof memory still holdeth shape,
> Time and the Muse hav purged of their unhappiness;
> with their bright broken beauty they pervade the abyss,
> peopling the Solitude with gorgeous presences:
> as those bare lofty columns, time-whiten'd relics
> of Atlanteän adoration, upstanding lone
> in Baalbec or Palmyra, proudly affront the waste
> and with rich thought atone the melancholy of doom.

And the genius with which he reveals to us the secrets of
art and nature does not fail him in his vision of the elemental emotions of humanity: as when he tells of a mother's
love for her child:

> The unfathomable mystery of her awaken'd joy
> sendeth her daily to heaven on her knees in prayer:
> and watching o'er the charm of a soul's wondering dawn
> enamoureth so her spirit, that all her happiness
> is in her care for him, all hope in his promise;
> and his nobility is the dream-goal of her life;

or when he sets before us the hopefulness of the child just
awakening to manhood

> as he rideth forth to do battle, a Chevalier
> in the joyous travail of the everlasting dawn,

or the ecstacy of spirit with which youth greets the
coming of first love:

> as the oceantide of the omnipotent Pleasur of God,
> flushing all avenues of life, and unawares
> by thousandfold approach forestalling its full flood
> with divination of the secret contacts of Love,—
> of faintest ecstacies aslumber in Nature's calm,
> like thought in a closed book, where some poet long since
> sang his throbbing passion to immortal sleep—with coy
> tendernesses delicat as the shifting hues
> that sanctify the silent dawn with wonder-gleams,
> whose evanescence is the seal of their glory,

consumed in self-becoming of eternity;
till every moment as it flyeth, cryeth "Seize!
  Seize me ere I die! I am the Life of Life."

All this is great poetry; our century, at least, has not
heard its like before. In eloquent discourse which has 'all
the colours, music, imaginative life and passion of poetry',
and which at the same time expresses a mind delicately
sensitive to the varied conditions and interests of our
strange modern world, Bridges has revealed to a generation, which more than any other had need to listen,

How Natur . . . teacheth man by beauty
and by the lure of sense leadeth him ever upward
to heav'nly things.

   .   .   .   .

Verily by Beauty it is that we come at WISDOM.